THE BANKERS' BLACKLIST

A volume in the series
Cornell Studies in Money
Edited by Eric Helleiner and Jonathan Kirshner

A list of titles in this series is available at
cornellpress.cornell.edu.

THE BANKERS' BLACKLIST

Unofficial Market Enforcement and the Global Fight against Illicit Financing

Julia C. Morse

CORNELL UNIVERSITY PRESS   ITHACA AND LONDON

First published 2021 by Cornell University Press

Library of Congress Cataloging-in-Publication Data

Names: Morse, Julia C., author.
Title: The bankers' blacklist : unofficial market enforcement and the global fight against illicit financing / Julia C. Morse.
Description: Ithaca [New York] : Cornell University Press, 2021. | Series: Cornell studies in money | Includes bibliographical references and index.
Identifiers: LCCN 2021009273 (print) | LCCN 2021009274 (ebook) |
    ISBN 9781501761515 (cloth) | ISBN 9781501761539 (ebook) |
    ISBN 9781501761522 (pdf)
Subjects: LCSH: Financial Action Task Force. | Banks and banking, International. |
    Money laundering—Prevention. | Terrorism—Finance—Prevention.
Classification: LCC HG3881 .M646 2021 (print) | LCC HG3881 (ebook) |
    DDC 364.4—dc23
LC record available at https://lccn.loc.gov/2021009273
LC ebook record available at https://lccn.loc.gov/2021009274

For my parents,
Duane and Diane Morse

Contents

Figures

Tables

x FIGURES AND TABLES

Preface and Acknowledgments

When I started this project in 2014, transnational terrorism was one of the most pressing international cooperation problems. In today's world, it shares the stage with numerous other challenges, including the COVID-19 pandemic, climate change and related environmental disasters, the rise of global populism, and the renewal of geopolitical rivalries. Yet the insights contained in this book are perhaps even more significant for this broader set of policy challenges.

As a scholar of international cooperation, I became interested in the international effort to combat terrorist financing because it appeared so unusually effective. I first learned about the issue area while working on the sanctions team at the US Mission to the United Nations. For someone with a lifelong interest in international organizations, this position was a dream job. Yet as I learned more about the Security Council's counterterrorism efforts, I was surprised to discover that another organization was perhaps even more crucial for fighting terrorist financing. This organization was the Financial Action Task Force (FATF).

The FATF is a small intergovernmental body that sets standards and monitors compliance with its rules, yet it has achieved a level of deep and widespread policy change that is extremely rare in international politics. Three decades ago, few countries had laws criminalizing money laundering; two decades ago, few states had laws criminalizing the financing of terrorism. Today, nearly every country in the world has an extensive legal and regulatory regime governing both areas. These are not just cosmetic changes; the FATF's monitoring structure assesses both rules and implementation. Indeed, the FATF's current round of evaluations is one of the first international monitoring efforts to assess effectiveness as well as technical compliance.

Part of the FATF's impact is undoubtedly tied to its membership. The organization's thirty-nine members include the most powerful economies in the world. The United States is closely aligned with the FATF's agenda and has reinforced FATF standards with its own domestic regulations and enforcement. Yet these features are not unique to the FATF. The United States has traditionally taken a leadership role in many international organizations, and in the realm of international finance, many club organizations consist primarily of powerful economies.

What, then, makes the FATF so effective at diffusing its standards? This book contends that the FATF's impact is tied to its reliance on unofficial market enforcement. Rather than directly coercing compliance, it produces a noncomplier list that serves as an organizing signal or focal point for cross-national banking. Banks around the world use the FATF list to identify countries that pose a high risk of illicit financing. They charge higher transaction costs to clients in such countries and, in some cases, terminate business relationships. As listed countries experience rising banking costs, the banking sector and other industry groups advocate for improved compliance with the FATF standards. Listed countries are pressured into changing their laws and regulations, and the FATF's guidelines spread across the globe.

The FATF story contains several lessons for policy makers looking to solve pressing cooperation challenges. States pay large political and economic costs for imposing economic sanctions on other countries. Unofficial market enforcement, in contrast, requires much lower enforcement costs and therefore can be deployed against a much broader cross-section of states. But, as the conclusion highlights, unofficial market enforcement can also generate unintended consequences and perverse economic impacts. International cooperation on combating illicit financing thus offers both policy lessons and cautionary notes.

This book is the culmination of a project that began at Princeton University. I was fortunate to have mentors who provided exceptional advice throughout the research process. I extend my gratitude to Robert Keohane, Christina Davis, and Kosuke Imai, all of whom were invaluable to my professional training and the development of my research agenda. Robert Keohane was, from my earliest days, an unwavering source of support. He encouraged me to look beyond a narrow issue area for its larger theoretical contributions, to borrow from other disciplines, and to always probe scope conditions. His ability to combine insightful critiques with steadfast confidence in my abilities allowed me to push the project forward while never losing faith. Christina Davis provided crucial guidance on merging theory with empirics and on integrating existing literature. She was always generous with her time and delivered thoughtful advice, both on professional issues and work-life balance. Finally, Kosuke Imai's methodological guidance helped me make careful empirical decisions and understand the strengths and limitations of quantitative analysis with observational data. Through Kosuke's feedback and the support of his research group, I also learned the importance of writing and presenting research in a way that makes it interpretable and interesting to nonspecialists—an insight that I will carry with me in the future.

Numerous individuals deserve gratitude for their guidance on this project. My Princeton writing group, which at various times included Amanda Kennard, Tyler Pratt, Christoph Mikulaschek, and Anna Schrimpf, reviewed many early drafts of these chapters and provided significant feedback. Tyler Pratt, in particular, deserves special acknowledgment for his willingness to talk through theory and offer useful empirical advice. I also thank Ryan Brutger, Allison Carnegie,

Tom Christensen, Zack Cooper, Aaron Friedberg, Jeff Frieden, Joanne Gowa, Judith Kelley, James Lee, Melissa Lee, Helen Milner, Andy Moravcsik, Mark Nance, Lauren Peritz, Yuki Shirato, Beth Simmons, Keren Yahri-Milo, the Imai Research Group, and participants in the Assessment Power in World Politics conference for comments and feedback. All of these individuals shared thoughtful critiques and advice; any errors in the manuscript remain my own.

While working on this book, I was fortunate to hold a fellowship at the Christopher H. Browne Center for International Politics at the University of Pennsylvania. I offer my sincere thanks to the Browne Center for its financial support, which allowed me to hold a book conference while in residence. I thank my three discussants, Abraham Newman, David Singer, and David Steinberg, who read the text closely and shared thoughtful and constructive suggestions about how to improve the manuscript. I also extend my gratitude to Ryan Brutger, Julia Gray, Michael Horowitz, Ed Mansfield, Beth Simmons, and Alex Weisiger for their guidance and feedback. Finally, I thank my colleagues at UCSB, who have helped me navigate the world of book publishing and provided significant encouragement, and Pinn Siraprapasiri, who provided research assistance with the case study on Thailand.

Portions of this project were presented at the International Political Economy Society Conference (2016, 2017), the International Studies Association Annual Conference (2016, 2017), and the American Political Science Association Annual Meeting (2016, 2017). Earlier versions of the ideas in this manuscript appeared in "Blacklists, Market Enforcement, and the Global Regime to Combat Terrorist Financing," *International Organization* 73, no. 3 (2019): 511–45, copyright © the IO Foundation, and in a chapter of *The Power of Global Performance Indicators* (Cambridge University Press, 2020), edited by Judith Kelley and Beth Simmons. A revised version of the material appears with permission from Cambridge University Press.

Over the course of my research, I interviewed government officials from a number of different countries, as well as bureaucrats from the FATF and its regional affiliates, the UN Office of Drugs and Crime, and the UN Security Council Secretariat. I also conducted many telephone interviews with banking and compliance executives. Most of these people requested anonymity, but I offer them my thanks for sharing their experiences and insights. I extend my gratitude in particular to Gordon Hook, executive secretary of the Asia/Pacific Group on Money Laundering (APG), for speaking with me on three separate occasions and to Daniel Glaser and Chip Poncy for their detailed insights on the inner workings of the ICRG process.

I was also fortunate enough to attend the plenary sessions of the two FATF regional bodies: the September 2016 meeting of the APG in San Diego, California, and the June 2017 meeting of MONEYVAL in Strasbourg, France. I'd like to thank APG executive secretary Gordon Hook and the US government delegation to the APG for assisting me with attending the September 2016 meeting, and the MONEYVAL Secretariat for allowing me to attend the June 2017 meeting. These experiences were invaluable for my overall project.

I am grateful for the financial support that I received throughout this project, and in particular, for financial assistance from the Christopher H. Browne Center for International Politics, the Niehaus Center for Globalization and Governance, the Bradley Foundation, the Center for International Security Studies, the Harold W. Dodds Fellowship, and the Fellowship of Woodrow Wilson Scholars at Princeton University.

It was a delight to work with Cornell University Press on this manuscript. Roger Haydon provided timely feedback and advice, as did one of the series editors of the Cornell Studies on Money team and an anonymous reviewer. Their close readings of the manuscript and insightful comments have improved the book in countless ways.

Two final notes of gratitude are in order. A robust network of people provided advice, emotional support, and sometimes even childcare over the course of this project. To friends and family in northern Virginia, Princeton, Seattle, Santa Barbara, Tampa, and elsewhere: thank you. I feel lucky to have all of you in my life.

Finally, my biggest thanks go to my family. They are the foundation on which everything else is built. My husband, Roy Hwang, has been a source of emotional and professional support for two decades. He has encouraged me to pursue my dreams, even when they require moving our family up the coast or across the country, while his humor and perspective remind me how lucky I am to be doing something that I love. My children, Lincoln and Eleanor, help me stay balanced, appreciate little joys, and end each day on a good note. They also drive me to read countless productivity hacks, and perhaps deserve credit for any workplace efficiency.

My final acknowledgments go to my parents, Diane and Duane Morse. They raised me to believe that I could sit at any table, challenge any argument, defend any conviction. Their unwavering love and unshakable confidence in my abilities have been the greatest gifts. This book is dedicated to them.

Abbreviations

AML	anti–money laundering
APG	Asia/Pacific Group on Money Laundering
BIS	Bank for International Settlements
CFT	combating the financing of terrorism
FATF	Financial Action Task Force
ICRG	International Cooperation Review Group
IMF	International Monetary Fund
NCCT	Non-Cooperative Countries and Territories
UNODC	United Nations Office on Drugs and Crime
UNSC	United Nations Security Council

CROSS-BORDER BANKING IN A GLOBALIZED ERA

How would you steal one billion dollars? In an era where banks rarely stockpile cash and their security measures rival the military, it seems an impossible feat. Yet in February 2016, North Korean hackers almost pulled it off. Exploiting time-zone differences, technological vulnerabilities, and weak points in financial regulation, they went after USD 951 million at the Bangladesh central bank. The heist was a partial success: 81 million vanished in a matter of days. Money moved from the New York Federal Reserve to a bank in the Philippines. Within forty-eight hours, conspirators had withdrawn the funds and taken it to a casino—a black box for illicit funds.[1] The money disappeared into untraceable banknotes; to date, the majority has not been recovered.[2]

In one sense, the "billion-dollar bank heist" was all about technology. Malware allowed the hackers to sneak into the Bangladesh central bank's computer system. Once inside, they learned how the bank operated, stole employee passwords, and eventually found the cornerstone of global finance: the SWIFT messaging system.[3] SWIFT allows banks to communicate with each other, protecting money transfer requests with military-grade security. The hackers mastered the system and waited until a bank holiday to send false transfer orders to the Federal Reserve. Fed officials processed the first few requests but stopped when compliance software flagged some messages as suspicious.[4]

But while technology was the vehicle for the crime, the larger story is about the strengths and vulnerabilities of global finance. Cross-border ties between banks facilitate trillions of dollars in transfers each day.[5] Open electronic borders

1

allow migrants to send money home to their families, make it easy for tourists to use ATMs in foreign countries, and smooth the way for Apple to build an iPhone with materials from six continents. Yet organized crime syndicates, drug cartels, terrorists, and dictators can make use of these same financial pathways. Because finance is so globalized, unsavory actors need only a few countries with weak financial regulation to exploit cross-border banking for criminal purposes. In the case of the Bangladesh bank heist, North Korean hackers chose the Philippines, which allowed its gambling sector to preserve financial secrecy. One loophole, and it was easy to make the money disappear.

If the theft suggests cooperation is urgent, it also highlights why international policy coordination may be so challenging. For nearly a decade, the Financial Action Task Force (FATF), an anti-illicit-financing international organization (IO) of thirty-nine powerful economies, warned the Philippines that the country needed to regulate its gambling sector.[6] A casino without anti–money launder-ing controls is an easy target for criminals wanting to make "dirty money" seem clean.[7] But the Philippine gambling industry was concerned that increased finan-cial regulation would deter investors and tourism, and thus lobbied hard against changing the rules.[8] When the Philippine Congress passed new laws to resolve major gaps in the country's ability to combat illicit financing in 2013, it intention-ally excluded casinos and internet gambling. The FATF called on the Philippines repeatedly to address the omission, to no avail.[9] Even after the 2016 bank rob-bery, the government remained opposed to reform. It was only when the FATF threatened to place the Philippines on its noncomplier list that the Philippine government finally took action.[10]

The Philippines closed its gambling loophole because the FATF list could have meant major disruptions to cross-border financial flows. In a globalized econ-omy, the flow of goods, services, and capital across borders creates opportunities and vulnerabilities that affect government policy (Keohane and Milner 1996).[11] If capital is mobile, governments may compete with each other to secure foreign investment, adopting policies that align more clearly with market preferences (Simmons 2000a; Elkins et al. 2006; Allee and Peinhardt 2011); market actors may intensify such incentives through threats of exit (Hirschman 1970; Good-man and Pauly 1993). Markets may pressure governments to adopt convergent economic reforms that de-emphasize social welfare in favor of open trade and monetary policy (Gill and Law 1989; Cerny 1990; Kurzer 1993; Rodrik 1997). In other cases, globalization may drive diversification, as governments pursue different regulatory and tax policies that attract certain types of firms (Garrett 1998; Cai and Treisman 2005). Investor attention to domestic policy may depend in part on global financial liquidity: when markets are flush with capital, inves-tors are more risk tolerant (Ballard-Rosa, Mosley, and Wellhausen 2019).

This book analyzes the link between cross-border financial flows and domestic policy by examining how unofficial market enforcement via global banking alters compliance with international rules. Banks are a particularly formidable force for policy change. Transnational bank channels facilitate trade financing, provide start-up capital for foreign direct investment, and allow individuals to send remittances across borders. For developing economies, bank-facilitated financing is particularly crucial for economic growth and poverty reduction (World Bank 2018). For developed economies, cross-border banking spurs investment and trade. Every country in the world relies on bank-to-bank networks for some type of commerce, and it is this near-universal dependence that makes it a uniquely powerful tool of pressure. Countries may be able to forgo foreign investment or sell bonds to domestic markets, but governments cannot afford to be cut off from the global banking community. For this reason, bank networks and operating practices can have profound effects on the domestic policies of states.

A significant body of literature has examined how international financial standards have diffused across states. While many scholars have focused on explaining the politics of standard creation and promotion,[12] others have examined when and why states adopt policies that meet such standards. Explanations for compliance typically depend on the type of state examined. Economic powers like the United States and the United Kingdom may comply because standards reflect preexisting preferences or agreed-upon outcomes.[13] When passive adopters[14]—countries that were either excluded from the standard-setting enterprise or failed to influence the outcome—follow suit, compliance may occur because such standards have gained widespread transnational acceptance as "best practices."[15] More often, however, dominant states or markets pressure passive adopters to change their regulations.

Such outside-in policy transformations can take many forms. Drezner (2007, 77) describes how the United States and the European Union used a mixture of "cajoling and coercion" to export anti-bribery standards to developing countries. Simmons (2000b, 2001) argues that the United States used the FATF to spread anti–money laundering standards because the US government anticipated significant externalities and that passive adopters would have few incentives to emulate policy. Dominant states may threaten to close off market access to nonconforming states (Kapstein 1992, 1994; Singer 2007). Alternatively, if market actors themselves view a standard as desirable, they may reward firms that meet such standards, regardless of domestic policy. The 1988 Basel Accord, for example, set minimum capital-asset ratios in order to reduce banking risk; as a result, well-capitalized banks viewed country adoption as a way of improving their global competitiveness (Ho 2002). Market actors may use international financial standards as a focal point—a coordination device that tells actors how to behave even in the absence of communication.[16] In such cases, financial standards serve as a guidepost against which market actors can evaluate firm behavior (Simmons 2001), similar to how international investors may use specific economic metrics to judge a government's creditworthiness (Mosley 2000).

Narratives focusing on dominant state pressure and market incentives pair uneasily, however, with more in-depth studies of international financial standards and compliance. Whereas the former often assumes that powerful countries and market actors can easily manipulate policy in passive adopter states, a small but robust body of work challenges this narrative. Through detailed case studies of Indonesia, South Korea, Malaysia, and Thailand, Walter (2008) shows that domestic politics (rather than external pressure) drove compliance with international financial standards after the Asian financial crisis and, perhaps more significantly, compliance was typically low when costs were high and third-party monitoring was difficult. In the face of international pressure, countries may engage in "mock compliance" (Walter 2008) or "cosmetic compliance" (Chey 2014), adopting enough policies to appear compliant but then manipulating implementation "in ways that . . . in practice still defeat its objectives" (Chey 2014, 3).[17] These important works suggest that when international standards require significant policy change, direct coercion may be little match for intransigent domestic politics. Such findings align with the "enforcement school" view of compliance: states are unlikely to adopt costly laws and regulations to meet international obligations unless they face a risk of stringent enforcement (Downs et al. 1996; Goldsmith and Posner 2005).

This book accepts the importance of domestic buy-in but argues that unofficial market enforcement offers an effective way of shifting domestic politics. In emphasizing how an IO may quietly leverage market behavior, it reimagines the relationship between international standards, market pressure, and compliance. Traditionally research on market pressure suggests international financial standards provide a focal point that market actors can use to evaluate individual financial institutions' competitiveness (Ho 2002; Kapstein 1994; Simmons 2001). Competitive market pressures thus drive countries and financial institutions to meet international standards. But as Chey (2014, 11–12) points out, this logic assumes that market participants share a clear and detailed understanding of the rules and accept the desirability of the international standards. In reality, financial standards are often ambiguous and highly contentious. Many countries and financial institutions profit from the financial secrecy that enables money laundering and terrorist financing; international standards may create new norms around these issues, but market actors are unlikely to use such rules as a focal point unless their own profit structures shift significantly. The FATF established guidelines for decreasing money laundering in casinos, but countries like the

Philippines were unlikely to suffer any consequences for (and indeed, might even benefit from) failing to regulate their gambling sectors.

Yet the FATF overcame this resistance by using its noncomplier list to engage global banks in *unofficial market enforcement.* Unofficial market enforcement occurs when information drives market actors to act as de facto punishers of countries that fail to follow international rules. While the idea of market actors as enforcers is not new,[18] the FATF process is tangibly different in several ways. First, global banks have no natural profit-based incentives to avoid illicit financing; they make such choices due to regulatory and reputational concerns. The FATF case therefore has much larger policy lessons because it demonstrates how government policy and public opinion can shift market incentives in crucial ways. Second, while market-based accounts often emphasize how international rules themselves serve as a focal point, the FATF standards are ambiguous as to how banks should judge country risk. Instead, the FATF itself provides a timely, frequently updated focal point—its noncomplier list—and assumes that banks will use its information accordingly. The unofficial nature of this process is crucial to its success: by relying on an informational focal point to influence market decision-making, FATF member states minimize their own enforcement costs and maximize the probability that market processes incentive domestic policy change.

The FATF noncomplier list showcases the power of globalized finance. The same channels that allow criminals and terrorists to send money across borders can be harnessed as tools of pressure to force reluctant governments to adopt new laws. By avoiding sanctions or direct coercive action, the FATF's noncomplier list preserves a veneer of bureaucratic authority and technocratic monitoring that protects it from easy critiques. Governments must reconfigure their political priorities to pass new legislation or risk being cut off from the global financial system.

The Bankers' Blacklist examines the effects and implications of this unofficial market enforcement process. The FATF noncomplier list has been an unparalleled success in driving countries to comply with the FATF recommendations. Rarely in international politics has an IO been able to generate such rapid and widespread policy change. Countries all over the world have adopted laws and regulations to meet FATF standards on keeping criminals and terrorists out of the financial system. For scholars of international organizations, the illicit financing issue area offers unique lessons on how IOs can drive policy improvements even in the face of significant domestic opposition.

Two cautionary notes are in order, however. First, while this book has important implications for policy makers interested in global solutions to transnational threats, the research cannot answer crucial questions about the ultimate impact of

FATF standards on illicit financial flows. The project sheds light on how and why states adopt the FATF's prescribed policies but leaves unaddressed the query of whether the standards actually reduce money laundering and terrorist financing. The latter question is not simply one of cosmetic vs. true compliance—regulators could be implementing the FATF's standards but the standards themselves might not do what policy makers intend.[19] The guidelines, for example, are designed to regulate transactions through the formal banking network, but an even larger amount of capital moves through "shadow banking" intermediaries like hedge funds and unregulated activities like credit default swaps.[20] As countries tighten financial regulation for banks, criminals may redirect money to other parts of finance. While these are important inquiries, they are beyond the scope of this analysis. Instead, the project focuses on the long-standing debate among political scientists and practitioners who work on international cooperation: under what conditions can an international organization engender deep compliance with its rules?[21]

A second caveat is also important for understanding the FATF's ultimate impact. When states work through an IO to enlist market actors as enforcers, they relinquish some control over the enforcement process. In the words of Daniel Glaser, the former assistant secretary for terrorist financing and financial crimes at the US Department of Treasury, "part of the power of market processes is that it creates dynamics you don't fully control, where small actions have systemic resonance . . . you can't easily escalate or de-escalate."[22] States may rely on IOs to leverage market processes, but it is bankers and investors themselves who decide the specific form and content of market enforcement. The FATF may intend for banks to treat each client as an individual, but in practice, banks often adopt indiscriminate "de-risking" practices that leave entire categories of clients without easy access to formal finance. The implications of this challenge are discussed at length in the conclusion.

Cross-Border Banking and Domestic Policy

The link between domestic policy and transborder flows of goods, services, and capital is well established in political science literature.[23] When market actors can move capital freely around the globe, governments are likely to adopt policies favored by the market in order to compete with each other to secure foreign investment (Simmons 2000a; Elkins et al. 2006; Büthe and Milner 2008). Research on sovereign debt markets suggests international investors are attuned to a small set of country-specific policy indicators like inflation and deficit (Mosley 2000), a government's repayment record (Tomz 2007) and political institutions (North and Weingast 1989; Schultz and Weingast 2003; Beaulieu et al. 2012), its memberships in economic IOs (Gray 2013), and the actions of similar, "peer" countries (Brooks et al. 2015). In the realm of international finance, regulators may be incentivized to set global standards due in part to competitive market pressures (Singer 2004, 2007), while other states may adopt the standards in response to pressure from domestic and international banks, which want to attract business (Ho 2002). But while scholars have posited that market forces may drive improvements in compliance, this book outlines a causal chain linking an IO's rules and monitoring to cross-border banking and policy change.[24]

Bank-to-bank relationships are the foundation of international finance. When an immigrant in the United States wants to send money to her family in China, she need only go to her local bank branch, fill out the necessary paperwork, and initiate a transfer.[25] The same process allows parents to send money to children studying abroad, foreign businesspeople to purchase stakes in local companies, and international charities to support relief efforts overseas. Access to global finance is thus a type of equalizer; regardless of an individual's wealth or power in the world, cross-border banking relationships facilitate sending money around the globe.

In most cross-border transfers, money moves through well-established ties between banks. For hundreds of years, such transfers have occurred primarily through correspondent banking relationships. In correspondent banking, one bank (the correspondent) holds deposits that are owned by other banks (the respondents) and provides payments and services on their behalf. Such processes ease globalized finance, reducing the time and costs for sending money across borders.

Banks have historically maintained broad correspondent networks, but in recent years, international financial cooperation has led to thousands of correspondent account closures. Following the 2008 financial crisis, the G-20 economies[26] sought to address some of the roots of the crisis through international soft law (Shaffer and Pollack 2009; Helleiner 2010, 2014; Kirton et al. 2010; Brummer 2010). In particular, the G-20 used intergovernmental bodies like the Basel Committee on Banking Supervision and the FATF to promulgate voluntary standards and policy recommendations for global finance. These IOs took steps that profoundly altered how banks do business with banks in other countries. Under the new Basel guidelines, for example, banks must meet minimum liquidity requirements, maintaining more cash on hand. As a result, banks have fewer resources for lending and have sought to shift away from high-risk, low-yield clients.

While the Basel requirements have made banks more circumspect with loans, the FATF guidelines have made correspondent banking more expensive. A core component of the FATF recommendations is the principle that banks and financial institutions are the first line of defense against illicit financing. Banks are expected to implement stringent "know-your-customer" rules to root out criminals and terrorists from the financial system. As part of this process, banks must create illicit financing risk profiles for their customers, taking into account each client's identity, business, source of funds, and country of origin. Higher-risk customers require greater scrutiny and attention; in other words, they cost more. And depending on how high these costs go and the profitability of transactions, a bank may decide that the costs of maintaining a correspondent relationship with a riskier country are simply not worth it.

Of course, rigorous international standards on stopping illicit financing would have had little impact if banks did not also face strong regulatory and reputational incentives to avoid dirty money. Since the 2008 financial crisis, regulators in many large economies have begun to levy penalties against banks for anti–money laundering failures. While the United States and the United Kingdom are responsible for the majority of high-value penalties, regulatory enforcement has diversified in recent years. In 2019, for example, regulator anti–money laundering fines totaled more than USD 8 billion, with US and UK officials responsible for little more than a quarter of the total penalties.[27] Government fines are crucial to spurring bank action because they increase the potential costs of allowing dirty money. Banks have also become more risk averse because of the possibility of reputational harm; public revelations of bank noncompliance have led to significant declines in share prices, even absent major regulatory punishment (Jamieson 2006).

What does all of this mean for globalized finance? At the micro level, different categories of people face different barriers in sending money across borders. For those fortunate enough to be in low-risk countries sending money to other low-risk countries, the costs of compliance are small. US customers must provide identity documents to open accounts and explain their business. If a US citizen sends money to Europe, the bank will screen the transaction, but probably not too closely or for too long. For citizens of higher-risk countries, however, the effects are more extreme. A bank might require more identity documents or delay the transfer for several days. In some cases, the bank might refuse to do business with an entire class of customers. In the United States, for example, money transmitters have traditionally facilitated the flow of remittances to economically vulnerable states like Haiti, Liberia, Nepal, and Somalia. While these services used to rely on banks as intermediaries, many transmitters have lost banking access over the last ten years and now rely on nonbanking channels, such as cash couriers, to send money across borders.[28] Immigrants from these countries face higher costs and delays in sending money back to their families, not to mention the additional risks of corruption or expropriation.

Shifts in the global bank network take on even more significance at the macro level. Because international banks consider a country's illicit financing risk profile, governments face strong incentives to establish a positive reputation in this area. The US dollar remains, at least for now, the dominant currency in international finance;[29] if banks in the United States restrict business with a country because of its risk profile, domestic banks and firms could lose access to the dollar. Even the threat of market punishment can drive a country to pass stricter laws and increase regulatory guidelines for the financial sector. If international banks in the United States and Europe identify defensible standards or criteria for judging a country's illicit financing risk, countries must work to keep themselves above any high-risk threshold. And if a country ends up on something like the FATF noncomplier list, its government will face strong pressure from the banking sector to improve domestic policy quickly before banks decide to cut network ties.

IOs and Focal Points

The FATF drives behavior through its noncomplier list, which serves as a type of focal point for global banks. In our current information-abundant era, an IO blacklist might seem like a relatively weak tool of influence. In many issue areas, information competition is intense—IOs, nongovernmental organizations, and even some states release metrics evaluating and comparing countries' policies (Kelley and Simmons 2019)—and audiences can choose their preferred monitoring scheme. Even if an IO releases a monitoring report or a targeted list, its impact will be minimal unless states and nonstate actors have a reason to be interested in the information. Why, then, is the noncomplier list so powerful? And, more generally, how do IOs generate demand for their monitoring? Answering these questions is core to understanding power and influence in the world today.

IOs promote cooperation between states in part by acting as focal points that shape expectations about acceptable behavior.[30] International law can shape how states approach negotiations (Allee and Huth 2006; Huth et al. 2013), while IO adjudication can resolve disagreements about facts, underlying rules, or how to interpret the terms of a negotiated agreement (McAdams 2005; Powell and Mitchell 2007; Ginsburg and McAdams 2004; Huth et al. 2011). IOs also have normative influence over states; they may influence perceptions of when a certain behavior is politically or socially acceptable (Voeten 2005; Lebovic and Voeten 2009). An emerging literature on global performance indicators has brought renewed attention to these debates (Cooley and Snyder 2015; Kelley and Simmons 2015, 2019).

Scholars of international soft law highlight additional explanations for why an IO might serve as a focal point for states and nonstate actors. Soft law bodies like the FATF, the Basel Committee, and the International Association of Insurance Supervisors exist outside of legally binding treaties.[31] Rather than formal rules, these bodies establish "voluntary standards, best practices, and recommended guidance" (Newman and Posner 2018, 3) and rely on technical experts rather than high-level politicians. Because of this technocratic nature, some scholars see soft law bodies as filling a demand for concrete policy solutions to ongoing cooperation challenges (Slaughter 2004; Sabel and Zeitlin 2010). In this vision, soft law serves as an effective focal point for coordination problems (Zaring 1998, 2019; Guzman and Meyer 2010): it may lack any clear enforcement mechanism (Boyle 1999), but it can nonetheless influence domestic policy through bureaucratic networks (Andonova and Tuta 2014; Shaffer and Pollack 2009; Eberlein and Newman 2008).

An alternative view of international soft law emphasizes the role of state power in forming standards and driving compliance (Kapstein 1992; Oatley and Nabors 1998). Kirshner (2003) highlights how even though the global financial system is perceived as imposing "best practices" on states, in reality, policies reflect political choices rather than underlying economic truths. Soft law bodies that establish focal points for financial actors may accomplish this feat because they reflect the preferences of powerful economies and industries (Drezner 2007). In this view, states and nonstate actors look to an IO for a signal about behavior not because of institutional legitimacy or authority but rather because it is a guidepost for learning about how powerful countries view the world. Even seemingly technocratic organizations may be influenced by domestic political preferences, creating winners and losers among states (Verdier 2009; Mattli and Woods 2009; Büthe and Mattli 2011). Powerful countries may use bureaucratic networks as tools of leverage against other states (Farrell and Newman 2019).

While this literature significantly enhances our understanding of how IOs function as focal points, it devotes less attention to explaining how an IO becomes a focal point in the first place. For an IO to provide an organizing solution, there must be some uncertainty about how states or nonstate actors should behave, and there must be a reason why these parties look to an IO to clarify the situation. But often such conditions are taken as starting points for analysis. Johnston (2001, 490) notes that when rationalist scholars model cooperation, they assume that state preferences—including states' underlying demand for a focal point—are fixed. Martin and Simmons (2012, 333) make a similar point, writing that "the concept of 'focal point' is frequently relied upon as a way to reduce transactions costs, but just why some solutions are accepted as focal is rarely discussed."

This book sheds light on this topic through a discussion of how an IO may develop the institutional prominence necessary to serve as a focal point. Three conditions enhance an IO's salience within an issue area. First, when an IO develops comparative advantages like technical expertise and unique access to government policy, it is more likely to become a valuable source of information. Second, when IO member states leverage coercive pressure against those governments or nonstate actors who refuse to follow rules, the IO's informational signals become more costly to ignore. Third, when an IO takes steps to enhance its perceived legitimacy, perhaps by expanding membership or adopting more inclusive procedures, it is less likely to encounter entrenched opposition to its rules or monitoring. While these conditions need not go together, in combination, they provide a solid foundation for an IO to become a noteworthy source of information in an issue area.

When an IO is salient in an issue area where market actors are also searching for information about country performance, IO monitoring can shape market behavior. Market actors may reallocate resources away from poorly performing countries, creating new incentives for compliance improvements. This book focuses specifically on how an IO focal point in the form of a blacklist leads international banks to change how they do business with publicly identified noncompliant countries. Banks terminate correspondent accounts or raise the costs of capital for banks in listed countries, leading domestic banking and other industry groups to become advocates for policy reforms.

Market enforcement can be a powerful driver of policy change because it creates a domestic constituency, often where none existed before. In issue areas like human rights, trade, or environmental policy, international agreements empower individuals to mobilize and advocate for their preferred policy outcomes (Moravcsik 1995; Gurowitz 1999; Simmons 2009; Chaudoin 2016; Mansfield et al. 2002; Dai 2002, 2007). But in many other issue areas, particularly more technical ones, states do not have an incipient community of activists ready to pressure the government to comply. Market enforcement generates new domestic allies. When banks and companies have difficulty accessing international capital, they will seek the most direct pathway to overcome these obstacles in order to reduce their costs and improve their profit margins. If such difficulties are related to something country-specific, market actors will pressure the government to remedy the situation so that domestic firms can engage once more in international finance. Thus, an IO, by simply publicizing the results of its monitoring, creates a ripple effect that leads to deep and widespread compliance improvements.

The FATF List, Unofficial Market Enforcement, and Soft Law Compliance

The FATF and its member states have worked to keep illicit funds out of the financial system for more than three decades; however, the FATF's reliance on a noncomplier list and unofficial market enforcement is relatively new.[32] FATF standards themselves are relatively ambiguous on how exactly banks should determine which countries constitute the greatest illicit financing risks. Moreover, banks themselves face diverse risk calculations, depending on their geographic footprints and profit patterns. Absent a clear signal from the FATF, banks have few incentives to align their decision-making in ways that penalize a uniform set of countries.

Following the 2008 financial crisis, FATF members decided that the organization needed a more effective approach for pressuring reluctant governments to adopt FATF standards. Beginning in February 2010, the FATF issued triannual public announcements identifying countries that had yet to meet key standards. The process was designed to appear noncoercive: most countries were identified on a list titled "Improving Global AML/CFT Compliance," which noted that the countries had made written high-level political commitments to address the identified problems.

On the surface, the FATF's new noncomplier list was simply an informational signal about which countries were falling short of FATF standards. The FATF has several institutional advantages that make it a meaningful source of information on anti–money laundering policy. It is primarily a technocratic body, relying on a small secretariat and a network of government bureaucrats who have expertise and unparalleled access to information; as a result, the FATF is not only the most knowledgeable standard setter in this issue area but also the most credible assessor of state policy. The FATF also has a previous (somewhat controversial) history of using economic coercion to make states and nonstate actors more attentive to FATF recommendations and reporting. Finally, over the last decade, FATF members have sought to enhance the organization's perceived legitimacy among states and private actors by expanding its membership, giving more voice to regional actors, and developing more robust bureaucratic procedures.

Bank reaction to the noncomplier list, however, depends not only on the FATF's ability to provide a focal point but also on bank demand for information about illicit financing risk. Historically, banks had few reasons to consider whether a country was vulnerable to money laundering or terrorist financing. While the FATF's standards diffused across powerful economies throughout the 1990s and the early 2000s, the organization's ambiguous guidelines meant that banks could take minimal efforts to screen high-risk clients and still claim compliance. But during the same period, FATF member states also worked to enhance the organization's credibility and legitimacy, and to draw attention to its standards via direct coercion. Such efforts were so successful that banks could not ignore it when in 2010 the FATF began to issue a new precise signal about countries that constituted significant illicit financing risks. Since that time, banks have worked to integrate the FATF list into their compliance systems in order to demonstrate to regulators, shareholders, and customers that they are taking compliance seriously. Indeed, it does not matter that the FATF itself rarely calls on banks to punish listed countries; instead, the FATF's credibility as a monitor means that banks must take action in response to listing in order to demonstrate compliance.

The FATF noncomplier list leads the global banking network to punish countries that fail to comply with the FATF's standards. Although market enforcement in the FATF context is primarily through the banking system, it is one version of a larger process where market actors maximize profits and minimize risks by allocating resources away from countries that fail to meet international standards.[33] In the case of illicit financing, the FATF is able to leverage bank pressure in a more timely and directed fashion as compared to many other types of market enforcement. Bank pressure is not static; instead, the FATF harnesses it over and over, redirecting focus through triannual updates to the noncomplier list.

This looming threat is a strong incentive for policy change. As international banks restrict capital flows to banks and individuals in listed countries, domestic banking and business associations become strong advocates for meeting the FATF standards. Political priorities are reconfigured and governments encounter strong pro-compliance political pressure. As a result of this process, governments in listed countries pass new laws, strengthen bureaucracy, and implement regulations in ways that improve compliance with the FATF recommendations.

Interstate Power and the Role of the United States

In the FATF context, powerful economies facilitate unofficial market enforcement. IO scholars have long emphasized the role of interstate power disparities in driving international cooperation. Some view international organizations as mere reflections of state power (Mearsheimer 1995), while others argue dominant states with financial market power create international rules and regulatory regimes to reflect their own preferences (Drezner 2007). This tradition emphasizes how the United States and the United Kingdom have relied on power disparities and the threat of market closure to force nondominant states to agree to international financial standards like the 1988 Basel Accord (Kapstein 1992, 1994; Simmons 2001; Singer 2007; Oatley and Nabors 1998). As these large economies use global regulatory networks to diffuse their preferred standards, the network itself becomes its own source of power that states can use to gather strategically valuable information and deny access to adversaries (Farrell and Newman 2019).

While buy-in from powerful economies intensifies the impact of unofficial market enforcement, it is an insufficient condition in an issue area like illicit financing where private actors have profit incentives to ignore international standards.[34] Government policy determines how market actors calculate profit margins, and countries with large financial systems have disproportionate influence over firm decision-making. But even if powerful economies support an international rule or standard and hold financial actors accountable for meeting that standard, this process may not lead to unofficial market enforcement in any meaningful sense. In the case of illicit financing, UK and US regulatory efforts to penalize banks for anti–money laundering failures increased bank incentives to create compliance systems, but banks interpreted the regulations in different ways. The FATF's rules on customer due diligence leave it largely up to banks as to how they should evaluate geographic risk. Historically, even if one bank decided that a country was too risky, clients in that country usually had access to other financial institutions, which meant that market pressure was never concentrated enough to incentivize policy change.

The FATF noncomplier list changed these calculations for banks because banks could not plausibly maintain strong anti–money laundering systems and ignore the FATF's signal. The FATF secretariat and its network of bureaucrats spent decades establishing the organization's credibility as a technocratic standard setter and monitor of government policy. Its standards and monitoring have grown more sophisticated over time, and today, the FATF has one of the most robust peer evaluation and compliance assessments systems of any international organization. The FATF has also increased its engagement and collaboration with the private sector in recent years, so much so that private actors may even be supplanting state influence within the organization (de Oliveria 2018). The FATF's expertise and credibility meant that banks could not plausibly ignore its list when determining country risk.

The FATF noncomplier list is a powerful signal in part because it is *not* a direct proxy for US interests or preferences. The FATF's listing procedures are built around a compliance threshold, above which countries are automatically eligible for listing. This technocratic approach was intentional—FATF members wanted "automaticity baked in" so that listing decisions would not be subject to political squabbles.[35] The list's bureaucratic procedure makes it more difficult for powerful countries to prevent listing and for would-be listed countries to lobby effectively against listing.

Why would the United States make such a trade-off, giving up some amount of control over listing decisions? Because unofficial market enforcement is a more effective and wide-reaching tool for policy change than direct coercion. By relying on the FATF to provide a focal point for global banks, the US government avoids some of the political enforcement costs of unilateral lists or direct coercion. Moreover, because the FATF as a whole must agree to remove countries from its list, listed governments are incentivized to undertake deeper policy improvements. This incentive structure is intensified by market pressure: ultimately, listed governments must convince banks that they are no longer high-risk environments for illicit financing.

Why Analyze Policy Change on Combating Illicit Financing?

Over the last two decades, international financial regulation has become the centerpiece of global security and economic policy. Following the 9/11 terrorist attacks, the United States opted to make the suppression of terrorist financing the cornerstone of US counterterrorism efforts (Zarate 2013). The US government pursued this objective first through the United Nations Security Council (UNSC), which adopted a far-reaching resolution that required all countries in the world to criminalize terrorist financing.[36] But not long after the UNSC took action, the United States convinced other FATF member states to expand the organization's mission to include combating the financing of terrorism. Although the UNSC was the first to act, the FATF has been the heart of the global effort to combat terrorist financing. Indeed, the UNSC even references the FATF standards in some of its counterterrorism resolutions (Pratt 2018).

The global campaign to keep terrorists and criminals out of the financial system has been less visible to the public than the wars in Iraq and Afghanistan, but it has affected the day-to-day lives of people around the globe. Banks spend billions of dollars each year trying to implement know-your-customer requirements that are designed to prevent illicit financing.[37] Creating accounts for new customers takes longer today than ever before, and customers must provide increasingly detailed personal information. As the costs of doing business rise, banks charge customers more for sending money across borders or in some cases drop relationships with low-yield clients.

International financial regulation on illicit financing is also part of the G-20's post-crisis financial reforms. As early as the fall of 2008, the G-20 statement highlighted the importance of "protecting against illicit financing risks from noncooperative countries" (G-20 2008). As G-20 countries attempted to address the roots of the crisis by reforming the Basel banking standards, they also focused on increasing incentives for countries and banks to meet the FATF's standards. Responding to the G-20's call, the FATF created its new noncomplier list procedures in 2009 and issued its first revamped list in February 2010. Around this time, countries like the United States and the United Kingdom also began to levy large fines against banks for illicit financing violations. By 2017, banks globally had paid USD 321 billion in fines.[38]

Despite the obvious importance of this topic, it remains understudied by scholars of international political economy and international organizations.[39] In devoting this book to understanding how the FATF enlists global banks to act as its enforcers and improve policy outcomes, this book sheds light on a topic that is substantively significant and sometimes overlooked.[40] This book will hopefully encourage future research on the subject and also broaden awareness of the myriad of unexpected ways that countries cooperate on pressing security issues.

Theoretical, Empirical, and Policy Contributions

The Bankers' Blacklist makes several types of theoretical contributions. Most significantly, it highlights the importance of the global bank network as a tool of international pressure. As previously discussed, cross-border bank-to-bank transactions undergird many aspects of economic activity. Migrants cannot send remittances without access to the formal financial sector. Firms gain a third of all financing for exports through bank-intermediated transactions. Individuals, companies, and banks around the world depend on access to foreign banks and currencies to participate in the global economy, and this dependency makes it a powerful tool of influence. The correspondent bank network facilitates all of these transactions and, as such, is a powerful lever that can incentivize compliance with international rules.

By examining how unofficial market enforcement reconfigures domestic politics, this book also bridges the gap between scholars who adopt outside-in approaches to understanding financial harmonization and scholars who emphasize the importance of domestic buy-in. Interstate power matters, but it cannot fully explain the FATF noncomplier list's impact; similarly, market forces are important, but in large part because they impose costs on influential domestic actors like the banking industry. Ultimately, listed countries meet FATF standards because their political calculations shift, and continued noncompliance becomes significantly more costly.

For scholars of international organizations, this book also sheds light on the origins of IO focal points. It theorizes that an IO's ultimate ability to provide an organizing solution for outside observers is tied to the institution's prominence, which can be developed through informational advantages, coercive pressure, and legitimacy, as well as how the IO disseminates information. This argument supplements the emerging literature on global performance indicators by identifying the scope conditions for when ratings and rankings are most likely to generate substantive policy improvements.

The Bankers' Blacklist also makes several empirical contributions. Scholars often encounter difficulties when trying to test the causal impact of information on state behavior because the source and content of information do not vary over time. The over-time variation within the FATF case, however, provides a unique opportunity to explore and test the boundaries of IO monitoring and focal points as drivers of compliance. Chapter 3 shows that monitoring and information in the years immediately following 9/11 failed to generate reputational effects or lead to widespread improvements in compliance. In contrast, once the FATF created its noncomplier list, monitoring harnessed market forces to generate significant policy change.

The empirical chapters rely on a mix of quantitative and qualitative analysis that lend strong support to the theory. The book assembles original data on when countries criminalize terrorist financing in line with the FATF standards and uses regression analyses to demonstrate that the FATF noncomplier list is linked to deep and widespread policy change. Additional quantitative analyses illustrate that listed countries experience declines in cross-border bank-to-bank lending. To hone in on the causal mechanism, the book relies on more than thirty interviews with government, IO, and financial industry professionals, as well as participant-observation at two FATF regional affiliate meetings, to illustrate how listing has affected banking and government compliance across a variety of contexts. Two detailed case studies, which draw on interviews and local news articles, further support the analysis.

Finally, this book makes several important policy contributions. For policy makers who work on combating illicit financing, it shows that the FATF noncomplier list has been a useful tool for incentivizing countries to adopt the FATF's preferred policies. More broadly, this book illustrates that global challenges can be addressed through nontraditional forms of cooperation. In an age where US hegemony is on the decline and formal IOs seem incapable of responding to current problems, organizing cooperation less around legally binding commitments and more around technical expertise, monitoring, and assessment may be the best path forward. Information is a source of power, one that IOs can wield to great effect.

Plan of the Book

The book continues in chapter 1 with a brief primer on international financial regulation and a discussion of cross-border banking as a mechanism to influence domestic policy. Chapter 2 builds on this foundation, laying out a general theory of focal points and unofficial market enforcement. By relying on an IO's signal to influence market behavior, states mitigate enforcement costs and also set into motion processes that can generate deep and widespread compliance improvements. Chapter 3 applies this theory to the FATF, exploring the conditions under which the noncomplier list drives global banks to penalize listed countries and incentivize policy change.

Three empirical chapters explore the theory's central claims through a series of quantitative tests, qualitative discussions, and case studies. Chapter 4 examines the relationship between listing and compliance improvements, while chapter 5 explores the causal mechanism for this policy change: market enforcement via global banking. The final empirical chapter shifts the analysis to case studies of Thailand and the Philippines, demonstrating the different pathways of market enforcement. The FATF's listing of Thailand in February 2010 caused Thai banks to experience delays and higher costs in cross-border banking, eventually leading to significant lobbying by industry groups. In the Philippines, listing affected the remittance industry, bank flows, and potentially even stock prices.

The book concludes with a discussion of the theory's significance for political science scholarship and policy. In one sense, the FATF story is an ideal cooperative outcome: member states worked through an international organization to generate widespread policy change. In other respects, however, the FATF noncomplier list offers a cautionary tale. Global bank networks have shifted dramatically in response to international soft law regulations, and even when listed countries undertake policy change, international banks may not resume doing business. Banks are powerful tools of pressure in part because neither states nor international organizations fully control them; reversing some effects may be impossible. These implications are discussed in greater detail in the conclusion.

1

A PRIMER ON INTERNATIONAL
FINANCIAL STANDARDS ON
ILLICIT FINANCING

They met in an online chat room. The forum was a place where native-born Somalis, living in far-flung lands that felt strange and unfriendly, could connect. They talked about home and current events, and in particular, the Somali government's ongoing battle against the terrorist insurgent group Al-Shabaab. People disagreed about who should win. Sometimes, Al-Shabaab leadership went on the site to try to engage them and win their support. Fervent supporters were invited to join a smaller, private chat room known as the Group of Fifteen. It was here that political support was transformed into a vehicle for financing terrorism.

The Group of Fifteen upped the stakes for Al-Shabaab supporters. Participants not only pledged monthly financial commitments but were held accountable for meeting them. Two American women, Hinda Osman Dhirane and Muna Osman Jama, collected money and sent it to Al-Shabaab contacts in Somalia and Kenya. Between 2011 and 2013, these women transferred thousands of dollars to the organization. The money went to safe houses and transportation, but funds are fungible: support for Al-Shabaab convoys meant that the group could spend other money on weapons and recruitment. Eventually, US law enforcement discovered the effort. The chat room was shut down and in 2016 a US court found Dhirane and Jama guilty of providing material support to a foreign terrorist organization. They were sentenced to more than a decade of jail time.[1]

The story of the Group of Fifteen illustrates the complexity of combating terrorist financing: cross-border flows are small, difficult to track, and rarely go directly to pay for terrorist attacks. But the broader context of such funding is even more complicated. The world's most powerful economies want to keep terrorists and other criminals out of the financial system. As part of this effort, they've worked through the Financial Action Task Force (FATF) to set guidelines for how banks should weed out illicit financing. But how do banks evaluate such risks? For every Somali who funnels money to Al-Shabaab, there are many more who send funds to their families for food and medical care. In 2015 Somali workers worldwide sent USD 1.4 billion to Somalia; this money accounted for nearly 25 percent of the country's gross domestic product. At any given moment, banks must weigh humanitarian and profit considerations against the risk of fueling terrorism or organized crime. Banks make these decisions amid little guidance and large reputational and regulatory penalties for failure.

This chapter explains how international financial standards have reshaped bank incentives related to illicit financing. It begins from the premise that international and domestic factors interact to shape how governments make policy decisions (Oatley 2011; Chaudoin et al. 2015). Decisions taken at the international level can have feedback effects on the configuration of interests and institutions within countries (Gourevitch 1978; Lake 2009b) just as the domestic policies of powerful economies may produce competitive advantages internationally.[2] International relations today are characterized by "complex interdependence" (Keohane and Nye 1977), where one state's policies and actions affect the policy options of its partners. In interdependent settings, international institutions can shape how countries conceptualize their own interests (Katzenstein 2009) and provide opportunities for issue linkage that counteract domestic obstacles (Davis 2004).

Domestic-international interactions are particularly pronounced in the realm of finance. Networks of bureaucrats involved in regulating global finance can shape domestic preferences and activate different coalitions (Farrell and Newman 2015, 2016; Newman and Posner 2016, 2018). Cross-border capital mobility allows international financial actors to exert structural power over states, making it increasingly costly for governments to adopt policies that run counter to market interests (Andrews 1994). Regulators in dominant economies may shape international standards to reflect their interests and then use these principles to exert influence over developing countries' domestic policies (Helleiner and Porter 2010). While international standards can be understood as "a self-interested political choice by powerful states" (Sica 2000, 58), the creation and implementation of such rules can also have feedback effects on dominant economies, reshaping domestic incentives.

In the issue area of combating money laundering and terrorist financing, international and domestic interactions have significantly altered how countries regulate the banking sector. Banks have few natural profit reasons to scrutinize financial transactions. Over the last three decades, however, powerful economies have worked to develop international standards on stopping illicit financing, and this effort has, in turn, forced banks to consider each client's risk of illicit financing. Banks spend billions of dollars each year on such safeguards[3] and evaluate client risk based in part on an individual or firm's country of origin. Yet banks face significant ambiguity about how to assess and evaluate country risk. This uncertainty creates an opening for the FATF to influence bank operations through its noncomplier list.

Cross-Border Banking and the "Lifeblood" of Global Finance

Bank influence over domestic policy is distinct from other types of cross-border capital flows. Bank transfers connect a wide variety of economic activities, touching many different aspects of daily life. The tight network structure of global banking also means that powerful interests can weaponize banking by threatening loss of access (Farrell and Newman 2019). Compared to foreign direct investment (FDI) flows or sovereign debt markets, transnational banking is highly regulated at the domestic and international levels. While some amount of domestic deregulation in the 1980s and 1990s boosted cross-border flows and contributed to the consolidation of financial institutions in the European Union and the United States,[4] the banking sector remains, in general, a highly regulated industry. Domestic banking regulations may be affected by electoral rules (Rosenbluth and Schaap 2003) or internal bureaucratic divisions. Singer (2007) argues that domestic regulatory agencies may use the harmonization of regulatory standards at the international level to manage domestic financial instability. In the realm of banking, international standards both reflect domestic interests and influence how banks do business globally.

A sizable literature in economics examines the determinants of cross-border bank lending.[5] While both global and domestic financial conditions are key to understanding bank finance, most analyses suggest that "supply push" factors dominate "demand" factors as determinants of banking sector capital flow (Borio and Disyatat 2011; Obstfeld 2012; Gourinchas and Obstfeld 2012). Bruno and Shin (2015a) argue that the bank leverage cycle—that is, the process by which bank leverage, assets, and a country's gross domestic product (GDP) move up and down together—helps determine bank-to-bank flows across borders.[6] Cerutti et al. (2015) caveat such findings, showing that while global factors such as market volatility are important in explaining cross-border flows, recipient country characteristics like stronger institutions and weaker government regulation are associated with higher gross flows. The authors also find that more stringent banking regulation, more government supervision, and more restrictions on foreign bank presence can reduce the cyclical impact of global liquidity on cross-border flows to banks. Such research suggests that banks consider country-specific factors when making decisions about cross-border transfers.

Most cross-border bank transfers occur through established, ongoing relationships with banks in other countries. As trade barriers have decreased and transportation costs have declined, demand for international financial services has increased significantly (Berger et al. 2000). Financial institutions can use a variety of channels to deliver services to customers in foreign countries. While large international banks like Citigroup or HSBC may have branches in foreign jurisdictions, particularly in those countries with lower regulatory restrictions on foreign bank entry (Cerutti et al. 2005), banks of all sizes rely most often on correspondent relationships to transfer money across borders.

Correspondent banking dates back to at least the sixteenth century (Norman et al. 2011, 10). This practice allows one bank (the correspondent) to hold deposits that are owned by other banks (the respondents) and to provide payments and services on their behalf; such relationships are typically reciprocal.[7] In cases where a payer's bank does not have an account with a receiver's bank, banks may use an intermediary bank with whom both the payer and the receiver banks have correspondent banking relationships (Committee on Payments and Market Infrastructures 2016). Longer payment chains, however, are likely to increase the costs of cross-border transactions, which means that it is advantageous for customers if domestic banks have direct correspondent relationships with final-destination countries.

Correspondent banking is the foundation of the global economy. IMF director Christine Lagarde described the correspondent banking network as "like the blood that delivers nutrients to different parts of the body," noting that the network "is core to the business of over thirty-seven hundred banking groups in two hundred countries" (Lagarde 2016). Through correspondent banking, a bank may provide third-party payments and trade financing, as well as cash clearing and short-term borrowing needs in a particular currency. While interbank networks are important for all countries, they are particularly crucial for developing economies, where economic growth is likely to be tied to financial flows that rely on banking, such as trade, remittances, or humanitarian aid.

While banks may charge clients in some countries higher costs for doing business, the global bank network has historically been broad and open (Bank for International Settlements 2016). Large international banks in particular might hold thousands of correspondent accounts all over the world.[8] Until recently, nearly all banks were connected to the formal financial system in this way.[9] Since the financial crisis, however, the costs of maintaining a basic correspondent relationship have risen significantly due to changes in financial regulation. Cross-border banking activity in advanced economies has diminished (Lane and Milesi-Ferretti 2017), stalling a decades-long pattern of growth. This financial regulatory regime and its implications for cross-border banking are discussed in the next section.

International Financial Regulation and Bank Policy

International finance is governed by a dense web of technocratic regulations that are typically termed "international soft law."[10] International soft law standards operate outside of formal treaties or contracts between states and are thus "non-binding."[11] State-led IOs, informal intergovernmental bodies like the G-7 and the Basel Committee, and even private standard setters can issue soft law standards (Kirton et al. 2010; Brummer 2015; Green 2013; Vabulas and Snidal 2013, 2020), and although such rules are not binding under international law, they nonetheless shape state behavior (Vabulas forthcoming). Unlike formal international agreements, which are negotiated by diplomats, soft law is often produced by IOs that are populated by technical experts and government bureaucrats. This distinction has led some scholars to emphasize informal financial regulatory networks as largely coordination mechanisms (Deeg and O'Sullivan 2009; Raustiala 2002; Dehousse 1997), with some scholars going so far as to argue that soft law networks are a new type of global governance (Slaughter 2004; Coen and Thatcher 2008; Sabel and Zeitlin 2010).

Despite the technocratic basis, regulators from wealthier countries may still play an outsized role in rule development (Kapstein 1992, 1994; Oatley and Nabors 1998; Zaring 2004, 552). Many financial regulatory bodies have historically allowed little to no role for developing countries (Porter and Wood 2002; Pagliari and Helleiner 2010; Helleiner and Porter 2010). Some scholars have argued that soft law purely reflects the interests of powerful countries (Goldsmith and Posner 2006; Drezner 2007), while others have suggested that private industry heavily influences the formation of transnational regulatory standards (Baker 2010; Laurence 2001; Tsingou 2008, 2015; Underhill and Zhang 2008; Lall 2012). The growing importance of transnational nonstate actors may limit the ability of individual states to control political processes (Cerny 2010).

International financial regulation covers a wide range of topics, including banking, securities, corporate governance, and auditing.[12] Different IOs govern distinct issue areas. Within each set of standards, there are specific codes and principles. The FATF, for example, has issued forty recommendations on how to keep illicit funds out of the formal financial system, while the Basel Committee on Banking Supervision has issued twenty-five core principles on regulating risk in the banking sector. Many financial standards were issued within a few years of the 1997 Asian financial crisis. Policy makers blamed weak financial and corporate regulation in East Asia for the crisis, and this interpretation strengthened the argument for international standards (Walter 2008, 16–17).

Following the 2008 financial crisis, the G-20 emerged as a key global actor in international finance (Walter 2010).[13] The centerpiece of the G-20's strategy for economic stability and recovery was international soft law (Newman and Posner 2018, 3). At the G-20's urging, international regulatory bodies governing banking and securities expanded their membership to include strategically important developing countries. The G-20 also transformed the Financial Stability Forum, which had coordinated the various international standards, into the new, more robust Financial Stability Board (FSB). The FSB has a wider membership, including all members of the G-20, a larger secretariat, and a more expansive mandate (Helleiner 2010; Arner and Taylor 2009); it also has a stronger role in promoting compliance (Gadinis 2012; Moschella 2013).[14]

Another key change in financial architecture was the Basel Committee's adoption of the Basel III Framework. The Basel Committee on Banking Supervision is one of the oldest and most developed financial regulatory bodies (Kapstein 1994; Singer 2007; Walter 2008). Established by G-10 central bank governors at the end of 1974,[15] its goals are to enhance financial stability through improvements in banking supervision, and to provide a forum for coordination among its members. In the aftermath of the 2008 financial crisis, the Basel Committee adopted a new set of reforms, collectively dubbed Basel III. This agreement sets out stricter requirements for the quality and quantity of regulatory capital,[16] creates additional capital buffers, sets forth minimum liquidity requirements and a minimum leverage ratio,[17] and stipulates additional requirements for systemically important banks.

The 2008 financial crisis also shifted how large economies approached the international effort to stop illicit financing. The G-20 noted the importance of responding effectively to illicit financing risks from uncooperative countries (G-20 2008). These countries looked to the FATF, the central standard setter in this issue area, to reform its process for dealing with noncompliant jurisdictions. While the FATF is less well known than the Basel Committee in terms of financial governance, its standards and post-2008 actions have had a significant effect on the global banking system and in particular on correspondent banking.

The FATF and the Global Effort to Fight Illicit Financing

The FATF has worked to keep "bad money" out of the financial system since 1989. Established by a small group of mostly developed economies as part of the "war on drugs,"[18] the FATF began by developing forty recommendations on the legal and regulatory steps that governments should take to combat money laundering. After the 9/11 attacks, the FATF's mission expanded to include combating terrorist financing. Although the FATF currently includes only thirty-seven member jurisdictions and two regional organizations,[19] it has a network of nine regional affiliate organizations that it uses to disseminate its standards to more than two hundred economies worldwide.[20]

The FATF standards focus on how governments can best keep criminal proceeds and terrorist financing out of the formal financial system.[21] The recommendations treat banks as the front line of national security, particularly when it comes to terrorist financing (De Goede 2017). Of the forty recommendations, the FATF's requirement that banks and other financial institutions verify customer identities has had a particularly significant impact on how banks do business. Banks and other financial institutions are responsible for implementing stringent "know-your-customer" measures that include asking for identity documents and obtaining information about the intended purpose of business.[22] The requirement is ongoing; over time, financial institutions must continuously monitor business relationships and scrutinize transactions in accordance with each customer's risk profile.[23]

While the FATF's significant impact on cross-border banking may seem surprising given its soft law nature, FATF standards are backed up by the financial power of the world's largest economies. A robust literature in political science has documented how economically powerful states influence domestic politics in other countries. A hegemonic state may use its market power to change the incentives of political actors in other countries, leading them to advocate for alternative policies (James and Lake 1989). When powerful countries agree on regulatory standards and act in concert, widespread policy harmonization is likely to occur (Drezner 2005, 2007). US economic power has contributed to the diffusion of US regulatory standards in other areas of global finance (Simmons 2001; Posner 2009), and powerful countries can weaponize global economic networks for coercive gain (Farrell and Newman 2019). Even in highly institutionalized issue areas like international trade, large economies like those of the United

States and the European Union dominate bargaining and shape dispute settlement (Steinberg 2002; Brutger and Morse 2015).

The FATF's influence is reinforced by its relationship with powerful economies. The United States has been at the forefront of efforts to combat money laundering since the organization's inception in 1989 and has incorporated most of the FATF standards into domestic law.[24] A sizable portion of scholarship views the FATF's agenda as closely intertwined with the United States and its impact as linked to US market power (Jakobi 2015, 2018; Roberge 2009; Drezner 2007; Sharman 2008, 2011). The EU has also adopted significant measures to implement FATF recommendations;[25] this process may help "harden" the FATF's soft law standards into a more certain and durable form of guidance (Newman and Bach 2014).

The United States, the United Kingdom, and other large economies have also penalized banks for anti–money laundering compliance failures (Verdier 2009).[26] In 2012, for example, the US government fined HSBC USD 1.256 billion for what US Department of Justice assistant attorney general Lanny Breuer described as "stunning failures of oversight—and worse—that led the bank to permit narcotics traffickers and others to launder hundreds of millions of dollars through HSBC subsidiaries" (US Department of Justice 2012). De Goede (2017, 128) describes the HSBC case as influential because the US Senate argued its jurisdiction was not bound by geography, but rather applied to all transactions denominated in US currency. As a result, HSBC's corporate headquarters was held responsible for the decisions of local bank branches in Mexico.

Banks also implement FATF standards because they are likely to suffer reputation damage if they are involved in an illicit financing scandal. Reputation damage can lead to financial costs or, for smaller banks, complete collapse. When the US government discovered that Riggs Bank was helping several dictators launder money, for example, it levied relatively small financial penalties against the bank, but the scandal ultimately led to the bank's demise.[27] Thomson Reuters, which sells compliance software to banks, uses such concerns to market risk management systems to financial actors, many of whom view reputation damage and regulatory issues as equally important.[28]

Although banks have regulatory and reputational incentives to implement FATF standards, and in particular, know-your-customer obligations, they face significant practical challenges with this task. Neither FATF standards nor member states' implementing regulations specify precisely how to measure illicit financing risk. In the United States, for example, the Department of Treasury advises that "assessment of customer risk factors is bank-specific, and a conclusion regarding the customer risk profile should be based on a consideration of all pertinent customer information. . . . Any one single indicator is not necessarily determinative of the existence of a lower or higher risk customer."[29] The FATF advises countries and financial institutions that certain types of clients, products, and countries may be lower risk[30] but does not clarify or specify precise guidelines or penalties for high-risk environments.

Banks build risk assessment systems that rely in part on the customer's country of residence. Notably, in the case of cross-border banking, country risk *does not* equate to traditional economic and political risk. Rather, the FATF recommends that financial institutions evaluate country risk based on the effectiveness of a country's system for combating money laundering and terrorist financing, as well as its levels of corruption and criminal activity (FATF 2018, 64). Assessing such risks is not straightforward. Large banks spend millions of dollars each year on compliance departments and related technology, and even with such measures in place, compliance officials operate amid considerable ambiguity about how to assess country attributes.

Effects of Financial Regulation on Correspondent Banking

International financial regulation has drastically reconfigured cross-border banking. Basel III requires banks to have more liquidity and be more risk averse, which creates incentives for banks to terminate low-yield relationships. While the precise effect of Basel III on global banking is a subject of much debate,[31] Basel III's minimum liquidity requirements have almost certainly contributed to the contraction of correspondent banking. Minimum liquidity standards require that banks maintain more cash on hand; as a result, banks have fewer resources for lending and are more risk averse. The FATF's push toward stronger know-your-customer requirements and more stringent penalties for failed enforcement has also raised the costs of cross-border banking. Compliance with such policies is extremely expensive; in the last decade, the average cost of maintaining a correspondent account has increased from around USD 17,000 to close to USD 84,000 (International Chamber of Commerce 2017, 19).[32]

As costs have risen, the global banking network has begun to change. Correspondent banking relationships are profitable when they are linked with other banking products. With increased costs, banks maintain relationships only to serve corporate customers, support the cross-selling of other products to respondent banks, or preserve important reciprocal relationships (Bank for International Settlements 2016, 13). As profitability decreases and costs increase, banks restrict business because there is little to no payoff to compensate for increased risk. In the post-financial-crisis world, banks have sought to downsize and deleverage, eliminating high-risk, low-yield clients (Committee on Payments and Market

Infrastructures 2016). Even leading international banks find it no longer profitable to maintain large, widespread correspondent bank networks (Denecker et al. 2016). Correspondent banking relationships have fallen by 25 percent;[33] between 2011 and 2015 alone, the total number of active correspondent accounts decreased by forty thousand, with declines in more than a hundred countries.[34]

When a bank is deciding how to reconfigure its correspondent network or whether to charge certain clients additional fees, it faces a dilemma similar to that of an investor looking to purchase government debt: it has many options but not enough information. Like other market actors, banks have strong incentives to rely on country reputation when making decisions about correspondent banking. But while investors might focus on aspects of a country's political and economic system that could affect profitability, banks consider compliance with global regulations as a guidepost for good business. Criminals and terrorists might be lucrative clients, but if banks have too much exposure to illicit financing, they are likely to suffer reputation damage and regulatory enforcement. For this reason, banks look for information that provides a defensible standard of behavior for how they should evaluate a country's illicit financing risk. This underlying demand for information creates an opportunity for the FATF to provide an informational signal that influences bank behavior.

Conclusion: Banking as a Tool of Pressure

States have leveraged cross-border economic ties to pressure and coerce each other for more than two thousand years. In ancient Greece, Athens imposed economic sanctions on city-states that failed to join its side in the Peloponnesian War.[35] In more modern times, market actors like international investors and multinational corporations have become independent forces in international politics, incentivizing governments to undertake new policies in order to attract capital. With globalization driving international finance to new levels of interdependence, the cross-border bank network is a powerful market force for influencing domestic policy.

This chapter showcases the power of cross-border banking as a tool of pressure. Government policy makers, aided by the technological changes driving globalization, have created a transnational banking system where individuals can easily send money across the globe. This expansion of global finance provides new opportunities for economic growth. But the same pathways that allow migrant workers to send money to their families also allowed two women to send money to Al-Shabaab. Without global policy coordination, the cross-border banking network is easily exploited for illicit purposes.

The world's most powerful economies use international soft law to respond to such vulnerabilities. The FATF's know-your-customer requirements have transformed how banks weigh the costs and benefits of doing business with foreign clients. As governments adopt and implement the FATF standards, banks increasingly look for ways to evaluate a client's illicit financing risk. The next chapter will show how, under certain conditions, an IO can leverage this type of underlying demand for information to harness the power of market enforcement.

2

A THEORY OF UNOFFICIAL MARKET ENFORCEMENT

In February 2019, the Financial Action Task Force (FATF) and the European Commission each published a list of economies that posed a high risk of illicit financing. These two intergovernmental bodies had overlapping memberships and similar goals, yet they encountered very different reactions. The FATF's update to its noncomplier list garnered little public pushback or direct bilateral appeals, despite the inclusion of strategically important economies like the Bahamas, Ethiopia, and Pakistan. The European Commission's list, on the other hand, led to a diplomatic crisis and the list's eventual implosion.[1]

Why did the Commission's effort fail while the FATF met with few difficulties? Part of the problem was the choice of targets. The European Commission, the executive arm of the European Union (EU), went beyond the FATF list to identify its own expanded set of targets that included Saudi Arabia, Panama, and four US territories. As soon as the Commission announced its proposed list, diplomats from Saudi Arabia, Panama, and the United States began to lobby EU member states to veto the list when it came to the Council for final approval.[2] But while pressure from powerful countries like the United States and Saudi Arabia could explain a shift in the list's contents, it does not explain why the Commission's entire endeavor collapsed. The Council rejected the Commission's approach, criticizing the list as "not established in a transparent and resilient process."[3] The Commission spent more than a year rethinking its process even as the FATF, only a few months later, placed Panama on its noncomplier list with little fanfare.[4] And when the Commission finally proposed a new list in May 2020, it chose to adhere closely to the FATF list.[5]

The story of the Commission's failed blacklist illustrates the importance of institutional context for understanding how international organizations (IOs) can use informational signals to generate unofficial market enforcement.[6] The EU, despite being broadly committed to anti–money laundering policy, was unable to go further than the FATF's effort. As a monitoring body, the Commission lacked the FATF's expertise and legitimacy to justify a more expansive list. Moreover, the EU's three-branch structure meant that the Commission's proposal was subject to approval from the European Parliament and the Council; its actions were less insulated from political concerns. This latter point is particularly important because, unlike the FATF, the EU's list explicitly requires market action against listed countries.[7] The EU's requisite market punishment and its openness to lobbying meant that EU bureaucrats could not move beyond the FATF's list without encountering significant pushback, which ultimately destroyed the whole endeavor.

The theory developed in this chapter describes in general terms the conditions under which an IO can use unofficial market enforcement to incentivize policy improvements. Market enforcement is "unofficial" when an IO drives market decision-making through an informational signal or focal point rather than direct coercion. Focal points, as first articulated by Thomas Schelling in *The Strategy of Conflict*, provide a shared expectation about how to behave.[8] Building on Schelling's work, the theory argues that an IO can establish its salience by developing comparative advantages in information provision, leveraging economic coercion (or other tools of power), and enhancing its own perceived legitimacy. Narrowing the focus to focal points and market actors, the theory addresses how IOs and states can reconfigure market incentives to encourage complementary decision-making.[9] For an IO, influencing market behavior via focal point effects rather than explicit economic coercion has numerous strategic advantages. It reduces enforcement costs and is a more effective pathway for generating long-term policy improvements.

Unofficial market enforcement improves compliance. Cross-border banking patterns activate new domestic constituencies to support comprehensive policy reform. Building on accounts that emphasize the domestic effects of cross-border networks (Keck and Sikkink 1998; Risse-Kappen 1995) and the ways in which international soft law restructures politics (Farrell and Newman 2015; Newman and Posner 2016, 2018; Büthe and Mattli 2011), the theory emphasizes how unofficial market enforcement reconfigures legislative agendas and executive priorities. Because punishment does not come directly from an IO or a powerful country like the United States, policy reform advocates can argue for new laws or regulations without discussing the underlying coercive process. In this context, the politics of new legislation are much less contentious than if reform was directly tied to an explicit IO-sponsored coercive threat, thus producing deeper and more widespread policy change.

IO Focal Points and Institutional Prominence

IOs shape state expectations about how to interact in the international arena. Institutional rules, monitoring, and dispute settlement may all function as focal points in this context. International law, for example, can shape the resolution of territorial disputes by signaling each side's reservation point (Allee and Huth 2006; Huth et al. 2013). In a similar vein, international adjudication can resolve ambiguity about facts or underlying concepts (McAdams 2005; Powell and Mitchell 2007), or about how to interpret the terms of a bilateral or multilateral agreement (Ginsburg and McAdams 2004; Huth et al. 2011). In regulatory issue areas, nonbinding international standards may serve as focal points because they structure future incentives for cooperation.[10] Standards may offer countries a middle ground, producing policy harmonization by pulling toward leniency as well as stringency (Perlman 2020). Experimental tests of how information produces focal points have found that even random, nonstrategic signals can influence equilibrium outcomes in coordination games (McAdams and Nadler 2005);[11] this finding suggests that even noncostly IO signals (known in game theory as "cheap talk") may still influence state behavior.

IOs also shape norms about what constitutes "acceptable" behavior, serving as focal points for how states should interact or implement policy.[12] Both rationalist and constructivist scholars emphasize the importance of "common knowledge" in shaping cooperative outcomes (Katzenstein et al. 1998). Fearon (1998, 298) points out that international regimes are the result of repeated multilateral bargaining, and as such they may "legitimize focal principles" because they are "the concrete products of visions of world order." Even when IOs reflect shared understandings, this "common knowledge" may be shaped (and reshaped) by a highly political process of contestation between states (Finnemore and Sikkink 1998). Political institutions and concomitant norms of behavior can create a "civic culture" that generates consensus values and limits uncooperative behavior (Weingast 1997). Voeten (2005) demonstrates such a process in his analysis of the United Nations Security Council (UNSC), which he argues creates elite focal points about when the use of force is socially acceptable. Even when IO focal points are "constructed," in that an IO intentionally chooses and promotes a certain principle or policy, it may acquire normative significance (Garrett and Weingast 1993). Governance arrangements may also generate policy feedback effects, shaping actors' interests, resources, and capabilities over time (Pierson 1993, 2006; Newman and Posner 2016).

Interestingly, even IOs that are clearly politically biased may be able to serve as focal points. The United Nations Commission on Human Rights, for example, was disbanded after many years of allegations that its member states targeted adversaries and ignored abuses in their own countries. Despite such perceptions, Lebovic and Voeten (2009) show that the commission's judgments signaled to the international community which human rights violators were politically acceptable targets for cuts in multilateral aid.

If the literature is clear on the ways that an IO can serve as a focal point for states, little has been written on exactly how an IO becomes a focal point (Martin and Simmons 2012; Johnston 2001, 490). One likely reason for this oversight is that much of the work on IOs as focal points comes from legal scholars who examine issue areas where an international court or adjudication body explicitly serves as a focal point. In these cases, states have clearly anticipated that governments may implement rules in different ways and that these differences may create distributional costs across states. Delegating adjudication authority to an IO is thus an integral part of the regime, without which the IO might not exist.

IOs serve as focal points, however, across many different contexts, and in most cases, the link between institutional design and an IO's focal point status is much less clear. Governments act as though the World Bank's ease-of-doing-business index is a focal point for foreign investors (Pinheiro-Alves and Zambujal-Oliveira 2012; Schueth 2015; Kelley et al. 2019), but why should firms rely on this index as opposed to the *US News & World Report*'s "Open for Business" ranking? Israel responded strongly to the UN's Goldstone Report alleging possible war crimes[13] but largely ignored similar reports from Human Rights Watch. As the number of IOs governing each issue area continues to increase, the origins of IO focal points become even more important.

In Schelling's original discussion of how a focal point may help solve a coordination game, he notes that focal points are context dependent. People "can often concert their intentions or expectations with others" (Schelling 1960, 57) so that they arrive at the same solution, but doing so requires a focal point with some kind of prominence for all actors. A tourist who is asked to meet a stranger in New York City without any advance communication might pick Grand Central Station because of the location's prominence in Hollywood movies, but a student at New York University who is asked to meet another Lower Manhattan resident might pick the arch in Washington Square Park. Previous experiences and relationships determine what qualifies as a focal point.

Schelling's emphasis on salience suggests that an IO's ability to serve as a focal point for states and nonstate actors will depend on the degree to which it has first established itself as a prominent authority in a particular issue area. An IO is a prominent authority in an area when states and nonstate actors notice, and are motivated to follow or at least acknowledge, its rules or decisions. Hurd (1999) suggests three possible pathways by which an IO might motivate compliance: self-interest, coercion, and legitimacy. In a similar vein, this book argues that IOs can become salient focal points under three conditions: developing comparative informational advantages, drawing on coercive pressure, and enhancing institutional legitimacy. Informational advantages may enable agreements to be what Beth Simmons (2009, 116) describes as "self-enforcing": states continue to cooperate because the expected long-term benefits outweigh the present value of noncompliance.[14] Coercion and legitimacy, however, may also be important in establishing an IO's prominence, particularly if authority is viewed through a relational framework (Lake 2010). Each pathway is discussed in turn.

Condition 1: Informational Advantages

An IO's comparative informational advantages depend in large part on technical expertise and access to information.[15] States delegate authority to an IO in part to divide labor and take advantage of gains from specialization (Hawkins et al. 2006); as a result, IO secretariats may have the expertise and resources to perform tasks like rule clarification and policy monitoring better than many other international actors. In the process of carrying out daily responsibilities, IO experts can shape legal and even scientific knowledge (Bonneuil and Levidow 2011). In some contexts, this creates a feedback process where IO bureaucrats become the foremost experts on a new strand of international law. In the World Trade Organization (WTO), for example, states behave as though dispute settlement body decisions establish precedent, despite the fact that WTO precedent has no formal authority in international law (Busch 2007; Pelc 2014; Davis and Shirato 2007).

Although many IOs have technical experts, international soft law bodies in particular tend to embody this strength as they draw on bureaucratic networks to make agreements (Zaring 1998; Slaughter 2004; Brummer 2010, 2015). Soft law agreements rely on technocratic expertise to establish the legitimacy of nonbinding rules, as experts are presumed to know more and therefore be more legitimate sources of information and guidance than nonexperts (Jacobsson 2000). Networks of technical experts may also have unique material and ideational assets that help increase incentives for rule adoption and implementation (Andonova and Tuta 2014). Such networks can be drawn upon for monitoring and assessing state policy. The Organisation for Economic Co-operation and Development's (OECD) monitoring process, for example, relies on bureaucratic networks to assess state policies and motivate cooperation through a combination of peer review and peer pressure (Schafer 2006, 74).

IOs can also develop comparative advantages when it comes to accessing information about government policy. While state or nonstate actors may provide information about domestic policy when a government's noncompliance is highly visible (Dai 2007),[16] certain types of policy challenges make it easy for a government to hide uncooperative behavior. Regulatory agreements, for example, may be too complex and technical for nonexperts to monitor behavior, or they may require such extensive policy changes that outside observers cannot easily develop a comprehensive picture of compliance. Some international agreements also govern highly sensitive topics like weapons systems, where it is impossible for any third party to assess domestic compliance without significant cooperation from a monitored government. In these contexts, states may delegate monitoring powers to an IO to leverage the organization's specialized expertise, credibility, and legitimacy (Hawkins et al. 2006).

Condition 2: Coercive Pressure

IOs may also draw on coercive pressure to cement their prominence and salience. Realist scholars argue that IOs generally reflect the interests of powerful countries (Mearsheimer 1995), which may act as third-party enforcers for international rules. The United States has punished countries that violate the nuclear nonproliferation treaty and worked unilaterally to sanction would-be proliferators. Dominant economies like the United States and the EU may also use their economic clout to establish international regulatory standards and coerce recalcitrant states into cooperative behavior (Drezner 2007). Intergovernmental networks themselves can be a source of social power between states (Hafner-Burton and Montgomery 2006, 2009). Farrell and Newman (2019) highlight how powerful nations like the United States can weaponize regulatory networks to strategically gather information and deny network access to adversaries.

In some cases, an IO itself may have the ability to leverage financial resources as tools of coercion. If member states are willing to delegate such power to an IO, it is often a formal, legally binding IO with a standing charter and large secretariat, and powerful members typically retain some control over enforcement. The UNSC, for example, has the authority to impose sanctions on countries, companies, and individuals that violate its rules or resolutions. In recent years, the UNSC has used targeted sanctions to punish rule violators like Iran and North Korea; the UNSC's five permanent members, however, have veto power over such decisions. Another example is the IMF's use of conditionality, which requires would-be borrower countries to commit to certain policy reforms prior to receiving financial support. Conditionality allows the IMF to dictate monetary policy in borrower countries. Governments often require IMF funding to address balance of payment issues and therefore may be pressured into undertaking economic reforms that are domestically unpopular. The United States, however, has mechanisms to formally and informally control this process (Stone 2011).

A third, quite distinct, form of coercion occurs through market pressure. While member states and IOs may be able to leverage market incentives to coerce states, this form of coercion plays out differently from intergovernmental pressure or explicit IO punishment. Market actors like banks and investment firms make decisions based on their profit structures, which reflect the domestic and international regulatory environment. Governments or IOs can adopt policies to alter profit structures, as has occurred with the adoption of labor standards and laws against child labor, but such laws serve primarily as a framework for decision-making. Ultimately, market actors will decide for themselves how to do business. This separated decision structure has strengths and weaknesses from a compliance perspective. Market actors may enforce government rules even without government encouragement, as occurs in US state bond markets (Kelemen and Teo 2014), or may channel resources toward countries with gaps in regulation (Oates 1972). Because states and IOs do not fully control market pressure, however, this approach runs a high risk of unintended consequences.

While coercion is undoubtedly a powerful mechanism for increasing an IO's prominence, states may find it more effective to use explicit coercive pressure to establish a focal point rather than as a long-term cooperation solution. Explicit coercion is often too costly to be deployed on a continuous basis. When states leverage economic penalties or deny market access to recalcitrant states, they incur political, financial, and social costs.[17] Indeed, this is one of the most fundamental differences between direct coercion, even when it occurs through markets, and the unofficial market enforcement process described in this book. When powerful countries use an IO to coerce behavioral change in weaker states, they often incur significant political costs. The United States' push for UNSC sanctions against Iraq in the 1990s not only failed to motivate cooperation from Iraqi leader Saddam Hussein, it also caused a massive humanitarian crisis that generated significant international backlash against the UN and the United States. Similarly, the FATF's early attempts to generate compliance improvements through explicit coercive pressure were widely criticized as illegitimate and, as a result, targeted only a small number of states. In contrast to these examples, unofficial market enforcement provides IO member states with political cover and plausible deniability.

Given the consequences and costs of explicit coercion, states may use it as a short-term solution to draw attention to rules and generate normative change. Cooter (1998) shows that law can create new norms without shifting individual moral values; people internalize the norms because there are rational advantages to acting in accordance with the law. Similarly, when an IO's policies are supported with coercive pressure, states and nonstate actors may shift their approach to a policy issue to align more closely with the IO's mission. This normative shift may last even absent coercive pressure, particularly if the possibility of such pressure remains present.

Condition 3: Institutional Legitimacy

An IO's prominence in a particular issue area is also linked to legitimacy. IOs are legitimate to the extent that their actions are perceived as "desirable, proper, or appropriate within some socially constructed system of norms, values, beliefs, and definitions" (Suchman 1995, 574). When an IO has stronger legitimacy, state decision-making is more likely to be influenced by a "logic of appropriateness" where governments follow rules because they have internalized an IO's associated norms and roles.[18] For an IO, legitimacy is an important subcomponent of prominence because coercion and self-interest are often insufficient for sustaining long-term cooperation: self-interest can change as circumstances change and coercive threats may not always be credible (Buchanan and Keohane 2006, 410). Legitimacy will be particularly important if an IO's rules require costly policy changes that run counter to a state's political or economic interests. Kelley (2009, 61) argues that legitimacy makes it more difficult for governments to ignore the results of international monitoring, enhancing both international and domestic pressure on monitored states.

Legitimacy enhances an IO's authority over states. This book follows Lake (2009a, 55) in adopting a relational definition of authority, where an IO possesses authority to the degree that states "acknowledge an obligation to comply" with its rules. As Lake notes, authority may be reinforced by coercion, but even in such cases, the perception that coercion is used legitimately will affect the overall level of satisfaction with an authority structure. When an IO is viewed as legitimate, states have internalized its norms and begun to define their own interests in accordance with the IO's rules and framework (Hurd 1999).

IO legitimacy may evolve over time as a by-product of participation. Actors can "enter into new relationships for instrumental reasons but develop identities and rules as a result of their experience" (March and Olsen 1998, 953). Bernstein and Cashore (2007) describe such a process in their analysis of nonstate market-driven governance, where strategic, self-interested logic dominates the initiation of governance mechanisms but a combination of norms and self-interest establish political legitimacy and cement the governance infrastructure. Political legitimacy is crucial to this process because it works in part to silence dissent: as Chinkin (1989, 866) points out, even nonbinding international standards can make it difficult for opposition forces to argue that behavior in conformity with standards is illegitimate.

IO legitimacy may also reflect an institution's unique strengths and weaknesses. IOs with significant expertise, accountability, and transparency are more likely to be perceived as legitimate (Karlsson-Vinkhuyzen and Vihma 2009). Eckersley (2007) argues that legitimacy should also be tied to institutional effectiveness. But adopting such an outcome-oriented measure may pose challenges in an area like international finance. Capital markets are not abstract entities that follow objective scientific criteria but rather are embedded in a social, cultural, and moral context (De Goede 2005). Since the 9/11 terrorist attacks, US and other Western policy makers have increasingly viewed Islamic finance as less legitimate and operating outside "normal" financial spheres (De Goede 2007; Warde 2007); as a result, Islamic countries have sought to create a regulatory framework for Islamic finance that reproduces much of the existing financial governance structures (Rethel 2011). Tying legitimacy to effectiveness in such contexts is challenging because no clear criteria exist for judging a regime's impact. Instead, some scholars argue for a process-oriented approach to legitimacy: inclusive, democratic policy-making processes are more likely to lead to efficient and legitimate policies (Underhill and Zhang 2008).

An IO can also take steps to strengthen its legitimacy. It may strengthen democratic accountability, giving voice and representation to a wider cross-section of states. The United Nations has taken this approach on several occasions, expanding Security Council membership from 11 to 15 countries in 1965, and expanding representation on the UN Economic and Social Council from 18 to 27 countries in 1965, and then later from 27 to 54 countries.[19] An IO may also try to build a normative basis for its legitimacy, relying on "norm entrepreneurs" to call attention to issues and construct cognitive frames in a way that aligns with the IO's mission and operations.[20] Finally, an IO may double down on technocracy in order to legitimate itself through bureaucratic authority. Barnett and Finnemore (1999, 707), drawing on earlier work from Weber, emphasize that bureaucracies gain power from both "the normative appeal of rational-legal authority in modern life and the bureaucracy's control over technical expertise and information." Bureaucratic expertise is, by its very nature, knowledge that is asserted to be correct, and because it is highly technical, nonexperts have difficulty challenging such claims (Hülsse and Kerwer 2007). Soft law bodies that govern global finance often work to develop technocratic authority as a source of legitimacy.

IO Focal Points and Market Actors

An IO's ability to establish itself as a prominent authority in a particular area depends in part on context. As noted earlier, focal points are rarely universally salient, but rather reflect the qualities and experiences of specific individuals (Schelling 1960, 58). An IO may develop informational advantages, coercive pressure, and legitimacy with states but not nonstate actors; in such cases, it will exert influence primarily through governmental channels like laws and regulation rather than by changing market behavior or increasing civil society activism. In the early years of the UNSC's targeted sanctions against Al-Qaeda, for example, many governments failed to issue domestic regulations requiring financial institutions to freeze the assets of listed individuals; as a result, the sanctions had a limited impact.[21] Conversely, an IO may be more salient for nonstate actors than for states, increasing incentives for pro-compliance mobilization (Hafner-Burton and Tsutsui 2005) or even leading to activism on both sides (Chaudoin 2016).

An IO's salience for market actors depends on how its rules or information link to profits. In a capitalist economy, firm decision-making is, at least in theory, dominated by profit maximization: a firm weighs the costs and benefits of different policies and chooses the path that offers the most financial gains. But firm decision-making is embedded in a larger cultural and political context, where domestic laws and international standards shape market incentive structures.

International standards or rules can serve as focal points for firm decision-making. Soft law allows governments to coordinate domestic policies (Deeg and O'Sullivan 2009; Dehousse 1997; Raustiala 2002; Slaughter 2004) and may also empower a subset of domestic regulators in ways that shift domestic policy (Newman and Posner 2015, 2018; Farrell and Newman 2014). International standards themselves also reflect the preferences of market actors and signal their shared expectations about acceptable behavior (Baker 2010; Laurence 2001; Kurzer 1993; Tsingou 2008, 2015; Underhill and Zhang 2008).[22] Networks of regulators may operate as a type of "epistemic community" with common knowledge and shared norms (Kapstein 1989; Raustiala 2002; Slaughter 2004), leading financial institutions to follow espoused standards because they represent best practices or because they face competitive market pressures to conform (Zaring 2019).

Even as international rules shape market decision-making, they often also create new uncertainty surrounding implementation. Mosley (2003b) points out that for market actors to follow international standards, they must be aware of them and understand their value. But states may have strategic reasons for opting for ambiguous standards. Ambiguous rules are well suited to dealing with complex problems and an uncertain policy environment, and may even be a source of power for institutional actors (Best 2005, 2012).[23] Unfortunately for regulated market actors, ambiguous rules introduce significant implementation challenges. Increasing rule complexity over time intensifies this problem. Even when firms or investors accept a guideline's general desirability, they may be uncertain about how to implement it in line with existing business practices. Uncertainty can be particularly problematic for firms if they also face large, indeterminate costs from failing to align business practices with international standards. Such costs could occur due to an overt policy failure, such as a bank taking on too much liquidity risk and failing to meet short-term financial demands, or due to a problematic corporate policy that government regulators subsequently uncover.

Market Decision-Making among Uncertainty

Market actors like banks and investors operate amid significant uncertainty, regardless of government regulation. Information asymmetries and incentives to misrepresent are common across financial markets.[24] Moreover, market actors cannot rely exclusively on their own judgments because markets are interdependent—profitability depends in part on the actions of others. An international investor who evaluates sovereign debt risk differently from other investors will only gain from this judgment if others eventually realize their mistake; otherwise, he may be left holding government bonds that no one is willing to purchase. In many areas of finance, market actors are engaged in this type of guessing game, where each company or investor is trying to anticipate what other companies, banks, or investors will think or do.[25]

Regulatory ambiguity can intensify market uncertainty, particularly when rule ambiguity is combined with uncertain but significant risks or penalties. A sizable literature in finance distinguishes between situations of risk (characterized by clear prospects with varying levels of known probabilities) and situations of uncertainty, where policy options are indeterminate and probabilities are unknown.[26] Individuals prefer known-probability risks and dislike uncertainty (Ellsberg 1961), creating ambiguity aversion. The nature of ambiguity aversion depends in part on the likelihood of uncertain events, the domain of the outcome, and the source of uncertainty (Trautmann and Van de Kuilen 2015). Experimental studies show that ambiguity aversion increases when peers observe an individual's actions (Curley et al. 1986; Trautmann et al. 2008) and is present in simulations of financial market trading (Sarin and Weber 1993; Kocher and Trautmann 2013).

In the context of international finance, ambiguous rules and uncertain penalties can cause market actors to take steps to avoid ambiguity. Firms or investors may avoid entire categories of customers or business transactions if potential upsides are few and downsides are high. Ambiguous rules can thus lead to a type of "hyperimplementation" where firms, banks, or investors overcomply with obligations to minimize certain types of risks. Such a process has occurred in the banking sector as banks try to comply with international and domestic regulations on reducing illicit financing risk. Guidelines provide no clear standard for judging illicit financing risk, and so some large banks have opted to just "de-risk" from low-yield customers. UK and US banks, for example, have closed the accounts of Somali money transfer operators, which channel critical remittances that support the Somali economy. Somali money transfer operations have struggled to find banks willing to open accounts, and existing providers have delayed or blocked transfers with little explanation (El Taraboulsi-McCarthy 2018).

Market actors may also reduce ambiguity by searching for a shared standard of behavior. A significant body of literature has highlighted the importance of focal points for financial markets.[27] Without a central organizing principle, each market participant runs the risk that their interpretation will differ significantly from others and put them at the risk of public shaming, censure, or punitive consequences. When market actors need information about country performance, IO monitoring and assessment is well suited to fill this demand.

IO Monitoring and Global Performance Indicators

IOs monitor and assess state policy across a variety of contexts, producing everything from detailed, lengthy monitoring reports to country ratings and blacklists. While all types of IO monitoring can provide useful information, ratings and performance indicators are likely to be particularly effective at reducing ambiguity. A key aspect of any focal point is that it must provide a *unique* signal about expected behavior (Schelling 1960). In today's information-abundant environment, how an IO sends a signal may be as important as the actual content of information. If an IO is evaluating state conduct, a precise and unambiguous report about the quality of domestic policy is likely to have a much stronger impact than a detailed but unquantifiable report. Precision facilitates comparisons across countries (Kelley and Simmons 2019). It also reduces uncertainty about a state's specific behavior and about how others are likely to view the state. This reduction in uncertainty about others' views is important because, for information to generate a focal point, observers must update their own beliefs and their beliefs about others' beliefs—what Dafoe et al. (2014, 374) term "first-order" and "second-order" beliefs.[28]

IOs can enhance the precision of monitoring through the use of global performance indicators—regularized, publicized reporting routines that facilitate peer comparisons, such as indexes, categorical assessments, or blacklists (Kelley and Simmons 2019). Evaluation exercises often shape outcomes through participant reactivity: the very act of being evaluated tends to lead to behavior change (Espeland and Saunder 2007). Recent research suggests that global ranking and performance indicators can be influential tools of social pressure (Kelley and Simmons 2015, 2019; Cooley and Snyder 2015). Empirical analyses of the effects of global performance indicators illustrate their impact across diverse policy domains, including education (Bisbee et al. 2019; Kijima and Lipscy 2020), development (Honig and Weaver 2019; Skagerlind 2020), business (Kelley et al. 2019), political and civil liberties (Roberts and Tellez 2020), labor rights (Koliev et al. 2020), terrorism (Jo et al. 2020), and human trafficking (Kelley and Simmons 2015; Kelley 2017).[29] By design, global performance assessments are likely to lead to "uncertainty absorption" (March and Simon 1958): although an IO may have assembled an index from a large body of evidence, the final product communicates only the IO's inferences, not the original data. Unlike long, detailed monitoring reports that leave ample room for interpretation, audiences can use indicators and ratings as heuristics that guide decision-making in predictable ways. Through quantification, IO evaluations appear more certain and objective (Merry 2011, S84).

This process of uncertainty absorption masks the degree to which focal points are constructed and privilege certain norms and conceptions over others.[30] Martin and Simmons (2012, 335) highlight this point, writing that "international rules and the forums in which actors hammer them out in turn become key focal points for discursive struggles over legitimate political agency and action (internationally and domestically)." Even when states institutionalize preexisting norms, such efforts often mask divergent normative understandings and underlying power dynamics. Formal rules may be biased in a way that privileges powerful countries. Informal agreements between IO member states may also provide channels for powerful countries like the United States to have unusual amounts of influence over top priorities (Stone 2011). These formal and informal power dynamics mean that IO monitoring of noncompliance often reflects underlying power dynamics.

Focal points can be understood as tools of informational power even under conditions of strict delegation. While states may opt to delegate authority to an independent IO body in order to reduce direct state control (Abbott and Snidal 2000), even technocratic processes can reflect normative power dynamics. As Susan Engle Merry writes in her article on the expansion of indicators in global governance, monitoring can obscure what is fundamentally a political decision. Outcomes appear "as forms of knowledge rather than as particular representations of a methodology and particular political decisions about what to measure and what to call it" (Merry 2011, S88). Gross domestic product becomes the primary indicator of a country's wealth. Freedom House's conceptualization of "free" begins to characterize a liberal democracy. The initial debate over an indicator's concept or underlying data is lost, and the indicator begins to seem like unbiased empirical knowledge.[31]

Unofficial Market Enforcement and Compliance with International Rules

Why would states rely on an IO focal point to harness market power rather than opting for direct economic coercion? At first glance, this choice might seem puzzling. The causal chain linking an IO focal point, unofficial market enforcement, and compliance improvements rests on two hard-won scope conditions: (1) a prominent IO and (2) market demand for country-specific information. Each condition requires states to invest significant time and resources in supporting an IO's mission internationally and domestically. In contrast, powerful economies like the United States and the European Union might quickly leverage their market power to coerce bilateral policy change or pressure an IO to sanction uncooperative countries. Indeed, in the months after the 9/11 terrorist attacks, the US government pursued this approach, giving the US Department of the Treasury the power to designate and impose countermeasures against foreign jurisdictions and institutions of "primary money laundering concern" (Zarate 2013, 151).[32]

Yet direct coercion has clear downsides for states. Governments pay economic, political, and normative costs for penalizing or stigmatizing other states. Unilateral action risks isolating a country or being ineffective, while multilateral action may require the leading state to make a costly demonstration of commitment (Martin 1992). Both types of action force governments to weigh the benefits of coercion on a specific policy issue against other important priorities. For these reasons, states acting in isolation or through an IO are often reluctant to rely on strong coercive pressure to force policy change. Even the United States, which holds disproportionate market power and influence, has relied on market pressure more indirectly than overtly. Dominant economies shape international regulation in ways that favor their own preferred standards, and other states follow because they do not want to lose market access rather than because they are overtly threatened (Kapstein 1992, 1994; Simmons 2001; Singer 2007; Oatley and Nabors 1998).

If powerful economies opt to coordinate official coercion via multilateralism, they face two additional challenges that may limit the effectiveness or impact of such action. First, IO member states must agree on how to distribute consequences for noncompliance. Larger consequences will correlate with more contested negotiations. Interstate relations depend on cooperation across many different issues areas; many states are reluctant to disrupt bilateral relations unless a policy issue is highly salient or the target country is relatively unimportant. Member states will also fight to avert or weaken economic penalties against their allies. For these reasons, formal IO enforcement is likely to be relatively weak and target only a small number of states.

Second, when powerful countries rely on direct multilateral coercion to drive compliance improvements, they are also likely to encounter significant resistance from the targets of coercion. For some types of cooperation problems, states share similar preferences; as a result, institutional rules are likely to reflect convergence and states will comply easily with such mandates. Indeed, a primary insight of institutionalist literature is that international institutions are designed according to the interests of states, and as a result, the rules themselves provide incentives to comply (Keohane 1984). But powerful countries may exert disproportionate influence over rules, such that many countries find themselves subject to standards that do not reflect their priorities or are beyond their capabilities. While domestic interest group behavior and transnational civil society activism can support compliance with international commitments in issue areas like the environment (Raustiala 1997; Von Stein 2008; Dai 2007) and human rights (Keck and Sikkink 1998; Simmons 2009; Hafner-Burton and Tsutsui 2005; Risse and Sikkink 1999), interest groups can also oppose compliance (Downs and Rocke 1995; Rosendorff and Milner 2001) or work in both directions (Chaudoin 2016).

Strong external pressure does not automatically reconfigure domestic preferences. Targeted governments may become more entrenched in their views or complain that they are being victimized by powerful countries. They will lobby for IO enforcement to cease and attempt to negotiate a new interpretation of compliance. Targeted countries may also engage in "cosmetic compliance," adopting minimal reforms in order to appear compliant but avoiding deep policy change (Chey 2014).

Unofficial market enforcement overcomes several of these downsides. When states rely on an IO's monitoring scheme or rating indices to generate shifts in market behavior, they reduce their own enforcement costs. They also harness market forces to reconfigure domestic politics in ways that support compliance. While unofficial market enforcement is not without downsides, it has the potential to be a potent driver of widespread and deep policy reform.

Overcoming Enforcement Costs

IO secretariats and member states face fewer enforcement costs for influencing behavior via international monitoring as compared to direct coercion. IO monitoring and assessment is relatively low stakes for most states. Because

IOs have monitoring powers across a wide variety of issue areas, government bureaucrats are usually familiar with monitoring procedures. Moreover, these procedures often have high levels of legitimacy because IO secretariat officials work to develop technical expertise and become resources for policy implementation. While monitored countries may still want to avoid the reputational harm of being "named and shamed," they are unlikely to expend significant resources to lobby the IO for a better rating. If lobbying does occur, it may even facilitate information exchange and norm transfer because the monitored government is engaged with bureaucrats rather than politicians.[33]

Because of its technocratic nature, IO monitoring gives states and IO bureaucrats some amount of political cover for negative country assessments. Even if an evaluated state is unhappy with its rating, IO bureaucrats and member state governments can respond that the assessment is purely informational. In contrast, when an IO or a group of countries authorizes direct coercive action, the targeted country has a better claim to argue that it has been victimized and to challenge the legitimacy of such endeavors. While states may be willing to pay the enforcement costs of such action if it pertains to extremely high-value political issues (like nuclear proliferation) or for non-allies, governments are often unwilling to spend political capital on punishing friendly states for other types of cooperation problems.

IO monitoring may also reduce enforcement costs because it influences targeted state behavior indirectly, functioning as a type of indirect speech. Indirect speech occurs when a speaker "communicates to the hearer more than he actually says by way of relying on their mutually shared background information, both linguistic and non-linguistic, together with the general powers of rationality and inference on the part of the hearer" (Searle 1975, 61). Indirect speech is particularly common in situations characterized by a mixture of cooperation and conflict, such as international diplomacy. It provides speakers with plausible deniability and helps preserve social relationships, even in the case where an indirect request is clearly understood (Pinker et al. 2008).[34] When an IO relies on its monitoring (rather than explicit coercion) to drive market behavior, monitoring becomes a type of indirect speech that signals potential financial consequences but limits the political enforcement costs for sender states.[35]

Reconfiguring the Domestic Politics of Compliance

Unofficial market enforcement is powerful in part because of its impact on domestic politics. Existing literature has highlighted how global market actors react to information about country performance (Mosley 2003a; Tomz 2007; Schueth 2015) and how IO signals can change market behavior (Kucik and Pelc 2016; Bechtel and

Schneider 2010). When market actors rely on an IO's signal about country performance and reallocate resources based on this information, they serve as de facto enforcers for the IO's rules. Unofficial market pressure via the cross-border banking network is particularly effective at reconfiguring domestic interests.

In nearly every country in the world, the banking sector is a powerful political and economic actor. Either through central banks or private-sector lending, domestic banks typically have direct access to the leader's "winning coalition," that is, those people whose support is essential to maintaining power (Bueno de Mesquita et al. 2003). As banks have become increasingly reliant on international business to generate profits, these actors have become more sensitive to noneconomic (political) considerations and influences (Cohen 1986, 59). If international banks rely on an IO focal point to make decisions about resource allocation across countries, this unofficial enforcement process can transform domestic politics.

Unofficial market enforcement via cross-border banking is likely to reconfigure domestic politics through three channels. First, banks themselves are more likely to advocate for policy change. Second, key bureaucratic actors like central banks or finance ministries are more interested in pursuing compliance. Third, rising bank costs increase costs across numerous economic sectors, broadening the pro-compliance coalition. Each point is addressed in turn.

When an IO's monitoring report leads international banks to raise the costs of business for domestic banks in noncompliant countries, this action creates strong incentives for the domestic banking community to lobby for policy change. To operate in the modern economy, banks need to be connected with banks in other countries. If international banks start to close correspondent accounts or hike up costs, the banking sector has a strong motivation to push the government to adopt new laws or procedures in order to improve the country's image. Many countries in the world have a banking association, which serves as a lobbyist for industry interests. The banking industry may lobby the legislature directly or approach officials at the ministry of finance, central bank, or regulatory agencies. Regional banking associations may also lobby governments. While the political influence of the banking sector may vary across countries (Grossman and Woll 2014), its intensive lobbying in support of compliance is likely to shift a government's policy calculations.

Second, bank-to-bank enforcement may lead parts of the government, such as the central bank or the ministry of finance, to advocate for new policies. In some cases, these parts of the bureaucracy may already be supportive of policy reform. Central banks and finance ministries are connected through bureaucratic networks, which can provide incentives for policy emulation (Slaughter 2004).

Transnational standards may also serve as a political resource for reform-minded domestic actors who are dissatisfied with the status quo (Newman and Posner 2016). Central banks also have incentives to monitor and proactively address any processes that could reduce economic growth. Grittersová (2014, 2017) argues that the presence of reputable foreign banks in developing countries decreases investor uncertainty and has positive reputational spillovers that affect sovereign bond markets. If reputable international banks change their lending habits, close branches, or restrict lending, such processes may negatively affect sovereign spreads. As a result, a central bank may lobby the executive to take steps to avoid restrictions on cross-border banking.

Third, bank-to-bank enforcement may mobilize a cross-section of additional economic actors. International rules can impose compliance costs on both government and private industry. In the realm of international finance, compliance costs are likely to be particularly diffuse because financial institutions act as intermediaries, linking many sectors of the economy. Chey (2014, 16) notes that diffuse costs may be an important reason why governments fail to implement international standards—if numerous, politically influential sectors view international regulations as damaging, they will mobilize against effective compliance. But the flip side of this argument is also true. If IO monitoring acts as a catalyst for bank-to-bank enforcement, the IO will (indirectly) impose costs across the economy. This is particularly true when US and European banks are the external enforcers. Although globalization allows capital to move freely across borders, local currencies operate within a clear hierarchy, where the US dollar and the euro are the most important modes of exchange (Cohen 1998, 2011).[36] If market enforcement causes domestic banks to lose easy access to such currencies, the costs of business will increase across the economy. The business community may find it more costly to engage in trade or more difficult to attract foreign direct investment. Migrants abroad may encounter difficulties sending remittances back to a home country. Faced with such challenges, these constituencies will advocate that the government change its policies.

Unofficial market enforcement via global banking profoundly alters the incentives of punished governments. As global financial institutions restrict business with banks in targeted countries, the targeted country's financial industry has strong incentives to demand more government regulation. Banks advocate for more oversight because they need the government to signal to foreign banks, investors, and firms that the risks have decreased. While a single bank can (and often does) put in place its own systems to reduce risk, an individual bank can rarely send a credible signal to outside audiences. Banks have incentives to misrepresent their own risk management practices; in the face of such uncertainty, external financial actors will act to reduce their own risk exposure. If a government changes its policies, however, this action sends a positive signal to banks around the world.

Countries will vary in how susceptible they are to unofficial market enforcement. Because domestic banks typically suffer the earliest costs from changes in international banking, countries that are highly integrated into international markets via global banking are likely to be the most responsive to market pressure. This link between bank pressure, market integration, and policy change occurs not because such countries suffer the most from market enforcement but rather because the banking sector tends to have more influence in countries with many cross-border transactions. The banking industry often has ties to the government because it plays a central role in the global economy; larger banking sectors are more likely to exert influence over government policy (Pepinsky 2013). Governments may be particularly inclined to listen to the financial sector because international banking failures can generate outsized ripple effects.

Higher levels of market integration could correlate with domestic policy in several ways. Domestic political pressures influence a government's basic approach to financial internationalization (Haggard and Maxfield 1996; Brooks 2004; Chwieroth 2007), which suggests that a stronger banking sector might advocate for more financial openness. Conversely, if a government is working to expand its banking sector and integrate more closely with international finance, it may invest in policies that match best practices or consensual knowledge (Kapstein 1989; Slaughter 2004).[37] Regulators in developed economies may also help shape international regulatory standards, as part of an effort to balance the objectives of financial stability and competitiveness (Singer 2007). Regardless of whether market integration causes or results from the banking sector's influence, market integration should make countries more susceptible to unofficial market enforcement.

Reputation Costs and Spillover Effects

For IO member states, a secondary benefit of relying on an IO focal point to influence market behavior is that the focal point may impose additional reputation costs on noncompliant states. A substantial body of literature has highlighted the role of "naming and shaming" in international politics.[38] Kelley (2017, 12) suggests comprehensive rating exercises have more validity than typical naming-and-shaming approaches because they focus on all countries, facilitate comparisons, reward positive behavior, and subject countries to recurrent evaluations. An IO may also opt to combine comprehensive monitoring with stigmatization of noncompliant countries, creating a more legitimate and precise focal point for outside observers. This approach may generate reputation costs at the bureaucratic level, as regulators lose prestige with counterparts in other countries, or for the country more generally (Kelley and Simmons 2019). Stigmatization or direct blacklisting may also generate a "lowest-common-denominator" effect (Morse 2019), where countries suffer additional reputational damage from being grouped together with particularly problematic states.

An IO focal point could also drive policy change through positive spillover effects. Just as international rules and standards signal acceptable behavior, so too can monitoring clarify which states are interpreting the rules correctly. Even non–publicly identified governments may make policy improvements under such conditions, either because government bureaucrats have more information about best practices or because they want to avoid the possibility of future stigmatization. Focal points might also reshape global norms, leading policy makers to internalize new standards of behavior and proactively change their policies.

Summary of Theory

The theory articulated in this chapter illustrates why unofficial market enforcement can be such a powerful tool for driving policy change. When market actors use an IO focal point to make decisions about resource allocation—and effectively penalize countries that fail to meet international rules—the costs of noncompliance increase. Domestic politics shifts, and governments have new incentives to comply.

Figure 2.1 illustrates the theory's complete causal chain. An IO sends an unambiguous signal about which countries are failing to meet international rules. Based on this information, market actors move resources away from (or charge higher transaction rates to) identified noncompliant countries. Domestic market actors in these countries suffer financial costs and become motivated to lobby for policy change. Governments, in turn, seek improved compliance with the IO's rules or standards.

The figure also highlights two scope conditions of the theory. In order for an IO monitoring report or blacklist to serve as a focal point, the IO must first establish its prominence or salience in a given policy arena. An IO may develop comparative advantages in information provision and take steps to enhance its technocratic expertise. It may also reinforce the importance of its rules through coercive pressure. Finally, it may enhance its authority by strengthening institutional legitimacy. Taken together, these three mechanisms help cement an IO's prominence within an issue area.

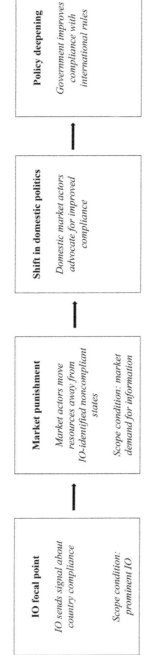

IO focal point

IO sends signal about country compliance

Scope condition: prominent IO

Market punishment

Market actors move resources away from IO-identified noncompliant states

Scope condition: market demand for information

Shift in domestic politics

Domestic market actors advocate for improved compliance

Policy deepening

Government improves compliance with international rules

FIGURE 2.1. A theory of unofficial market enforcement

Note: The figure illustrates how an IO may use unofficial market enforcement to incentivize compliance with its rules or standards. In order for an IO focal point to influence market behavior, the IO must first establish itself as a prominent or salient actor. In order for market actors to punish IO-identified noncompliant states, market actors must have unfulfilled demand for information about country compliance.

The second scope condition highlights the importance of market incentives. In order for market actors to integrate an IO focal point into their profit calculations, market actors must have an unfulfilled demand for information about country compliance. In some issue areas, market demand might arise organically because an IO's rules are complementary to market decision-making. In other areas, regulatory and reputational incentives might shift the underlying profit structure and encourage market actors to seek out new information. Regardless of the reason, market actors must need information about country compliance and also face barriers to finding such information on their own.

Conclusion: The Power of Unofficial Market Enforcement

States seeking to improve cooperation in a given issue area have numerous options for influencing other countries. Powerful countries can unilaterally pressure laggard states to change their policies. Countries can also use multilateral venues to punish uncooperative behavior and coerce compliance improvements. But both bilateral and multilateral pressure often stall under the weight of enforcement costs. Governments are willing to sacrifice economic or political capital only for top political priorities and only against a small subset of countries. As a result, when states or IOs rely on these traditional mechanisms to improve compliance with international rules, policy change tends to be shallow and concentrated in only a few states.

This chapter lays out an alternate path where member states drive cooperation via unofficial market enforcement. This pathway requires member states to invest initially in establishing an IO's salience by working to increase its informational advantages, cement its authority with coercion, and improve its legitimacy. It also requires governments to adopt regulation that reconfigures market incentives to support an IO's mission. Under these conditions, IO focal points can harness the power of market processes indirectly and to great effect. While all market actors can influence domestic policy, unofficial enforcement via the banking sector is particularly effective at reconfiguring domestic politics and increasing incentives for policy change. The next chapter applies these insights to international cooperation on combating money laundering and terrorist financing, illustrating how focal point effects and market enforcement have transformed the policy landscape in this issue area.

3

THE FATF'S FIGHT AGAINST ILLICIT FINANCING

The Sinaloa cartel is one of the most powerful drug operations in the world. Based in Mexico, the multi-billion-dollar syndicate spans two continents, stretching from New York City to Buenos Aires. The organization moves cocaine, synthetic drugs, and opioids with ease across countries and borders, aided by its close ties to the Mexican government and security establishment.[1] In addition to drug trafficking, it is known for having committed crimes of unimaginable brutality—a trend that has only increased since Mexican police arrested and extradited the cartel's former head Joaquin "El Chapo" Guzman to the United States in 2017.[2] In 2018, the Sinaloa cartel and competitor syndicates in Mexico were responsible for more than thirty-three thousand drug-related homicides, including the deaths of at least 130 Mexican candidates and politicians.[3]

Mexico's problems with organized crime have been well known for decades. A 2007 Congressional Research Service report describes how Mexican cartels dominate the illegal drugs market in the United States and details efforts by then president Felipe Calderon to request US assistance to stop money laundering (Cook 2007). Despite this established knowledge, however, British banking giant HSBC allowed Mexican funds to flow unchecked through its banking network for years. When US regulators finally discovered HSBC's lack of oversight, they found that the Sinaloa cartel and the Colombia-based Norte de Valle syndicate had used HSBC to launder at least USD 881 million. The US government fined HSBC USD 1.256 billion—the largest anti–money laundering penalty in US history.[4]

One of HSBC's most notable failures was how the company evaluated Mexico's illicit financing risk. International and domestic regulations require banks to scrutinize transactions with clients in high-risk countries, that is, those countries that pose a significant risk of money laundering or terrorist financing. Given the influence and power of cartels like the Sinaloa, HSBC clearly should have put Mexico into a medium- or high-risk category. But instead, HSBC placed Mexico into its lowest-risk category, allowing billions to move with little oversight or monitoring.[5]

HSBC's failure to screen its business risks in Mexico reflects the conflicting incentives that banks face when it comes to illicit financing.[6] Money laundering is a source of significant revenue, particularly for banks that operate in countries with large offshore sectors or criminal enterprises. But moving dirty money is also potentially costly. Regulators can levy fines and shareholders can punish public failures. In the aftermath of the HSBC scandal, the bank's share price lagged, diverging from much of the banking industry and only returning to 2011 levels in 2017.[7] Large international banks cannot avoid risk entirely since most major economies have some degree of illicit financing risk. Instead, they must make their own judgments about risk and create compliance systems that maximize profits but also demonstrate an attempt to minimize money laundering and terrorist financing.

The Financial Action Task Force (FATF) and its member states understand this conflicting incentive structure. FATF and domestic implementing regulations allow banks flexibility in how they assess each country's illicit financing risk profile,[8] even as government regulators sometimes levy penalties for failing to comply with anti–money laundering rules. Rather than telling banks directly how to mitigate such risks, the FATF directs market attention via its noncomplier list. Prior to creating the new noncomplier list, the FATF spent years developing its technocratic expertise and monitoring system, cementing its authority via coercive pressure, and enhancing its legitimacy. These institutional strengths allow the FATF to send a signal that cannot be ignored, providing a guidepost for how banks should identify high-risk countries.

The FATF noncomplier list drives the banking sector to engage in unofficial market enforcement. Ostensibly, the list has little coercive power, but banks use it as a focal point for identifying which countries to scrutinize. As banks restrict financial flows to individuals and firms in listed countries, this unofficial market enforcement process raises the costs of continued noncompliance.[9] Banks and businesses in listed countries find themselves suddenly facing higher costs and potential long-term consequences for government inaction. These actors cannot afford to be cut off from the international financial system, and so they become advocates for policy change, forcing governments to change their laws.

The FATF's reliance on unofficial market enforcement has numerous advantages over direct financial coercion. It reduces enforcement costs for the FATF member states, as compared to the FATF's previous coercive listing procedure. When an international organization (IO) takes action against an uncooperative country, the country's government is likely to lobby aggressively both the IO secretariat and member states to avoid any punitive measures. Countries with powerful allies may be able to avoid an IO's rules or enforcement actions (Stone 2011). In the illicit financing context, however, listed countries cannot directly lobby the FATF to stop market enforcement because the FATF is only indirectly responsible for the process. The FATF does not require banks to restrict capital to most countries on its noncomplier list; banks take this step on their own. The unofficial nature of the process means that the FATF's member states pay fewer enforcement costs and that listed countries are more likely to engage in deep policy change in order to be removed from the list.

This chapter describes how the FATF uses its noncomplier list and unofficial market enforcement to drive compliance improvements. The first section provides background on international cooperation to combat illicit financing and highlights the FATF's two main missions: setting global standards and monitoring compliance. The chapter then discusses how the FATF established itself as a prominent institution through a combination of informational advantages, coercive pressure, and legitimacy improvements; these underlying conditions enhance the power of the noncomplier list. The FATF uses its noncomplier list to signal how banks should evaluate a country's underlying illicit financing risk. Banks restrict lending to listed countries and charge higher premiums for services. This unofficial market enforcement process has been instrumental in transforming domestic politics in listed countries and has ultimately led to significant improvements in compliance.

The chapter also develops specific observable implications of the theory. Three key hypotheses probe the relationship between the noncomplier list and a country's level of compliance with the FATF standards. First, if the FATF noncomplier list is truly responsible for policy change in this area, then among the pool of countries that failed to meet a key FATF standard in February 2010 (the date of the first noncomplier list announcement), countries that were subsequently listed by the FATF should have complied more quickly compared to comparable nonlisted countries. Second, if market enforcement via banks is a key causal mechanism, then listed countries that are highly integrated into financial markets should be the fastest to change their policies. Third, if the FATF noncomplier list provides a focal point for banks, then listed countries should experience a decline in cross-border bank-to-bank lending, compared to nonlisted countries, and qualitative evidence should support the notion that international banks integrate the FATF list into their risk management models.

The chapter also discusses several hypotheses related to the theory's scope conditions. This book is an analysis of how a key aspect of international financial regulation has affected domestic policy; however, within-case variation provides a mechanism for exploring how an IO might establish itself as a focal point. Hypothesis 4 suggests that the FATF's impact on markets occurs primarily through its noncomplier list rather than through its comprehensive monitoring reports. Market actors need clear and precise focal points to organize expectations, and the FATF monitoring reports are too dense and difficult to quantify. Finally, hypothesis 5 proposes that the FATF's institutional legitimacy is core to understanding its impact on states.

Background on International Cooperation to Combat Illicit Financing

While criminals have used the financial system to store and transfer money for hundreds of years, the fight to preserve the integrity of the financial system is relatively new. The United States was the first country to criminalize money laundering in 1986,[10] with many European countries adopting similar laws in the 1990s. The effort to criminalize terrorist financing came even later, and cooperation expanded to include combating proliferation financing around 2008.[11] The robust regime that exists today reflects the degree to which policy makers have prioritized this issue area over the last thirty years.

In some ways, money laundering and terrorist financing are an unusual pairing. Many criminals commit crimes for the purpose of profit and need a way to "clean" the money so that they can use it without drawing the attention of law enforcement.[12] Money laundering is the process by which criminals attempt to disguise the illicit origins of funds. Terrorist financing, in contrast, usually occurs when legally acquired, nonillicit money is used to finance terrorist acts, individuals, or organizations. In money laundering terminology, terrorist financing occurs when "clean" money becomes "dirty."

Policy makers have linked money laundering and terrorist financing because the crimes affect the financial sector in similar ways. Both money launderers and financiers of terrorism might break up large amounts of money into smaller deposits to avoid suspicion. Similarly, both sets of actors might try to disguise the origins of money by wiring them through a series of accounts all over the world. As a result, if governments want to stop such activities, they need active cooperation from their own financial sectors as well as the financial sectors of other countries.[13]

Efforts to stop money laundering and terrorist financing also share a normative orientation that distinguishes them from many other policy issues. Both policy makers and the general public tend to view this issue area as tied to morality. As a result, policy solutions can sometimes be designed to make citizens "feel better" rather than based on an "accurate and rational" understanding of threats (Van Fossen 2003, 238). How policy makers understand the threat of money laundering reflects politics, economic interests, and social norms (Best 1989); similarly, how policy makers understand terrorist financing has changed significantly in the post-9/11 era (De Goede 2007). While money laundering and terrorist financing pose real threats to society and the financial system, the boundaries of such threats are not always easily identified or subject to universal agreement. Governments have never adopted a comprehensive treaty on terrorism, for example, because they do not agree on a single definition; the definition of "money laundering" has also changed significantly over time.[14]

The FATF has its origins in the US effort to stop money laundering related to drugs. Soon after the US government criminalized money laundering in 1986, policy makers discovered that domestic law was insufficient for controlling transactions in other countries. With the number of international transactions increasing exponentially, the United States needed a multilateral approach to address the problem. In 1988, the United States urged G-7 countries to take steps to prevent banks from being used for money laundering. Jakobi (2015) argues that the US government opted to seek G-7 support because of a lack of international alternatives and ongoing difficulties with bilateral law enforcement and mutual legal assistance treaties. The following year, the G-7 announced the formation of a financial action task force to assess ongoing efforts at combating money laundering and to consider additional preventive endeavors. The FATF held its first meeting a year later.

The FATF differs from formal IOs like the United Nations or the World Trade Organization in that it has no permanent charter or binding legal authority.[15] FATF members did not sign a treaty when they joined the organization, and for most of the FATF's history, members periodically reviewed and extended the organization's mandate for set periods of time. In 2019 the FATF's members opted for the first time for an open-ended mandate beginning in 2020. Member states still meet triannually but will now review the FATF's progress and goals every two years.[16]

Although the FATF started as a small IO, its membership has expanded over time, and today it includes thirty-seven member economies and two regional organizations.[17] The 2020 FATF membership is a diverse group that reflects the

TABLE 3.1 FATF member economies across time

COUNTRY	YEAR OF MEMBERSHIP
Australia	1989
Austria	
Belgium	
Canada	
European Commission	
France	
Germany	
Italy	
Japan	
Luxembourg	
Netherlands	
Spain	
Switzerland	
United Kingdom	
United States	
Denmark	1990
Finland	
Greece	
Gulf Cooperation Council	
Hong Kong, China	
Ireland	
New Zealand	
Norway	
Portugal	
Sweden	
Turkey	
Iceland	1991
Singapore	
Argentina	2000
Brazil	
Mexico	
Russia	2003
South Africa	
China	2007
Republic of Korea	2009
India	2010
Malaysia	2016
Israel	2018
Saudi Arabia	2019

Source: "FATF Members and Observers," FATF-GAFI.org (website), https://www.fatf-gafi.org/about/membersandobservers/.

organization's Eurocentric founding and its efforts to expand to include "strategically important countries."[18] Table 3.1 shows how the FATF's membership has changed over time. More recent additions to the membership have all been economically and strategically important countries, which may increase the perceived legitimacy of the organization. The FATF also maintains a network of FATF-style regional bodies that promote and monitor the adoption of FATF standards worldwide. A list of these bodies and their members is available in the appendix.

The FATF has two primary missions: standard setting and compliance monitoring. In 1990, it issued its first set of forty policy recommendations on legal, regulatory, and operational measures that governments could take to prevent drug money from moving through the financial system. Since that time, the FATF has revised its recommendations several times, and in 2001 it added new special recommendations on combating the financing of terrorism. In 2012, in order to prepare for its fourth round of country compliance evaluations, the FATF consolidated its separate money laundering and terrorist financing standards into forty comprehensive recommendations.[19] The FATF's current recommendations call on states to criminalize money laundering and terrorist financing in line with specific criteria, strengthen international cooperation, and provide legal assistance to other countries. Other recommendations target the financial industry, requiring banks and financial actors to keep records, verify customer identities, and establish their own programs to minimize illicit financing risk.

The FATF's second mission is compliance monitoring and assessment. Over its lifespan, the FATF has had four distinct monitoring approaches: self-assessment, mutual evaluation reports, cross-country reviews, and "naming and shaming" via some type of public list (Roberge 2011). Of these approaches, the majority of FATF monitoring occurs through mutual evaluations and public listing. The FATF mutual evaluation process engages bureaucrats from peer countries to work with the FATF secretariat as part of an evaluation team, which assesses compliance in member states. This form of monitoring is comprehensive, is directed at all countries, and often takes close to eighteen months per country. Peer review has been effective at promoting compliance improvements across the FATF's member states (Levi and Gilmore 2002; Sansonetti 2000). In contrast, the FATF's various listing processes are targeted monitoring endeavors focused exclusively on problematic jurisdictions. The FATF's history of listing is discussed in greater detail later in the chapter.

How the FATF Established Institutional Prominence

The FATF spent its first two decades working to establish itself as the central organization governing illicit financing. To cement institutional prominence, the FATF developed strong comparative advantages in information provision through technical expertise and unique access to government policy. It also leveraged economic coercion to draw attention to its recommendations and impose consequences on uncooperative states. More recently, the FATF has attempted to strengthen its institutional legitimacy, particularly among non-FATF member states. These three strengths—informational advantages, coercive pressure, and institutional legitimacy—have helped the FATF establish a reputation as a unique and salient authority on combating illicit financing.

Comparative Informational Advantages

The FATF's informational advantages come from the complexity of its standards and the strength of its bureaucratic network. Since the FATF first adopted anti–money laundering recommendations in 1990, its guidelines have grown more detailed and specific over time. In 1995, the FATF revised its standards after noting that "the dynamics of the global money laundering problem have changed" and that "the FATF's understanding of the efficacy of money laundering countermeasures has also changed" (FATF-GAFI 1996, 6). New guidelines included extending the money laundering offense beyond narcotics trafficking and requiring financial institutions to report suspicious transactions (FATF-GAFI 1996). The FATF has since revised its recommendations several more times. As a result, even longtime members are constantly working to understand and interpret new guidelines. Newer FATF members or regional affiliate countries may require extensive assistance with everything from drafting legislation to assessing their own country's risk profile.[20]

As the FATF recommendations have grown more complex, the task of monitoring compliance and policy implementation has become more difficult. The FATF began to evaluate how members were implementing its recommendations within a year of rule adoption. Between 1991 and 1994, the organization relied on an annual self-assessment exercise and a more comprehensive country evaluation modeled after the peer evaluation system of the OECD, called the mutual evaluation process. As previously discussed, the mutual evaluation process involves an on-site visit by a team of experts (drawn from peer countries), significant data collection, and a final detailed report. The FATF recognized almost immediately that the mutual evaluation process was a "particularly effective monitoring mechanism" because "the evaluations provide a very thorough scrutiny of the action taken against money laundering" (FATF-GAFI 1993, 7–8). After the FATF revised its recommendations in June 2003, the task force adopted an explicit methodology document for evaluating country compliance. By this time, the standards were so long and detailed that the FATF abandoned its self-assessment exercises and elected instead to focus on the mutual evaluation process (FATF-GAFI 2004, 10).

The FATF works to accomplish its two missions of standard setting and compliance monitoring through a network of bureaucratic experts and IO officials.[21] In the early 1990s, the FATF was primarily focused on getting its member states to adopt its forty recommendations, but this task alone was challenging.[22] Even very basic recommendations like criminalizing money laundering were new to most countries: before 1986, not a single country had a law criminalizing money laundering (Sharman 2008, 52). The FATF's initial institutional design was also built on the notion of voluntary cooperation, where members expected that information sharing and legal cooperation would strengthen domestic regulatory power (Helleiner 1998).

To assist with policy adoption, the FATF set up a small secretariat that is housed in the OECD headquarters in Paris, France. FATF members initially anticipated using this secretariat as a clearing house for information: the secretariat would produce summary reports and track technical assistance efforts by member states (FATF-GAFI 1992). Over time, however, the FATF secretariat has become an important source of both technical expertise and regime knowledge. At least one representative from the FATF secretariat attends all of the FATF's meetings and the meetings of the FATF regional affiliate organizations in order to align institutional knowledge across the global network. For example, during the September 2016 plenary of the Asia/Pacific Group on Money Laundering (APG, a regional affiliate of the FATF), member states debated whether one country had received too high a rating on a particular recommendation. In the middle of this discussion, the FATF secretariat representative spoke up to support the evaluation team's rating, reminding members that it was important to have consistency across mutual evaluation reports. In a subsequent discussion of another country's mutual evaluation report, the FATF official advocated for a rating change for similar reasons.[23]

The FATF's technical expertise is not just limited to secretariat officials. Instead, government officials from FATF member states work with secretariat officials to provide additional guidance and facilitate capacity building. Bureaucratic networks are strengthened through plenary meetings and the mutual evaluation process.[24] Bureaucrats from the FATF and regional affiliate member states participate in the evaluation process, joining with secretariat officials to conduct evaluations of peer countries. The FATF's 2016 evaluation of the United States, for example, had financial experts from Australia, Canada, and France, law enforcement experts from New Zealand and Spain, a legal expert from the United Kingdom, several FATF secretariat officials, and the deputy secretary for the APG. This networked approach to peer evaluation allows bureaucrats from other countries to gain invaluable knowledge by participating in the evaluation process.[25] It also lends credibility to the FATF's monitoring reports: the monitoring team spends a year interviewing local government and private-sector officials, studying regulation, and evaluating implementation. Final evaluation reports are extremely detailed, providing two to three hundred pages of information about each country's legal, financial, and regulatory system.

The FATF's apolitical reputation is core to its ability to gain access to state policy. Plenary meetings are staffed with bureaucrats from member countries' treasury departments or ministries of finance, rather than high-level political officials. The FATF makes decisions by "emerging consensus": if the FATF president notices that many countries are in favor of a proposal and few seem opposed, he or she deems it to be approved.[26] Consensus decision-making is possible in part because the FATF is primarily a technical body. According to Chip Poncy, former head of the US delegation to FATF, "The FATF relies on political bodies to address the most difficult political questions."[27]

The emerging consensus procedure delegates power to the FATF secretariat and president because in practice, a single state cannot overturn the proposal on the table. When an FATF monitoring team drafts a country's mutual evaluation report, for example, the assessors settle on what they consider to be fair ratings, albeit with some discussion with the evaluated country. While the report is subject to final approval in the plenary, the evaluated country must be able to convince a broad coalition of FATF member countries to upgrade a specific compliance rating in order for the rating to be changed.[28] Former FATF president Antonio Gustavo Rodrigues described this emphasis on expertise over politics: "In any organization with human beings, you have politics. But in FATF, politics is a secondary aspect."[29]

When political concerns do affect outcomes, the FATF's technical nature and bureaucratic procedures affect the way in which political influence is manifest. Countries like the United States or the United Kingdom might be more successful at advocating for ratings improvements, but they use technical justifications to explain their views.[30] And because plenary sessions provide time-limited opportunities for debate, powerful countries are only able to improve one or two ratings (out of forty). Of course, countries like the United States may exercise what Randall Stone terms "informal influence" to exert control over institutional outcomes behind the scenes (Stone 2011). Gordon Hook, executive secretary of the APG, reported that numerous factors come into play when an issue is a high priority to the United States and other strategically important countries.[31] Even in such cases, however, those other factors, including politics, often give countries a temporary reprieve rather than a permanent pass. The United States, for example, may have been influential in keeping the Philippines off of the noncomplier list despite the country's lack of oversight for its casino sector. After several years of threats from the FATF, however, the Philippine government finally passed new legislation with the understanding that failure to do so would mean an FATF listing (Ballaran 2017).[32]

The FATF's Previous Economic Coercion

The FATF has also used economic coercion to draw international attention to its standards. Although FATF members were initially focused on aligning anti–money laundering policies in member jurisdictions, by the late 1990s, governments realized that keeping illicit money out of the global financial system required more widespread policy change. A 1998 ministerial-level meeting held on the margins of the OECD led to a strategic shift in the FATF's priorities. The ministers agreed that "the major focus of FATF's future work should be to promote the establishment of a world-wide antimoney laundering network encompassing all continents and regions in the globe" (FATF-GAFI 1998, 9). The FATF's most powerful effort at spreading its standards was its decision to take action against offshore financial centers and other noncooperative jurisdictions.

In 2000, the FATF established the noncooperative countries and territories (NCCT) process to identify, assess, and penalize jurisdictions that were slow to adopt FATF standards. Member states worked with the FATF secretariat to set out twenty-five criteria for identifying detrimental practices and anti–money laundering policies. The criteria, which were consistent with the FATF standards, focused primarily on finding countries with loopholes in financial regulation, inadequate supervision of the financial sector, weak customer identification requirements, excessive financial secrecy, or ineffective systems for reporting suspicious transactions.[33] The FATF established four regional review groups to gather information and solicit input from jurisdictions of concern, none of which were FATF members. Based on this exercise, the FATF identified twenty-one countries as noncooperative in 2000 and 2001. Listed countries included Israel, Lebanon, Liechtenstein, Panama, the Philippines, and Russia, as well as many smaller tax havens (FATF-GAFI 2000a, 2000b).[34]

The NCCT process drew strength from explicit economic pressure. One of the FATF's forty recommendations requires financial institutions to give extra scrutiny to business relationships and transactions with individuals and companies in countries that do not meet FATF standards.[35] The FATF explicitly referenced this recommendation to pressure NCCT countries to change their policies. In its public statements, the FATF recommended that financial institutions "give special attention to business relations and transactions" with individuals, companies, and banks in noncooperative countries (FATF-GAFI 2000a, 12). The FATF also threatened explicit economic countermeasures against NCCT countries that failed to improve their anti–money laundering laws and regulations, and it ultimately took this action against two countries: Nauru and Myanmar (Gardner 2007).

The NCCT process forced offshore financial centers and other nonmember jurisdictions to accept the FATF's standards. Prior to the FATF's action, offshore centers and tax havens had few incentives to comply with the FATF recommendations. Countries build out offshore financial capacities as a route to economic development (Palan 2003); some governments even target criminal money in pursuit of this objective (Rawlings and Unger 2008). For local economies dependent on attracting international capital, the profit advantages of financial secrecy outweighed any tangential benefits of appeasing powerful FATF member states, even the United States. Indeed, throughout the 1990s, the US government highlighted concerns about money laundering in Pacific Island offshore centers like Nauru and Vanuatu, but the countries' governments were reluctant to take action.[36] Even after the NCCT process began, the four listed Pacific tax havens were slow to change course because governments felt that acquiescing would be the end of their financial sectors (Sharman 2005, 317).

The FATF grew in importance as countries became aware of the potential financial repercussions of uncooperative behavior. Listed governments experienced declines in offshore banks and other services firsthand (Sharman 2005, 319), while other countries learned about such effects through regional organizations, personal relationships, professional associations, and financial industry journals (Sharman 2008). Even countries not on the list improved compliance in order to avoid being listed (Doyle 2002; Drezner 2005; Sharman 2008). Within a few years, 73 percent of targeted countries had made major policy concessions (Drezner 2005, 852). Countries that failed to improve, meanwhile, suffered significant financial costs as banks withdrew or charged higher transaction costs for doing business. Perhaps the most extreme case occurred in the small Pacific island nation of Nauru. The government of Nauru refused to change its regulations without compensation, and as a result, FATF member states leveraged countermeasures against it. Countermeasures coincided with bad publicity related to a Russian money-laundering scandal, being listed as a tax haven by the OECD, and strong bilateral pressure from the United States (Sharman 2006, 125). Under such constraints, the Nauru government capitulated in December 2003, but the economic costs could not be undone. Sharman (2008, 645) describes how the FATF's action "led to a *de facto* financial blockade by private institutions and the complete collapse of the country's financial system. . . . Even after [Nauru's] complying with the FATF's demands, no bank is willing to take the reputation risk of opening a branch in the country."

The NCCT process made it clear that countries could not afford to ignore the FATF standards. Daniel Glaser, former assistant secretary for terrorist financing and financial crimes at the US Department of the Treasury, described this evolution in an interview: "Prior to the NCCT, the FATF asserted that it was the global standard, but there was nothing behind it—no force of international law and no global agreement. . . . Post-NCCT, you never had the argument that these standards don't apply."[37] The NCCT process encouraged prolonged engagement with the FATF: since being outside the FATF global network did not prevent a country from coercive action, governments learned that they were better off working within the system.

Although the NCCT process successfully coerced policy change, it also had negative reputational consequences for the FATF as an organization. Non-FATF member states viewed the FATF as unequal and illegitimate due to its lack of a legally binding charter, exclusive club membership, and unwillingness to list its own members. Many countries perceived the use of economic coercion as a violation of international norms (Hülsse 2008). The NCCT listing procedure lacked transparency and seemed arbitrary (Unger and Ferwerda 2008; Tsingou 2010) and also appeared highly politicized given obvious omissions, such as the exclusion of many offshore financial centers (Gordon 2010, 92). Targeted countries were those who lacked influential allies, while countries with close ties to France, the United Kingdom, and Canada were kept off the list (van Fossen 2003). Some countries even accused the FATF of having a hidden agenda, aiming to eliminate tax evasion rather than address money laundering (Mitsilegas 2003).

Negative perceptions of the NCCT process impeded other aspects of the FATF's agenda. The FATF needed its regional affiliate bodies to work to diffuse standards and monitor compliance, yet the NCCT list "had the unintentional effect of straining the relationship between the FATF and the FATF-style regional bodies" (FATF-GAFI 2001, 11). G-7 countries wanted the IMF and the World Bank to adopt the FATF standards (Schott 2003; Holder 2003), but neither IO had any interest in such an endeavor given the FATF's mixed reputation.[38] The IMF opposed the NCCT practice as "against the nature of the Fund" (Sharman 2006, 156).

FATF member states eventually determined that the NCCT approach was not the best way to create widespread compliance with the FATF standards.[39] The FATF could not threaten punishment against every state with deficient antimoney laundering regulations. FATF members might be willing to list Panama over its lax regulation but were unlikely to subject fellow FATF member Brazil to the same treatment. Furthermore, while coercion generated surface-level compliance, targeted governments needed to accept the organization and its rules as legitimate in order to make on-the-ground policy improvements (Hülsse 2008). IMF managing director Michel Camdessus advised FATF countries of this truth even before the NCCT process, arguing, "The regulatory policies to achieve both sets of aims (AML and economic growth) are by necessity those of sovereign nations and cannot simply be imposed on them. . . . And we as international bodies must ensure that the policies are perceived as being in the self-interest of all."[40] For these reasons and under pressure from the IMF, the FATF terminated the NCCT process, listing no new states after 2001 and ending the list in 2006. The IMF subsequently agreed to integrate the FATF recommendations into its technical assistance program, but only on the condition that the FATF emphasize consensus and cooperation and develop a more fair and transparent procedure for monitoring compliance (Tsingou 2010, 624).

Strengthening Perceived Legitimacy

Over the last two decades, the FATF has taken several steps to strengthen institutional legitimacy. Core to this approach are the FATF's effort to improve the representativeness of its membership and give more voice to its regional affiliate organizations. The FATF now includes important emerging market economies like Argentina, Brazil, Korea, Malaysia, Mexico, and South Africa. Most recently, the FATF expanded again to include Israel and Saudi Arabia. The FATF's more economically and regionally diverse membership makes it more difficult for non-member states to critique the FATF as simply a political tool of OECD countries.

The FATF has also built out its affiliate bodies to encompass every region in the world. These regional affiliate organizations provide countries with opportunities to learn about the FATF standards and receive technical assistance; one practitioner described the regional bodies as "a crucial link and validation/credibility provider for the FATF system. . . . [They act] as both enforcer [via the MERs] but also supporter via lobbying FATF to understand the perspective of lower-capacity countries."[41] They also provide channels for weaker states to influence the FATF's current listing process. Since 2009, the FATF's current review process has drawn on the work of four regional review groups (Africa/Middle East, Americas, Asia/Pacific, and Europe/Eurasia), each cochaired by an FATF member and a representative of an FATF regional affiliate (FATF-GAFI 2009, 6). These regional groups are responsible for reviewing countries that are eligible for listing and for making listing recommendations. By empowering non-FATF members to participate in the review process, the FATF has enhanced the democratic legitimacy of its eventual listing decisions.[42]

The FATF has also taken some limited steps to strengthen the normative power of its standards. While policy makers may not have considered the normative implications of expanding the FATF's mandate to include terrorist financing, linking anti–money laundering with the global war on terror has made it more difficult for countries to resist the FATF standards. The FATF added special recommendations on combating terrorist financing shortly after the 9/11 terrorist attacks, during a time when the global community was broadly supportive of counterterrorism cooperation. Even as country attitudes toward combating terrorism have grown more nuanced, most countries still support the mission of fighting terrorist financing. The FATF's normative appeal may also have grown when the UN Security Council de facto endorsed the FATF standards in 2005, urging all member states to implement the FATF's recommendations.[43] Finally, the FATF's mandate expansion to include countering proliferation financing has also strengthened its normative appeal.[44]

Perhaps the most significant way that the FATF has sought to enhance legitimacy is through technocracy. International standards, by their very nature, are "expert knowledge stored in the form of rules" (Jacobsson 2000, 41); when an IO regularizes or systematizes its reliance on experts, such steps are likely to improve institutional legitimacy. While its standards have long been expert-driven, the FATF has significantly enhanced the technocratic nature of monitoring over the last two decades. It has intensified cooperation with the IMF and the World Bank, and also with the private sector, signaling to observers that the FATF standards incorporate input from a variety of financial experts (Hülsse 2008). The FATF has also established a more robust and transparent methodology for evaluating countries' anti–money laundering regimes. In February 2004, the FATF adopted a seventy-nine-page methodology document for how evaluation teams should assess compliance in the third round of mutual evaluations.[45] Prior to the fourth round of evaluations, the FATF published even more detailed methodological guidance for evaluating technical compliance and effectiveness.

Perhaps the most significant technocratic improvement has occurred in the FATF's listing procedures. After the FATF abandoned the NCCT process, it set up the International Cooperation Review Group (ICRG) in 2007 to analyze and publicly identify high-risk jurisdictions. This process soon proved problematic, however, because it relied on FATF members or FATF regional affiliate organizations to nominate countries for inclusion. Few countries were willing to make nominations.[46] Daniel Glaser, who represented the United States at FATF meetings for nearly two decades, described the problems with this process and why it was eventually changed: "The ICRG ended up sitting in judgment of bilateral disputes between two countries. FATF is not really set up to do this. It was very awkward and uncomfortable. It was clear that the system wasn't working. We needed to establish a system that had automaticity baked into it."[47]

In response to this problem, the FATF adopted new ICRG procedures in June 2009 and established strict bureaucratic criteria for listing eligibility. After identifying sixteen of the FATF's 40+9 recommendations as "key and core," the

FATF determined that if a country received failing scores ("partially compliant" or "noncompliant") on ten or more of the sixteen recommendations in its third-round mutual evaluation report, it would automatically be eligible for listing. Member states reportedly arrived at this threshold organically, choosing ten because it represented "a preponderance of the key and core recommendations."[48]

The FATF's new ICRG threshold provided its subsequent listing announcements (hereafter referred to as the noncomplier list) with a veneer of scientific validity.[49] The new listing procedures allowed the FATF to list both FATF and non-FATF members—a change that enhanced the procedure's legitimacy.[50] Non-FATF members could provide input through the regional review groups, which made listing recommendations and monitored progress in listed countries (FATF-GAFI 2009). These various technocratic changes made it easier for countries to support the noncomplier list and reduced the enforcement costs for FATF members. Glaser described this effect, noting, "The genius of the ICRG is that countries early on make a decision that they are fully aware will lead to countries ending up on a blacklist, but they make a process-based decision. No one has to put their hand up to say, 'We want a country on that list.' It just begins a process that requires a country to intervene to prevent it from running its course."[51]

Even the nomenclature of the noncomplier list is designed to de-emphasize coercive pressure. The FATF chose the name International Cooperation Review Group with the IMF's previous critiques in mind.[52] Beginning in February 2010, the ICRG issued two separate listing announcements, placing most countries on a statement titled "Improving Global AML/CFT Compliance: Ongoing Process." This announcement, often referred to by policy makers and the media as "the grey list," identified noncompliant countries that had already made a "high-level political commitment to address the deficiencies through implementation of an action plan developed with the FATF." The language of the list was mild, apprising outside observers that the FATF would "closely monitor the implementation of these action plans" but never mentioning any possibility of countermeasures or market pressure. The FATF eventually added a second list to its "Improving Global AML/CFT Compliance" announcement, where it identified "jurisdictions not making sufficient progress" and gave them four months to make significant improvements or be placed on a different list. This warning list is known colloquially as the "dark grey list."[53]

The FATF also issued a second announcement, termed its "Public Statement," which included two stronger listing levels.[54] First, the FATF identified a small group of countries with significant deficiencies that had yet to commit to action plans and called on its members to "consider the risks arising from the deficiencies associated with each jurisdiction." This list, which eventually became known as the "blacklist," was more coercive than the grey list but still allowed countries,

TABLE 3.2 Countries on the FATF noncomplier list (February 2010–June 2020)

COUNTRY	LISTED	REMOVED FROM LIST
Afghanistan	2012	2017
Albania	2012	2015
	2020	—
Algeria	2011	2016
Angola	2010	2016
Antigua and Barbuda	2010	2014
Argentina	2011	2014
Azerbaijan	2010	2010
The Bahamas	2018	—
Barbados	2020	—
Bangladesh	2010	2014
Bolivia	2010	2013
Bosnia and Herzegovina	2015	2018
Botswana	2018	—
Brunei Darussalam	2011	2013
Cambodia	2011	2015
	2019	—
Cuba	2011	2014
DPRK	2010	—
Ecuador	2010	2015
Ethiopia	2010	2014
	2017	2019
Ghana	2010	2013
	2018	—
Greece	2010	2011
Guyana	2014	2016
Honduras	2010	2012
Iceland	2019	—
Indonesia	2010	2015
Iran	2007	—
Iraq	2013	2018
Jamaica	2020	—
Kenya	2010	2014
Kuwait	2012	2014
Kyrgyzstan	2011	2014
Lao PDR	2013	2017
Mauritius	2020	—
Mongolia	2011	2014
	2019	—
Morocco	2010	2013
Myanmar	2010	2016
	2020	—
Namibia	2011	2015
Nepal	2010	2014
Nicaragua	2011	2015
	2020	—
Nigeria	2010	2013
Pakistan	2010	2015
	2018	—

COUNTRY	LISTED	REMOVED FROM LIST
Panama	2014	2016
	2019	—
Papua New Guinea	2014	2016
Paraguay	2010	2012
Philippines	2010	2013
Qatar	2010	2010
São Tomé and Príncipe	2010	2013
Serbia	2018	—
Sri Lanka	2010	2013
	2017	2019
Sudan	2010	2015
Syria	2010	—
Tajikistan	2011	2014
Tanzania	2010	2014
Thailand	2010	2013
Trinidad and Tobago	2010	2012
	2017	2020
Tunisia	2017	2019
Turkey	2010	2014
Turkmenistan	2010	2012
Uganda	2014	2017
	2020	—
Ukraine	2010	2011
Vanuatu	2016	—
Venezuela	2010	2013
Vietnam	2010	2014
Yemen	2010	—
Zimbabwe	2011	2015
	2019	—

Note: Data coded by author based on FATF public announcements. The FATF removes countries from the noncomplier list due to significant policy change (with the exception of São Tomé and Príncipe, which the FATF decided was a low threat and no longer needed monitoring). Countries with two dates were listed under both the third and fourth rounds of compliance evaluations; each round had its own criteria for listing.

regulators, and banks a significant amount of leeway to respond as they deemed appropriate.[55] The FATF public statement also established an explicit countermeasures list, which to date has only ever included Iran and North Korea.[56]

The multitiered structure of the FATF noncomplier list enhances its legitimacy. In one sense, the list still operates in the shadow of economic power: the FATF maintains a countermeasures list, even if FATF members are reluctant to deploy such measures beyond Iran and North Korea. But the explicit political message of listing is much milder: listed countries should work with the FATF to improve their laws. This indirect communication is politically more palatable for FATF members because it provides plausible deniability. When the FATF lists countries as part of the "Improving Global AML/CFT Compliance" initiative, FATF member states can argue that this is peer pressure rather than coercion.

Moreover, because listing eligibility depends on a clear bureaucratic threshold, such decisions appear more technocratic than political.[57]

The large number of listed countries provides additional support for the idea that the FATF's bureaucratic process reduces the political costs of listing. Between February 2010 and June 2020, the FATF listed more than sixty different countries, with several countries listed during both the third and fourth round of evaluations. Table 3.2 shows all listed countries, the year of listing, and the year of removal from the list.

The Noncomplier List as a Focal Point for Banks

International and domestic banks use the FATF noncomplier list as a guidepost for identifying countries that pose a high illicit financing risk. As discussed in chapter 1, banks have regulatory and reputational incentives to mitigate exposure to money laundering and terrorist financing, particularly for low-yield transactions. But government and international regulations are relatively unclear as to which countries constitute the highest risks. Moreover, even if banks understand that a country is risky, banks may do little to avoid transactions if the country is also an important source of profits. Banks thus face a type of coordination problem where they look for a common solution or focal point to organize behavior. The FATF exploits this underlying demand to intensify the impact of its noncomplier list.

The FATF's Unclear Guidance on Country Risk

Since its first set of recommendations in 1990, the FATF has called for financial institutions to "give special attention to business relations and transactions with persons, including companies and financial institutions, from countries which do not or insufficiently apply these [the FATF] recommendations" (FATF-GAFI 1990, 22). Although the FATF has clarified many of its standards over the last three decades, this basic requirement remains vague.[58] Domestic regulations also allow for similar interpretational flexibility. The US government, for example, requires financial institutions to consider the geographic location where a customer does business, with the guidance that certain locations "may pose a higher risk of money laundering or terrorist financing" (Federal Financial Institutions Examination Council 2018, 3), but it provides limited guidelines for how to assess such risks.

Despite such ambiguity, banks have numerous incentives to identify a defensible standard for evaluating a country's illicit financing risk. The FATF's decades-long effort to stop money laundering and illicit financing has generated strong norms of behavior for governments and the financial industry.[59] The FATF's institutional prominence means that its standards are perceived as "best practice" by banks.[60] Regulatory and reputational incentives create profit incentives for banks to minimize illicit financing risk. As a result, banks mitigate risk in part by ensuring that their risk management strategies align with the actions of others.

Banks need to justify their behavior to regulators and shareholders in a way that accords with the actions of other financial institutions. In bond markets, information intermediaries such as rating agencies have arisen to remedy such asymmetries.[61] For banks, numerous companies offer similar services related to illicit financing risk. Such services often include complex data algorithms for detecting and investigating potential money laundering. Systems integrate information on geography, sanctions and other risk lists, nonmonetary events, and customer characteristics to identify high-risk transactions. Crucially, however, there is no single standard across the industry: each company assesses risk in its own way, and banks can also tweak proprietary software to consider different factors.

Banks can ensure that they are acting in concert with other financial institutions when they integrate the noncomplier list into their risk models. One investment services firm executive suggested that the list's value is tied in large part to how it is viewed by government regulators. "Regulators are liability, and even then, if they [banks] think they can effectively outmaneuver the regulators they will. . . . So the list's value rests in whether regulators will use it and at what cost."[62] While each bank makes its own cost-benefit calculations about how to interact with countries that pose a high risk of money laundering or terrorist financing, it would be impossible for banks to ignore the FATF noncomplier list in making these determinations because government regulators view the FATF list as an important indicator of risk.

The Noncomplier List's Precise Signal of Country Risk

The FATF noncomplier list's impact on global banking is linked to its ability to send an unambiguous signal about country risk. Since inception, the FATF has conducted detailed evaluations of each member's compliance with its standards. Due to the expansion of the FATF global network in the last two decades, the FATF and its affiliate bodies now monitor compliance in more than two hundred economies worldwide. Although the FATF monitoring process produces detailed country-specific evaluations, standard monitoring does not facilitate easy cross-country comparisons. Countries are evaluated only about once per decade, each at a different time by a different team of evaluators. The final evaluation report assesses compliance with each of the FATF's forty recommendations but does not provide any cumulative overall rating. As a result, most country reports have limited effects on outside observers.

The FATF list changes this dynamic by clearly signaling a country's overall risk. In the words of Chip Poncy, the former head of the US delegation to FATF, "When you publish three-hundred-page mutual evaluation reports that no one in the market really understands how to read and there are no cumulative ratings, markets don't know how to react. There's not enough depth, understanding, or expertise in the market yet to understand and react to these technical issues absent country lists for material noncompliance."[63] Interestingly, however, Poncy later noted that while the FATF list is unambiguous about *overall* country risk, it is a blunt instrument for dealing with more detailed risks pertaining to specific local banks or actors:

> The [mutual evaluation] reports have no clear cumulative "red, yellow, green" result, and the listing processes accomplish that objective, boiling it down to which countries are high risk. There's a second angle, though, which is that a risk manager at a bank might want to use the FATF reports, but feel like there's not enough detail. If a bank wants to understand if a correspondent bank in another country is subject to sufficient oversight, there's nothing in the FATF evaluation that tells them that at the granular level. You can't really tell what's going on in terms of current oversight, prevention, enforcement, and particularly in nonbank financial sectors.[64]

The FATF's noncomplier list may also be an effective focal point because it creates a "peer effect," whereby countries are judged not just for noncompliance but also by the other countries that are also included on the list or in the category (Gray 2013; Brooks et al. 2015). Gray and Hicks (2014) show that peer effects may depend on whether the better-known peer countries have positive or negative reputations—if a country forms an agreement with a perceived "bad country," it is more likely to be viewed as higher risk. Dolan (2020) suggests that when the World Bank places a country in a higher category of economic development, this process may create a type of "halo effect," where observers attribute to the country other positive but unrelated characteristics such as democracy or respect for human rights.

In the case of a blacklist, peer effects may be closer to a "lowest-common-denominator effect" (Morse 2019), where countries are judged by the worst of the group. When the *Financial Times*, for example, covered Turkey's time on the noncomplier list, it described how the country was on a list "with the likes of

Cuba, Ethiopia, Indonesia, Nigeria, Pakistan, Syria, and Yemen," explicitly drawing comparisons with some of the riskiest listed countries.[65] Similarly, after the
FATF included Antigua and Barbuda on its noncomplier list in February 2010,
the leading opposition leader criticized the ruling party for Antigua and Barbuda's listed compatriots: "The Labour Party government and its representatives
worked diligently in advance of the issuance of the FATF lists in 2000 and 2001 to
ensure that Antigua and Barbuda was in full compliance with required standards
before the FATF identified delinquent jurisdictions. . . . Now, under the UPP, we
are on a list with Nigeria, Sudan, Ukraine, and Myanmar."[66]

Unofficial Market Enforcement and
FATF Compliance Improvements

Banks use the FATF noncomplier list to decide how to allocate resources across
countries, and this process has direct implications for how listed countries make
compliance decisions. When the FATF lists a country, international banks subject
banks and clients in the listed country to additional scrutiny. They may delay
transactions or charge a higher cost for money transfers. For particularly low-
profit clients, banks may avoid business entirely. This unofficial market enforcement process influences domestic politics in listed countries. Domestic banks
and other affected industries become advocates for compliance, urging the government to adopt stricter regulations. Banking and business groups are likely to
be particularly influential advocates in countries that are highly integrated into
international markets.

The FATF's reliance on unofficial market enforcement has amplified the
success of the noncomplier list process. Because the FATF list is not explicitly
coercive, FATF members have been willing to take action against a broad cross-
section of states. Whereas the NCCT process identified twenty-one non-FATF
economies, the FATF noncomplier list had identified sixty-five noncompliant
economies as of June 2020, including two FATF members (Greece and Turkey).
Significantly, the FATF listing process has also generated spillover effects for a
second, larger group of countries that work to improve compliance so as to avoid
listing.

Bank Reaction to the Noncomplier List

Domestic and international banks use the FATF noncomplier list as a focal point
for assessing the illicit financing risk of different countries. Unlike the FATF's
monitoring reports, which are lengthy and highly technical, the noncomplier list

provides a cohesive, defensible standard for identifying the highest-risk countries. As a result, when the FATF includes a country on the noncomplier list, banks typically respond by integrating the information into their risk models and changing how they allocate resources across states. Banks may subject clients in listed countries to additional scrutiny, requiring them to provide more identifying information or delaying transactions for several days. When Bosnia was on the FATF list, for example, foreign counterparts closed Bosnian bank accounts, canceled transactions, and delayed payments to and from Bosnia.[67] Banks may also terminate correspondent relationships with banks in listed countries. In this case, banks in listed countries may be unable to do business in desired currencies or may be forced to route money through several different banks in order to conduct cross-border transfers.

Unofficial market enforcement varies across jurisdictions, depending on the profitability of a particular bank-to-bank relationship. Banks require relatively little information to terminate relationships with low-profitability countries. If a bank does minimal business with a small, high-risk economy that ends up on the noncomplier list, it may use the FATF noncomplier list as a rationale for raising the costs of cross-border banking or terminating correspondent banking relationships entirely.

Both large and small banks have incentives to restrict business with banks in noncomplier list countries; however, large banks are likely to close more correspondent accounts because they have wider networks and are often more concerned about third-party punishment. Such punishment can come in the form of regulatory action, reputation damage, or a loss of shareholder confidence. In recent years, domestic regulators have been particularly active in monitoring and enforcing violations of anti–money laundering laws. The US and UK governments have levied billions of dollars in fines against banks for violating money laundering laws. In April 2019, for example, US and UK authorities fined Standard Chartered USD 1.1 billion for violating sanctions and anti–money laundering laws.[68] Because the United States and the United Kingdom are home to the largest financial centers in the world, enforcement action by these two governments creates ripple effects throughout global finance, increasing incentives for market actors to pay attention to the risk of money laundering in foreign countries.

Banks may also be concerned about the reputation consequences of engaging in business with criminals or terrorists. As the 2016 Wells Fargo scandal revealed, when banks adopt normatively problematic policies, they suffer significant declines in customer support, even months later.[69] It is not hard to imagine a bank or investment firm facing similar, or perhaps worse, repercussions for facilitating terrorist financing. Reputation damage may also affect how other market actors interact with a bank or company; indeed, Verhage (2011) finds that many bank compliance officers worry most about interbank reputation protection.

Finally, large international banks may change resource allocation based on the noncomplier list because they are concerned about the possibility of shareholder punishment. While investors and shareholders often focus their energies on short-run profits, they may also care about exposure to different types of risks. It is for this reason that the financial services industry offers several different types of indices and ratings systems that evaluate a company's exposure to environmental, social, and governance risk. Large asset managers use such indices to judge risk exposure, often shifting resources away from companies that are near the bottom of the ranking. As a result, even when a company does not suffer a decline in profit, its leadership may still worry about shareholders divesting if the bank is assessed as mismanaging or overlooking potential environmental, social, or governance risks.[70]

Banks weigh these three types of incentives—regulation, reputation, and shareholder concern—against profit considerations related to illicit financing. A bank doing business with a nonlisted country may ignore the country's lax regulatory oversight if the economy has a high volume of transactions. Listing, however, ups the stakes of such decisions, creating strong incentives for banks to adopt new risk management strategies. Banks in listed countries may face higher costs or payment delays, or in some cases, correspondent account closures.

Historically, banks facing international scrutiny have still been able to access the formal financial system through a practice called "nested correspondent banking," where a respondent bank has no direct relationship with a correspondent bank but instead conducts business in a two-step process. A US-based bank may have no direct correspondent relationship with banks in Vanuatu (a formerly listed country), for example, but it may maintain relationships with banks in Australia. If these Australian banks still have ties to banks in Vanuatu, then the US bank remains exposed to risk in Vanuatu through this nested relationship (Bank for International Settlements 2016, 10). Increasingly, however, correspondent banks are even terminating relationships with respondent banks that have too many risky secondary relationships (Bank for International Settlements 2016, 11). As a result, even large regional banks have incentives to change how they do business with banks in noncomplier list countries.

From Market Pressure to Government Policy

Unofficial market enforcement via global banking profoundly alters the incentives of listed governments. As global financial institutions and banks in nonlisted countries restrict business with banks in listed countries, the listed country's financial industry has new incentives to demand more government regulation. Banks advocate for more oversight because they need the government to signal to outside investors and foreign banks that the risks of illicit financing have decreased. While a single bank can (and often does) put in place its own systems to reduce risk, an individual bank can rarely send a credible signal about such reforms to outside audiences. Banks have incentives to misrepresent their own risk management practices; in the face of such uncertainty, external financial actors will act to reduce their own exposure. If a government changes its policies, however, and if the FATF deems such policy change sufficient to remove a country from its list, this action sends a much more powerful signal to banks and investors around the world.

In the FATF context, unofficial market enforcement influences government policy through three channels. First, banks themselves may become advocates for policy change. The banking industry often has close political ties to the government and may seek to lobby legislatures or bureaucrats at the ministry of finance, central bank, or regulatory agencies. The banking sector played crucial roles in both the Philippines and Thailand during listing: banks advocated strongly for the governments to comply with the FATF recommendations and also publicized the potential adverse consequences of continued listing.[71] Regional banking associations may also lobby governments. In Guyana, for example, the Caribbean Association of Banks pressed the Guyanese government to pass legislation to avoid the FATF noncomplier list. The association's statement highlighted the benefits of such action for the country and the region.[72]

A second pathway to policy change is via direct government intervention, usually due to direction from the central bank or ministry of finance. Officials from a country's central bank and ministry of finance often attend the FATF plenary meetings, and therefore these parts of the bureaucracy tend to be the most attuned to the potential impact of listing. When Ethiopia was on the noncomplier list from 2010 to 2014, the central bank played a critical role in encouraging private banks to meet the FATF standards. In the words of one bank executive, "For private banks, it was a whole range of new requirements but the Central Bank wanted it done. . . . Even if the first reaction was to ignore it, they realized it is what had to be done."[73] In countries where legislative change may be slow to occur, the central bank may act independently to issue new regulatory guidance or improve compliance procedures. When the FATF was considering listing Pakistan in early 2018, for example, the State Bank of Pakistan pressured banks and foreign exchange companies to improve the implementation of anti–money laundering regulations. The central bank warned industry officials that mishaps could hamper the flow of trade financing, remittances, and foreign direct investment.[74] Government officials from a country's financial intelligence unit—a part of the bureaucracy set up specifically to receive information and cooperation with other countries about illicit financing risks—are also likely to advocate for policy change.

Finally, bank-to-bank pressure may lead to improved compliance indirectly by imposing direct costs on firms and consumers. If listing causes domestic banks to lose easy access to the US dollar or the euro, the costs of business will increase. Trade will become more expensive and investment will be less attractive. Higher bank costs from listing may raise the costs of remittances, a key source of income for many countries. In the Philippines, concerns about higher remittance costs have been major drivers of policy change to avoid listing. Senatorial aspirant Susan "Toots" Ople, a longtime advocate of labor and overseas workers' rights, cited concerns about remittances when advocating for the Philippine government to amend the Anti–Money Laundering Act in 2016: "Millions of overseas Filipinos will once again bear the brunt of any sanctions to be imposed by the FATF in terms of higher remittance costs, and more stringent requirements, in sending money back home."[75]

While unofficial market enforcement can work through all of these channels to change the compliance incentives of a government, some governments will require more intense pressure to change their policies because the costs of compliance are higher. Many jurisdictions benefit financially from lax regulation; it is a key competitive advantage that helps them attract capital (Palan 2003). By changing their regulations to improve financial transparency, such countries stand to lose significant capital as foreign investors opt to store their money in alternative destinations. When the FATF listed the Bahamas in June 2018, for example, a Boston tax law group advised its clients that the Bahamas may no longer be a viable investment option if it changes certain laws to improve compliance with international standards.[76] Countries that have historically benefited from financial secrecy may only change their laws under intense international pressure.

Market Integration

The FATF noncomplier list's impact on government policy is likely to vary across countries. Countries that are highly integrated into global financial markets typically have strong domestic banking sectors that are sensitive to rising external costs and are also influential political actors. In countries with large financial sectors or where a large portion of the economy depends on foreign direct investment, domestic banks and other financial institutions are more likely to be familiar with the FATF and its mission. Domestic actors may even participate in the FATF's outreach activities to the private sector. As a result, these actors are more likely to be aware of the potential consequences of the FATF noncomplier list and to advocate for governments to improve their policies even before banks begin to restrict financial flows.

Reputation Costs and Spillover Effects

The FATF noncomplier list not only drives policy change via unofficial market enforcement; it may also affect compliance by imposing other types of reputation costs. Although the FATF adopts cooperative language in its noncomplier list process, media coverage frequently refers to the process as a "blacklist." This "name-and-shame" approach can damage country reputations and the reputations of bureaucrats that participate in the global anti–money laundering regime. One anti–money laundering official from a formerly listed country identified reputational considerations as the primary motivation for policy change: "As far as markets, I'm not saying we're unaware of the side effects, but at least from my perspective, that's not the main motivation. We just wanted a clean reputation internationally."[77]

The FATF noncomplier list may also generate policy change by incentivizing nonlisted countries to change their laws in order to avoid the possibility of listing.[78] The FATF's clear listing criteria signal how countries should prioritize different types of policy improvements. During the third round of evaluations, governments focused their policy reforms on the sixteen key and core recommendations. Whereas before, governments worked to implement all of the FATF recommendations, the focal point effect of listing drove policy attention toward key areas. In some contexts, such focal point effects might drive "gaming the system" behavior, where a state aims to achieve targeted goals while ignoring the overall policy objective. In the FATF case, however, measurable outputs and the regime's effectiveness are closely linked. A country cannot have an effective anti–money laundering regime without achieving a minimal level of compliance on the FATF's key recommendations. In one interview, an official from the secretariat of an FATF regional-style body described the FATF's most important recommendations as the "building blocks of the regime, without which anything else would be pointless."[79]

Why Not the United States?

Given the FATF's close alignment with the United States, it is worth considering to what extent the United States is responsible for the noncomplier list's powerful effect on compliance. US power has promoted financial, economic, and monetary harmonization and interdependence,[80] and the United States has been the global leader in the fight against illicit financing since the FATF's inception. The United States was the first country to criminalize money laundering (Peinhardt and Sandler 2015) and one of the first countries to criminalize terrorist financing. The FATF's regulatory agenda aligns closely with US foreign policy objectives (Sharman 2008; Roberge 2009; Jakobi 2013, 2018), and US economic power has contributed to the diffusion of regulatory standards in other areas of global finance (Simmons 2001; Drezner 2007; Posner 2009; Levi-Faur 2005). Moreover, because anti–money laundering is an issue area where states have few incentives to emulate rules and noncooperation generates high externalities, leading countries have strong incentives to use unilateral pressure and sanctions to generate behavior change (Simmons 2001, 2000b).

The United States' focus on combating money laundering and terrorist financing is undoubtedly important for the FATF's success: without regulatory buy-in from the most powerful economy in the world, global cooperation on combating illicit financing would proceed at a much slower rate, if at all. US membership in the FATF also enhances the IO's ability to provide a focal point for financial institutions. Banks across the world are much more likely to use the FATF's standards and monitoring reports to shape behavior if the United States, which houses a major portion of global finance, is a member of the organization. Absent the United States, the FATF might still be a credible assessor of a country's risk of illicit financing, but international banks would have primarily reputation-based reasons to consider such information, rather than the current combination of reputation and regulation.

The United States, however, is also constrained by the FATF. Its technical nature and strong bureaucratic procedures have required the United States to relinquish direct control over much of the listing process. As discussed earlier in this chapter, the FATF's reliance on "emerging consensus" to overturn bureaucratic recommendations gives significant proposal power to the president, the secretariat, and the evaluation teams. The US government may, of course, informally influence such discussions, but because the FATF is a technocratic body, such interventions are narrowly targeted and couched in scientific language. The United States can work through its bureaucratic network to convince other countries to support its views, but even such efforts can be stymied. In the FATF's 2016 evaluation of the United States, for example, the FATF rated the United States as noncompliant on four recommendations and partially compliant on four recommendations. The monitoring team also critiqued the effectiveness of US laws and regulatory implementation in certain areas.[81] The FATF noncomplier list further supports the notion that US power has its limits: since 2009, the FATF has listed at least eighteen official US allies and several other economies with close ties to the United States.[82]

Unofficial market enforcement depends on support from, but not control by, the United States. In order for the FATF noncomplier list to influence bank lending, the FATF must be salient to global banks. US support for the FATF mission and standards, along with complementary US regulation, creates incentives for banks to care about reducing the risk of illicit financing. Given US market power, US regulations could undoubtedly lead banks to change how they allocate resources to noncompliant countries. But the FATF's ability to create deep and widespread policy change depends on an *unofficial* market enforcement process whereby the FATF provides a focal point, not sanctions, and for this reason, limits on US power are crucial. The FATF must be a credible assessor of state policy and have legitimacy in order for the noncomplier list to drive market behavior without explicit instructions. US direct control of listing would undermine this process.

The United States is willing to make this trade-off because there are political and strategic advantages of deep policy change in this issue area, and US government officials understand that to achieve such effects on a wide scale requires a different approach. The unofficial nature of market enforcement is crucial to its success. Daniel Glaser, former US assistant secretary for terrorist financing and financial crimes, highlighted this point in an interview explaining why other IOs have difficulty emulating the FATF's noncomplier list: "Over the years, people have tried to recreate this moment, but they don't realize that there was ten years of work first that went into establishing expertise, credibility, and standards, and then an enormous amount of work into assessing countries."[83] By relying on unofficial market enforcement, the FATF reduces enforcement costs for its member states and thus allows them to take action against a much larger pool of countries.

The FATF's more technical, apolitical nature also ensures that the list has a longer-term impact on policy improvements. Targeted countries struggle to lobby for removal based on political considerations. Although the FATF noncomplier list process clearly operates in the shadow of market power, the FATF has also managed to avoid the legitimacy challenges that plagued its earlier NCCT process because it abides by clear bureaucratic procedures and rarely recommends that financial institutions employ countermeasures. As a result, the current noncomplier list has been ongoing for a decade, providing a continuous incentive for countries to reform their policies. Moreover, because of the bureaucratic cut point and the lack of overt coercion, the FATF has listed more than sixty economies, while many more have been under threat of listing.[84] The FATF also maintains ongoing engagement and periodic reviews with both listed and nonlisted countries, encouraging deeper policy change.

From an empirical perspective, another possible concern for examining the FATF's impact on policy is that the noncomplier list might correlate with parallel unilateral actions by the United States. The US government maintains several sanctions lists, for example, such as the 311 Special Measures list or its list of designated foreign terrorist organizations. The former list imposes sanctions on jurisdictions or financial institutions that pose significant money laundering concern; however, in the nearly two decades since the list's creation, the United States has listed only five countries: Burma, North Korea, Iran, Nauru, and Ukraine. Politically, it would be extremely difficult for the United States to add more than sixty countries to such a list, particularly since the United States has diplomatic relationships with almost all listed or formerly listed countries. Formerly listed countries like Turkey, Greece, and the Philippines are also quite important allies for the United States and would be able to lobby effectively against any US attempt to subject them to unilateral sanctions. Empirical tests probe these possibilities in chapter 5.

Empirical Expectations: The Noncomplier List, Unofficial Market Enforcement, and Compliance

The theory set forth in chapter 2 highlights how an IO focal point can lead to unofficial market enforcement and generate long-term improvements in compliance. In international cooperation to combat illicit financing, the FATF's reliance on the noncomplier list has incentivized policy reform via changes in cross-border banking. The FATF is able to rely on this unofficial market enforcement process because it is a well-known organization with informational advantages, coercive power, and institutional legitimacy. Because of the FATF's prominence and the fact that powerful economies support the FATF standards, banks reallocate resources in response to the noncomplier list as a way of mitigating the possibility of regulator and shareholder punishment. As this unofficial market enforcement unfolds and international banks penalize domestic banks and firms in listed countries, the banking and business sectors of such countries become allies for policy improvements.

This theory suggests several empirical expectations. Three hypotheses address the relationship between the FATF noncomplier list, unofficial market enforcement, and compliance improvements. Hypothesis 1 articulates the core claim: listing leads to improvements in compliance with the FATF standards. Hypothesis 2 begins to probe the causal mechanism for this relationship, stating that the effect of listing on compliance should be strongest for countries with high levels of market integration. Hypothesis 3 unpacks this relationship further, expecting that the noncomplier list acts as a focal point for banks and leads to declines in bank-to-bank lending. These hypotheses are tested through qualitative and quantitative analyses in chapters 4–6.

A second set of hypotheses probes scope conditions. Hypothesis 4 states that the FATF's institutional prominence gives it a unique ability to generate policy change. Chapter 4 tests this proposition by examining whether US pressure and focal points on illicit financing risk might also lead countries to improve their compliance with the FATF standards. Finally, hypothesis 5 expects that the FATF's primary impact on cross-border banking occurs via the noncomplier list rather than comprehensive monitoring reports. Chapter 5 probes this relationship.

Hypothesis 1: Listing and Policy Change

If the FATF noncomplier list serves as a focal point for identifying countries with a high risk of illicit financing, then listed countries should view the list as costly and take action to be delisted. The FATF noncomplier list provides a description of deficient policies that must be addressed before a country can be removed from the list. The FATF focuses on the most important deficiencies, such as a country's failure to adequately criminalize money laundering or terrorist financing. Compared to nonlisted countries with similar levels of noncompliance, listed countries should have stronger incentives to address policy problems and improve compliance with FATF standards.

Evidence of the link between the noncomplier list and policy change could manifest in several ways. Governments in listed countries might adopt new legislation in the weeks prior to FATF plenary sessions in order to signal improved compliance and enhance the case for delisting. Political leaders might justify new legislation through references to the FATF and its list. At a minimum, if the FATF list increases the incentives for compliance, listed countries should pass laws that conform to FATF standards more quickly than their nonlisted counterparts.

> *Hypothesis 1*: Countries listed by the FATF should be quicker to adopt new FATF-compliant laws as compared to nonlisted countries, and policy makers should tie the passage of new legislation to the FATF.

Hypothesis 2: Compliance via Unofficial Market Enforcement

While the FATF noncomplier list's effect on bank-to-bank lending should incentivize policy change across states, countries that are highly integrated into international finance are likely to be the most responsive to this process. Countries with significant cross-border financial flows typically have a powerful banking sector; this industry should be more attuned to the financial consequences of listing and also more capable of lobbying for policy change. When the FATF lists a country with high levels of market integration, the listed country's banking community should have the requisite political and technical expertise to advocate for rapid improvements in compliance. In contrast, when listed countries have low levels of market integration, the domestic banking industry will generally not understand the impact of the FATF list as quickly and also take longer to advocate successfully for policy change.

> *Hypothesis 2*: The FATF noncomplier list should lead countries with high levels of market integration to adopt new FATF-compliant laws more quickly than listed countries with low levels of market integration.

Hypothesis 3: Listing and Unofficial Market Enforcement

International banks have competing incentives with respect to illicit financial flows. Customers and shareholders may move their money away from banks that are involved in well-publicized money laundering or terrorist financing scandals. Government regulators may also take action against banks that fail to mitigate the risk of illicit financing. While the FATF standards and domestic "customer due diligence" requirements mandate that banks consider a customer's illicit financing risk based in part on the country of residence, regulations do not specify exactly how this should be done. International banks might restrict business with high-risk clients, but banks also have profit-based incentives to continue business relationships. Illicit money is a source of income, and even licit corporate clients may be interested in directing money toward countries with few financial regulations.

Banks can manage these competing incentives by relying on the FATF noncomplier list as a focal point for anti–money laundering compliance efforts. Banks might charge higher interest rates or subject customers in listed countries to greater scrutiny, increasing the costs of borrowing and driving down cross-border flows. For low-profit, high-risk countries, banks might terminate correspondent banking relationships entirely in order to reduce their overall risk exposure. All of these shifts should affect cross-border financial flows.

> *Hypothesis 3*: When the FATF includes countries on its noncomplier list, banks should take internal actions that result in decreases in cross-border bank-to-bank lending to listed countries.

Hypothesis 4: Institutional Prominence vs. US Power

The FATF's multilateral nature and institutional prominence are key to explaining the success of the noncomplier list process. By relying on technocratic monitoring, adopting strict bureaucratic procedures for listing, and taking other steps to enhance legitimacy, the FATF has a unique ability to influence domestic policy in this area. If this is true, then US pressure or technical assistance should not be associated with major increases in compliance. The United States could also threaten economic sanctions against countries that fail to abide by FATF standards or act as the de facto enforcer for the FATF. If the FATF's institutional prominence is key to explaining its effect, none of these US indicators should be associated with significant policy change.

> *Hypothesis 4*: US bilateral pressure, technical assistance, and sanctions should not be associated with significant increases in compliance with FATF standards.

Hypothesis 5: The Noncomplier List as a Unique Focal Point

This book asserts that the FATF's noncomplier list acts as a unique focal point for bank behavior. In theory, the FATF could influence global banking through other channels. The FATF and its affiliate bodies produce detailed and lengthy monitoring reports about each country's level of compliance with the FATF recommendations. These mutual evaluation reports form the basis for most listing decisions. While the mutual evaluations are less timely than the noncomplier list, they are usually released first and provide a much more complete window into a state's policies on combating illicit financing. Because banks may interpret such information in a variety of ways, however, mutual evaluation reports create considerable interpretational ambiguity that are unlikely to lead to measurable shifts in market behavior.

If the FATF noncomplier list truly drives bank behavior via focal point effects, the FATF's longer mutual evaluation reports should have no effect on cross-border bank-to-bank lending. In particular, countries that were evaluated prior to the creation of the new noncomplier list and were subsequently listed by the FATF from 2010 on should not have experienced declines in cross-border lending during the prelisting period.

> *Hypothesis 5*: Noncompliant countries that were evaluated by the FATF between 2005 and 2007 should not have experienced declines in cross-border bank-to-bank lending prior to the creation of the noncomplier list.

Empirical Plan of Book

The remainder of the book assesses these hypotheses and explores their implications for understanding how an IO focal point can drive unofficial market enforcement and policy improvements. Chapter 4 examines the basic link between the noncomplier list and improved compliance, focusing on when states change their laws to criminalize terrorist financing in line with the FATF standards. Qualitative evidence and regression analyses show that listed countries comply with FATF standards on terrorist financing more quickly than nonlisted countries and that market integration moderates this relationship. Additional analyses find little support for US pressure as an alternative mechanism.

Chapter 5 probes the relationship between listing and market enforcement, relying on quantitative and qualitative evidence to test hypotheses 1 and 5. Interviews with financial industry professionals indicate that banks consider a country's illicit financing risk because of domestic regulatory requirements and reputation considerations. Multiple regression analyses examine the relationship between listing and cross-border bank-to-bank liabilities, finding a robust association.

Chapter 6 outlines the process of market enforcement in two countries: Thailand and the Philippines. In Thailand, the FATF noncomplier list imposed large costs on the domestic banking industry, and as a result, the banking industry was influential in convincing the government to change its laws. In the Philippines, the banking industry was also an advocate for policy change, but the government ultimately reformed its laws due in large part to concern about how listing would affect remittance flows into the country. Together, the case studies suggest that part of the power of unofficial market enforcement via banks is that banks are integral to many different aspects of global finance; regardless of how countries are integrated into the worldwide economy, banks have a lever to influence policy change.

4

HOW THE NONCOMPLIER LIST DRIVES FATF COMPLIANCE

In the early hours of 11 September 2001, Al-Qaeda operatives boarded planes to carry out what would become one of the most significant terrorist attacks in history. The deaths of close to three thousand people in New York, Pennsylvania, and northern Virginia sent shockwaves across the globe. Dozens of countries lost citizens. Governments everywhere felt vulnerable to future attacks.

Against this background, international cooperation seemed easy. The United Nations General Assembly opened its 2001 session with a call for urgent action. Within a month, the UN Security Council had passed its most expansive resolution, requiring that every country in the world adopt legislation criminalizing the financing of terrorism. Other international organizations like the North Atlantic Treaty Organization expanded their missions to incorporate countering terrorism into their core mandates.

But while international support for counterterrorism efforts was broad, this surface-level political commitment did not always translate into meaningful action. Legislatures were slow and frequently lacked the technical knowledge necessary to understand international standards. Governments proposed counterterrorism laws that were laced with controversial political agendas about suppressing minority rights or free speech (Whitaker 2007); such proposals served to galvanize domestic opposition. And within a few years, the Bush administration's decision to wage war on Iraq weakened many countries' desires to support the United States. Nearly a decade after the UN Security

Council first called on countries to criminalize terrorist financing, most countries had laws that were weak and ineffective.

In February 2010, the Financial Action Task Force (FATF) pushed back against this trend with a public noncomplier list identifying twenty-eight problematic countries. The list discussed gaps in each country's anti–money laundering and combating terrorist financing legislation and outlined specific steps that governments should take to be removed from the list. Within a year, the noncomplier list began to transform domestic politics. Governments rushed to pass new laws to avoid listing. Once listed, legislatures pushed through new laws that had previously been stalled for years. As the FATF continued to add new countries to the list, the list's impact intensified. By 2019, nearly every country in the world had an FATF-compliant law on terrorist financing.

The FATF noncomplier list motivated governments all over the world to change their laws. In Turkey, the government worked to pass new legislation on terrorist financing over resistance from opposition leaders, who objected to the government's far-reaching definition of "terrorism."[1] In Nigeria, President Goodluck Jonathan warned senators to pass necessary legislation or "some countries will not honor international financial instruments emanating from Nigeria, including letters of credit; international investors will be scared to invest . . . and Nigeria's international image will be highly dented."[2] Even in Ecuador, where the president and foreign minister publicly rejected the FATF's right to "dictate policy," government officials began drafting a bill to outlaw the financing of terrorism.[3]

Why do leaders care about the FATF noncomplier list? And how does the list actually lead countries to change their policies? The theory in this book suggests that the FATF's impact on policy change is linked to how the noncomplier list serves as a focal point for global banking. The FATF is the leading institution in the effort to combat illicit financing because of its informational advantages, coercive power, and legitimate authority. Banks have regulatory and reputational incentives to minimize illicit financing risk, and the FATF noncomplier list is a natural way for banks to coordinate their behavior with respect to illicit financing.

This chapter explores the noncomplier list's impact on domestic politics. Drawing on qualitative evidence assembled from FATF and government documents, news stories, and interviews with government officials, it highlights how FATF monitoring reconfigures the domestic politics of compliance. The chapter begins by discussing why countries may fail to change their policies prior to listing and then explains how the noncomplier list alters these compliance calculations. The chapter then sets the stage for a robust quantitative analysis. It discusses common empirical challenges of measuring compliance and explains the regression's main dependent variable: the month and year that a country adopts an FATF-compliant law that criminalizes terrorist financing. The regression relies on a Cox proportional hazards model, which examines compliance patterns among the group of countries that had not adopted FATF-compliant laws on terrorist financing as of 2009. The analysis probes whether noncomplier list countries are more likely to adopt FATF-compliant laws in a given period. Results show that listed countries are eight times more likely to criminalize terrorist financing in a given period, and that this effect is strongest for countries with high market integration. Subsequent robustness tests find no relationship between US bilateral or economic pressure and compliance improvements.

The Logic of Noncompliance

The FATF's monitoring and evaluation process is extremely effective at finding compliance failures; nevertheless, countries often fail to meet the FATF standards. Many governments lack the technical capacity to understand and implement international standards; both legislatures and regulators may be confused about what types of policy change are actually required. Capacity problems are particularly true for countries that have recently joined an FATF regional affiliate. Prior to 1999, the FATF global network was relatively small: five of the FATF's nine regional-style bodies were created in the last two decades. As a result, many newer members are still familiarizing themselves with the FATF system and relevant priorities. Numerous international bodies work to disseminate knowledge about the FATF standards, but such efforts may sometimes generate misunderstandings or implementation challenges. A 2011 report from the UN Office on Drugs and Crime (UNODC) found that while many countries have followed the FATF recommendations by establishing financial intelligence units (FIUs), "the vast majority of countries are yet to develop fully functional AML/CFT regimes," with FIUs "sometimes without any AML/CFT cases prosecuted so far" (27).

Among poorer states, noncompliance may also be related to financial considerations. Complying with the FATF standards can be extremely expensive.[4] The FATF recommendations require governments to pass new laws, create and staff a new bureaucratic agency (the FIU), regulate and monitor the financial sector, provide statistics about policy implementation, and improve international cooperation. Governments must invest significant resources to implement such policies. For government regulators to monitor the financial sector, for example, they need to assemble information on each bank's risk exposure (based on customers, products, and services), its compliance procedures and internal controls, and its links to risky jurisdictions overseas.[5] High levels of compliance are rarely achieved by low-income countries, which often have inadequate budgets even to train bureaucratic staff in this issue area (IMF Legal Department 2011).

Finally, many governments face competing political demands that make it more difficult to fulfill international obligations. The FATF's decision to link together terrorist financing and money laundering seems to have inadvertently led policy makers in some countries to view these problems as "developed world issues" (UNODC 2011, 20). Some countries like the Bahamas have no history of terrorism, so their governments may be reluctant to spend political capital and financial resources setting up a robust terrorist financing regime. Some small island nations like Fiji and low-income countries like Angola face relatively low illicit financing risks and may assess such policies as disconnected from their own direct interests. One representative from a small island country expressed such a sentiment on the sidelines of the September 2016 Asia-Pacific Group on Money Laundering plenary, noting, "This is not our priority. There is no threat of terrorist financing. Yet the FATF might blacklist [us] and then suddenly it becomes our priority."[6]

In larger economies, governments may encounter a different problem: organized opposition to meeting the FATF standards. Many countries have financial sectors that have benefited historically from financial secrecy, which allows money launderers and tax evaders to store money anonymously without legal repercussions. In Panama, for example, there was significant political resistance to meeting the FATF standards. Financial industry professionals viewed such measures as potentially cutting into a key source of revenue.[7] In the Philippines, the parliament passed a watered-down anti–money laundering law in response to the FATF's Non-Cooperative Countries and Territories (NCCT) process, but the government pointedly ignored the FATF's requisite $10,000 threshold for reporting suspicious transactions.[8] Lawmakers believed that adopting the FATF threshold would be unacceptable for their wealthy colleagues as well as their supporters in the business community (Brillo 2010a). When meeting FATF standards threatens powerful financial interests, governments are unlikely to adopt requisite reforms without significant outside pressure.

Laws on terrorist financing may encounter political opposition for an additional reason: political overreach. Several countries have used counterterrorism legislation to suppress their political opponents, while other countries have used different FATF recommendations to justify illiberal behavior. The FATF recommendation that countries scrutinize and regulate their nonprofit sector, for example, is sometimes used to justify the suppression of legitimate nonprofit and civil society organizations (Hayes 2013). In the United States, efforts to stop terrorist financing have sometimes targeted Islamic charities on a purely speculative basis, with laws and regulations designed to stop unknown future attacks and directed toward organizations with unclear ties to terrorist entities (De Goede 2012). Governments in several other states, including Azerbaijan, Bangladesh, Nigeria, Russia, Sri Lanka, and Turkey, have used this recommendation to justify quashing political opposition.[9] For these reasons, some leaders encounter strong civil society pushback when they attempt to comply with the FATF standards.

How the FATF List Transforms Compliance Calculations

The FATF's global network and its mutual evaluation process are effective tools for resolving certain underlying problems, such as rule ambiguity or lack of government capacity. Through the FATF global network, countries meet one to three times per year for plenary discussions that encourage information sharing across states. Governments become familiar with the content and interpretation of the FATF recommendations as bureaucrats attend meetings and listen to presentations by experts in other countries. At the September 2016 annual meeting of the Asia/Pacific Group (APG), for example, government officials from APG member countries attended a mini-seminar on how anti–money laundering supervisors can cooperate across borders, as well as a presentation by US officials on cyber threats to business email.[10] The FATF monitoring process is also essential for generating expertise. The FATF and its regional bodies train bureaucrats to serve on evaluation teams, which provide an invaluable learning experience for participants.[11] During a country's yearlong evaluation process, the evaluation team meets with dozens of government agencies, as well as the financial sector; this process improves familiarity with the FATF and its mission. The evaluation also raises the profile of a country's domestic anti–money laundering bureaucracy because the financial intelligence unit, treasury department, and central bank play key roles in interpreting and implementing the FATF recommendations.

Technical assistance and monitoring, however, are not able to address more intractable sources of noncompliance, and for that reason, the FATF aims to intensify its impact on domestic policy through a noncomplier list. Up until 2009, an FATF member or affiliate country would adopt new regulations and laws primarily in the run-up to its mutual evaluation—an assessment done only about once per decade. Most governments faced few consequences for receiving poor ratings and anticipated little scrutiny until their next evaluations.[12] The reputation costs of noncompliance were also relatively low, as the two-hundred-page mutual evaluation reports did not facilitate easy comparisons across countries.

In 2009 the FATF redesigned its process for dealing with problematic jurisdictions. FATF member states realized that the organization needed a more technocratic noncompliance procedure.[13] In June 2009 the FATF adopted new rules whereby all countries that received "failing" scores on ten or more of the FATF's sixteen most important recommendations would be automatically eligible for listing.[14] The FATF relied on this threshold for the remainder of its third-round evaluations and created similar bureaucratic criteria for its fourth round of evaluations (currently ongoing).[15]

The FATF noncomplier list reconfigures the domestic political incentives of states in part by increasing the reputation costs of failing to meet FATF standards. Former FATF president Antonio Gustavo Rodrigues described the effectiveness of this "name-and-shame" process, pointing out that the FATF noncomplier list draws the attention of many international organizations "because in the end, everything is connected."[16] When the FATF lists a country, its reputation is damaged internationally, both within the FATF global network and across other diplomatic contexts.

Because of the FATF's clear listing threshold, countries work hard to improve their policies enough to avoid being eligible for the noncomplier list. Many governments, particularly those with extensive anti–money laundering expertise, have sought to pass legislation or adopt reforms in the run-up to the FATF's plenary sessions in order to prevent possible listing. Indeed, in this data set, 40 percent of new FATF-compliant laws on terrorist financing were passed within a few weeks of an FATF plenary session. Tom Keatinge, director of the Centre for Financial Crime and Security Studies at the Royal United Services Institute for Defence and Security Studies, described how the FATF evaluation system motivates policy change: "[Countries] work hard in preparation of their evaluations, but often the evaluation actually ends up being a wake-up call. They do badly and then use the MER and input from the FATF/FSRB/IMF etc. as a road map for improvement. They could ignore all that but then they are likely to find themselves in the grey-blacklist doom loop if they don't do what is deemed to be right by those judging them."[17]

Relatively few eligible countries manage to avoid being listed. According to the FATF, as of October 2018, it had reviewed more than eighty countries and publicly listed sixty of them.[18] The FATF focuses its attention on larger financial centers (those with at least USD 5 billion in assets) and on strategically important jurisdictions (FATF-GAFI 2014, 3).[19] Its bureaucratic procedures typically give governments a year to demonstrate the necessary political will and policy improvements in order to avoid listing, but this time line is challenging for most countries. In rare cases, such efforts are sufficient. Monaco was eligible for listing in 2009, but the government adopted and implemented a new law on money laundering and terrorist financing in August of the same year. When the FATF issued its first listing announcement in February 2010, Monaco was not among the listed countries. Similar processes occurred in Liechtenstein and Taiwan. For most countries, however, a year is not enough time to undertake massive policy change, and thus listing is unavoidable.[20]

The Impact of Listing on Global Banking

The FATF noncomplier list's most powerful impact is linked to how it serves as a focal point for market actors. International banks integrate the noncomplier list into their risk models, which they use to evaluate the costs and benefits of doing business with customers in different jurisdictions. Banks may restrict business, charge higher premiums for transactions, or, in some cases, terminate a relationship with banks or entities in listed countries. International investors may also engage in market enforcement, interpreting a government's noncompliance as a negative signal about its ability or willingness to repay debt obligations. In both of these scenarios, the existence of market enforcement creates pro-compliance domestic allies who are influential in pressuring governments to change their policies.

PATHWAY 1: DOMESTIC BANK PRESSURE

When banks shift resources based on the noncomplier list, this process creates political and economic costs for governments in listed states. As discussed in chapters 1 and 3, most countries have laws that require banks to evaluate potential customers based in part on the risk of money laundering or terrorist financing. Banks assess such risks by considering the customer's country of origin. As a result, the FATF has a ready audience for its noncomplier list: the international banking community.

A substantial body of evidence suggests that international banks around the world have integrated the noncomplier list into their risk calculations for doing business with banks or clients in listed countries. Banks maintain complex risk models to assess country risk. International banks typically subject customers and businesses in high-risk countries to more scrutiny, requiring additional identifying documents, delaying transactions, and, in some cases, refusing to do business altogether. Because of the FATF's prominence and ongoing regulatory scrutiny, banks cannot justify ignoring the noncomplier list. One practitioner explained this effect as follows: "Imagine a risk committee meeting in a bank where someone wants to do business in an ICRG-listed country. Not having considered the implications of the FATF listing as part of your due diligence would seem negligent in that committee."[21]

The most direct negative effect of the FATF list occurs through transnational correspondent banking relationships. Correspondent banking relationships are bank-to-bank networks that allow financial institutions in other countries to provide services on behalf of other banks.[22] Every country connected through the international financial system relies on correspondent banking to do business across borders, but recent surveys of banks worldwide have found that correspondent banking relationships are declining (Erbenova et al. 2016; Bank for International Settlements 2016). A 2015 World Bank survey found that half of banking authorities, and more than 75 percent of large international banks, reported a decline in correspondent banking relationships between 2010 and 2014.[23] Recent work suggests that banks often withdraw from correspondent relationships due to concerns about the risk of money laundering or terrorist financing (Durner and Shetret 2015; Erbenova et al. 2016).

The banking sector has an unparalleled ability to sound the alarm about the potentially harmful repercussions of listing. At the start of the FATF noncomplier list, many banking officials were already attuned to the possibility of market enforcement due to the consequences of the FATF's previous listing process. When the FATF listed countries under its old NCCT initiative in 2000 and 2001, banks around the world restricted business with NCCT countries. Banking officials—regardless of whether their countries were listed under the NCCT process—are aware of how FATF listing might affect their institutions. The leaders of major banks may even remember instructing their offices to avoid transactions with NCCT countries. In the years following 2010, banking officials became reacquainted with such consequences.

Politicians often do not understand the potential costs of listing. Political leaders typically have less familiarity with the FATF and its mission since its technocratic meetings are attended by bureaucrats.[24] High-level leaders may engage with the organization during the mutual evaluation process but are likely to be focused on specific outcomes, not the broader organizational context or related developments in other countries. As a result, political leaders may be unfamiliar with the potential consequences of listing prior to ending up on the list.[25]

Qualitative evidence suggests that domestic banking communities and banking associations alert governments and the public to the consequences of listing through public statements, press releases, and testimonials. Such efforts often highlight financial repercussions for both individuals and companies. During Panama's time on the noncomplier list, the executive vice president of the Banking Association described how the list caused serious problems for banks and commercial customers and morally damaged the reputation of Panama's banking sector.[26] In the Bahamas, the governor of the central bank of the Bahamas proposed targeted reforms to reduce the Bahamas' illicit financing risk profile in order to protect domestic banks and avoid listing. The governor explained, "We need to avoid any risk of FATF blacklisting, which would materially constrain local banks in their ability to service customers," particularly those "who would like to invest, travel or otherwise engage internationally."[27]

In some countries, banking associations have also been politically active, lobbying government officials directly to push for improved compliance with the FATF standards. The Bankers' Association of the Philippines (BAP) is a longtime advocate for meeting FATF standards; the industry group has taken action during both of the country's listing experiences and when it was under threat of a third listing in 2017. The BAP's efforts date back to the country's first anti–money laundering bill, adopted in 2001. Brillo (2010b, 117) recounts how the BAP lobbied and attempted to influence lawmakers by arguing that "the banking system would face not only an increase in transaction costs but serious reputational risk, if the law was not passed." Sixteen years later, the BAP continued to push the government to comply with FATF standards, testifying in support of legislation to amend the Anti–Money Laundering Act of 2001 so that it covered casinos and the gaming industry.[28]

In Guyana, the banking sector has also advocated consistently for improving compliance with the FATF standards.[29] Prior to FATF listing, the Guyanese government and the opposition spent more than two years negotiating new anti–money laundering and combating terrorist financing legislation without reaching any agreement. During this period, the local banking community warned repeatedly about the consequences of listing. In January 2014, after the Caribbean Financial Action Task Force issued a public warning to Guyana, the Bankers Association of Guyana met with the president to report problems with transferring money and continuing correspondent banking relationships with other foreign jurisdictions.[30] Weeks before the FATF listed Guyana in October 2014, the Caribbean Association of Banks urged the Guyanese government to pass necessary legislation, issuing a statement that highlighted the benefits of such action for the country and the region.[31] The government and the opposition, however, failed to find common ground, due to the opposition's attempts to tie other legislative priorities to the anti–money laundering bill.[32] The FATF listed Guyana in late October 2014. When Guyana finally passed legislation the following year, major parts of the Guyanese banking community had already begun to abide by the amended requirements.[33]

PATHWAY 2: CENTRAL BANK ADVOCACY

Due to concerns about domestic banks and about market enforcement from foreign investors, central banks also play an important role in pushing governments to change their policies to comply with FATF standards. To understand why central banks care about the noncomplier list, it is helpful to consider the market for sovereign debt. Many governments finance their budgets by issuing sovereign debt, sometimes in the form of bonds that are denominated in a foreign currency like the dollar or the euro. Although both governments and central banks can issue sovereign debt, central banks have a particular interest in how sovereign bonds perform because the central bank is responsible for monitoring the country's money supply.[34] For this reason, a central bank has strong incentives to cultivate a positive reputation internationally. A central bank may work to implement domestic policies that follow best practices and make the country competitive with other countries.[35]

A central bank is likely to be particularly concerned about the country's reputation when its debt is purchased by foreign investors—a trend that is increasingly common in recent years. In 2010, emerging market governments sold $1.3 trillion in debt on the international market. Five years later, the number had nearly doubled to $2.2 trillion (IMF and World Bank 2016). Foreign investors are buying much of this debt. One IMF study indicates that between 2010 and 2012, foreign investors spent close to half a trillion dollars purchasing debt from emerging economies (Arslanalp and Tsuda 2014).

The FATF noncomplier list is useful for international investors because listing signals information about economic and political risk. From an economic standpoint, listed countries suffer clear financial penalties due to market enforcement from banks, with implications for trade and exchange rate stability. When banks close correspondent bank accounts with listed countries or restrict foreign transactions, it becomes more costly for listed countries to trade internationally. The majority of cross-border capital flows are conducted in US dollars or euros. If financial institutions close correspondent bank accounts, they often cut off access to these key currencies that are essential for international trading relationships (Durner and Shetret 2015, 19). For this reason, in regions like the Caribbean, where trade is between 70 and 130 percent of GDP for most countries, governments have been extremely concerned about the impact of the FATF list on de-risking and macroeconomic performance.[36] Credit rating services take note of these potential losses, cautioning investors about listed countries. In February 2020, for example, Moody's responded to Pakistan's continued inclusion on the FATF noncomplier list by calling the information "credit negative for Pakistani banks because it raises questions about potential additional restrictions relating to banks' foreign-currency clearing services, as well as their foreign operations."[37]

The FATF noncomplier list also provides information about political risk, that is, a government's willingness to repay its debt obligations. Previous research suggests that rating agencies like Moody's and Fitch consider political risk when assigning ratings to new sovereign bond issues (Biglaiser and Staats 2012). FATF listing status may influence such calculations. The FATF is one of the few multilateral institutions that sets global standards for the banking industry. When the FATF puts a country on the noncomplier list, this action signals that the listed government is failing to implement financial best practices. This signal is particularly strong in the case of the FATF noncomplier list because countries are given time to meet the FATF standards and avoid listing. At a minimum, countries have two years between the revision of FATF standards and ending up on the noncomplier list, and most countries have substantially more time.[38] Given the possibility of significant economic consequences, investors might view a government failing to take action as a signal of political failure or incompetence.

Because international investors increase the costs of listing, central banks work to improve their countries' compliance with financial integrity standards. Central banks, particularly in emerging markets, monitor their own progress and relative performance on these issues through comparative indices, such as the Basel Anti–Money Laundering Index. In some countries, "the central bank has gone beyond domestic regulation to ensure its financial institutions meet the FATF standards, regardless of whether such measures are enforceable."[39] The central bank's role in pushing for policy change may also increase over time, as bank governors become more aware of the significance of the FATF list. When the FATF listed Thailand in 2010, the Parliament and the Bank of Thailand did not realize initially the significance of the FATF or the listing process. Once Thai banks began reporting slowed transactions and halted business relationships, however, the government and central bank changed their approach. Thailand was removed from the list in 2013, and since that time, Thailand has significantly improved its legal and supervisory anti–money laundering framework.[40]

Descriptive Evidence of Compliance Improvements

The FATF noncomplier list has been a robust tool for improving compliance in listed countries. Nearly all listed countries eventually change their policies. Governments pass and implement new laws, strengthen their regulatory capacities, and improve bureaucratic expertise prior to removal. Not surprisingly, such changes often take multiple years to implement; on average, states remain on the noncomplier list for three years. Descriptive statistics suggest that the domestic characteristics of states—in particular, a country's level of democracy and its government capacity—are correlated with the length of time that a state is listed. Figure 4.1 shows these relationships. On average, higher levels of democracy and lower levels of state capacity (proxied with GDP per capita) correlate with longer listing times.

Countries that change their policies in response to listing fall into three general categories. A handful of countries are "quick compliers" that make policy improvements within a few months of listing.[41] Azerbaijan and Qatar, for example, were listed in February 2010; by June, both countries had enacted new laws, issued new regulations for freezing terrorist assets, and addressed all other deficiencies. While the countries' autocratic political systems no doubt aided their efforts to pass legislation so quickly, several democratic countries also undertook rapid policy change. Greece, Honduras, and Ukraine all enacted new legislation within six months of listing, and although it took slightly longer for these countries to adopt implementing regulations, all were removed from the list in under two years.

Quick compliers are a rarity; most countries take a more incremental approach to policy improvements. Argentina, for example, adopted a step-by-step approach since its problems were too numerous to remedy quickly.[42] A government may also adopt an incremental strategy toward policy improvement because the bureaucracy moves slowly and needs time to understand and adopt new policies. According to one official from a formerly listed country, everyone in the government saw policy change as a priority because "we didn't want to be stuck on the list for years. You've agreed with the FATF and you want to show that you're committed to the process. The landscape internationally changes very

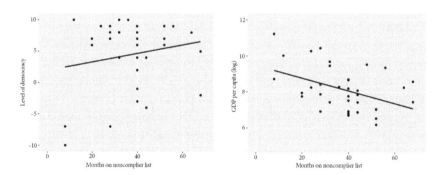

FIGURE 4.1.   Domestic characteristics of listed countries and average length of listing

Note: The figure illustrates the relationship between democracy (*left*) and government capacity (proxied with GDP per capita, *right*) and the months that a country remains on the noncomplier list. Data is shown for the forty countries removed from the FATF list as of December 2015. Democracy data is drawn from the Polity IV project. GDP per capita data is from the World Bank's World Development Indicators.

often for assessing countries; we wanted to be ready for the next step."[43] Nevertheless, the listed government spent three years modifying its policies before the FATF finally removed the country from the list.

A final set of countries are "reluctant compliers": governments that only implement changes after significant pressure from the FATF. In the early years of the noncomplier list, the FATF pressured reluctant compliers by moving them to stronger lists, referred to in the FATF global network as the "dark grey list" and the "blacklist."[44] The blacklist is part of the FATF's Public Statement, a listing announcement directed at more problematic jurisdictions.[45] The Public Statement includes a list of countries subject to countermeasures (since 2010, this list has only ever included Iran and North Korea) and a second list of countries where FATF members and affiliates should "consider the risks arising from the deficiencies associated with each jurisdiction." While the FATF's official language is quite mild, in practice, banks subject blacklisted countries to more oversight and scrutiny. The dark grey list is part of the FATF's "Improving Global AML/CFT Compliance" announcement, and it identifies countries that have not made enough progress; these countries have four months to demonstrate political commitment or face blacklisting.[46]

The FATF created the dark grey list and the blacklist to deal with reluctant compliers. Particularly in the early years of the noncomplier list, many governments struggled to find domestic support for passing stronger laws and regulations against illicit financing. Countries like Ecuador, Indonesia, Nigeria, Pakistan, Thailand, and Turkey all ended up on the FATF blacklist after failing to adopt sufficient legislation. In some cases, countries actually tabled legislation in advance of the blacklist but were unable to find domestic support for passing it. In Turkey, for example, officials from the Ministries of Justice, Interior, and Foreign Affairs worked quickly to draft a new terrorist financing law to align the country more closely with FATF recommendations.[47] The law stalled in Parliament, however, due to strong resistance from the opposition party. It was only after the FATF moved Turkey up to the blacklist and threatened to suspend its membership that the government eventually passed new legislation.[48] In Nigeria, the government passed relevant legislation but did not enact it until the country was put on the blacklist. Even in countries like Ecuador, which was listed for more than five years, the government eventually improved compliance.

As governments have become more familiar with the noncomplier list and its effects, the FATF has relied less and less on its blacklist to incentivize policy change. Between 2010 and 2012, the FATF placed twenty countries on the blacklist for at least a brief period of time; since that time, however, the FATF has only added one additional country to the list (Algeria in 2013).[49] When the

FATF removed Myanmar from the list in February 2016, the public statement became exclusively focused on Iran and North Korea, and nearly five years later, it remains this way.

Laggard States

The FATF noncomplier list has successfully incentivized policy change in nearly all listed countries. Only four countries listed today have been on the list for more than three years: Iran, the DPRK, Syria, and Yemen. Table 4.1 displays all the listed countries as of June 2020, organized by original listing date, and provides the reasons they have not yet been removed from the list. All the listed countries (with the exception of North Korea) have taken some measures to cooperate with the FATF and to implement their FATF action plans. Both Syria and Yemen have

TABLE 4.1 Countries on the FATF noncomplier list (as of June 2020)

COUNTRY	YEAR LISTED	REASON FOR CONTINUED LISTING
North Korea	2010	Noncooperative
Iran	2010	Insufficient progress
Syria	2010	No site visit (security)
Yemen	2010	No site visit (security)
The Bahamas	2018	Awaiting on-site visit
Botswana	2018	Implementing action plan
Ghana*	2018	Implementing action plan
Pakistan*	2018	Implementing action plan
Cambodia*	2019	Implementing action plan
Iceland	2019	Awaiting on-site visit
Mongolia*	2019	Awaiting on-site visit
Panama*	2019	Implementing action plan
Zimbabwe*	2019	Implementing action plan
Albania*	2020	High-level political commitment
Barbados	2020	High-level political commitment
Jamaica	2020	High-level political commitment
Mauritius	2020	High-level political commitment
Myanmar*	2020	High-level political commitment
Nicaragua*	2020	High-level political commitment
Uganda	2020	High-level political commitment

* Countries on the noncomplier list during the third round of evaluations; year shown is year of relisting.

Note: Data coded by author based on FATF public announcements. The FATF listed Iran and North Korea under its old listing process; in these cases, the year listed is the first year of the new noncomplier list procedures.

completed their actions plans; however, the FATF has been unable to conduct the necessary on-site visits in order to remove the countries from the list. Overall, the list appears quite effective at incentivizing policy change, even among the least cooperative of states.

Observing Compliance Improvements on Financial Integrity

Understanding the FATF's impact on states requires considering the counterfactual: what would each government's policies look like absent FATF guidance and monitoring? Significant policy harmonization can occur even if an IO has no independent effect on domestic policy. Countries could comply with international rules prior to joining an international agreement, or be incentivized to change their laws for other reasons. In the FATF context, however, the empirical evidence strongly suggests that most policy change is tied directly to the FATF. The technical complexity of the issue area makes it difficult for low-capacity countries to identify and implement best practices without the FATF's guidance. Moreover, FATF pressure is often necessary to counteract the financial incentives that encourage lax regulation in some countries.

To evaluate the FATF's impact on policy, this book focuses on one specific indicator of compliance: the criminalization of terrorist financing. The FATF considers the criminalization of terrorist financing to be a top priority and one of the six building blocks of the financial integrity regime.[50] Technical compliance is also substantively meaningful, as incomplete laws allow terrorists to exploit legislative gaps or engage in forum shopping, pushing bad money toward the weakest regulation. In terms of evaluating the FATF's independent effect on states, this dependent variable is also useful because it provides a clear indication of policy change. The FATF did not adopt the criminalization of terrorist financing as a recommendation until 2001, and prior to that time, only a handful of states had any type of law criminalizing terrorist financing.

Examining compliance by looking at legal change has some notable limitations. It is not a definitive measure of policy implementation. Analyses of global financial standards and domestic compliance have found that countries may engage in "mock compliance," reforming laws but failing to implement or enforce them (Walter 2008), or "cosmetic compliance," where authorities manipulate implementation to avoid the regulation's core objectives (Chey 2014). At a more micro level, policy failures may come from the unwillingness of firms themselves to follow international standards. Findley et al. (2014a, 2014b) probe the global implementation of international standards on anonymous shell corporations, finding that firms in developed economies often ignore international best practices on this issue. Both strands of scholarship suggest that simply examining legal change is insufficient for understanding the FATF's full impact on domestic policy. For this reason, the quantitative analyses are supplemented with more comprehensive case studies in chapter 6.

Another important limitation is that legal change may not correlate with policy success. The effectiveness of any counterterrorism policy is difficult to evaluate; a lack of attacks could indicate a successful policy, or it could indicate a shift in terrorist tactics or priorities. Even measuring the direct outcome—illicit financial flows—is not straightforward. Commonly used measures of illicit flows may not be reliable, as they lack a standardized methodology.[51] Although the primary goal of this book is to understand how an international organization like the FATF produces a focal point that increases compliance with its standards, the conclusion highlights the need for a more holistic approach in order to evaluate the normative consequences of the FATF's actions.

Concept and Operationalization

This book examines under what conditions the FATF noncomplier list leads to policy change, that is, the adoption of new laws or regulations that are tangibly different from existing laws and regulations. In theory, policy change could be either a deepening or a weakening of legislation: a country could repeal its laws or remove regulation. Within the realm of terrorist financing, however, policy change has been unidirectional. Countries adopt laws on terrorist financing and expand them over time, but to date, no country has repealed its laws. As such, the concept of policy change is one of policy *deepening*, where countries adopt more stringent or expansive regulations.[52] Moreover, because this chapter examines the effect of the FATF noncomplier list on state policy, policy change can be further specified as the compliance improvements that occur when a country deepens its laws in line with the FATF standards.

Three sets of international rules govern the issue area of combating terrorist financing. The UN General Assembly adopted the International Convention for the Suppression of the Financing of Terrorism in 1999. Two years later, the UN Security Council passed a resolution on terrorist financing, and the FATF adopted its special recommendations on terrorist financing. While all of these institutions have rules on terrorist financing, the rules differ in important ways. As can be seen in table 4.2, FATF Special Recommendation II,[53] which requires countries to create a stand-alone terrorist financing offense, is much more detailed than the Convention or the Security Council resolution. Specifically, the FATF recommendation requires countries to criminalize not only the financing of terrorist acts but also the financing of terrorist individuals and organizations. This expansion is important since funds are fungible. Differences in terrorist financing laws are also meaningful from an effectiveness standpoint since the majority of terrorist financing is used for broad organizational support (such as recruitment, training, subsistence, and travel) (FATF-GAFI 2008).

Given these differences, policy change is operationalized with original data on when a country adopts a FATF-compliant law criminalizing terrorist financing. Data comes from FATF reporting and mutual evaluation reports, news articles, and legal texts. Countries are coded as compliant in the given month and year when they adopt a law against terrorist financing that criminalizes this offense in line with the FATF standards. Drawing from section 5.2 of the FATF's methodology document,[54] compliant laws fulfill five specific criteria, criminalizing:

1. The collection of funds by any means, directly or indirectly;
2. With the intention or knowledge that funds should be used, in full or in part, to:
3. Carry out a terrorist act(s), defined to include all relevant Conventions;[55]
4. By a terrorist organization;
5. By a terrorist individual.

TABLE 4.2   International standards on the criminalization of terrorist financing

INSTITUTION	YEAR	STANDARDS
UN Convention for the Suppression of the Financing of Terrorism	1999	Criminalize the provision or collection of funds with intention or knowledge that they are to be used, in full or in part, to carry out an act defined in annex or intended to cause death or serious bodily injury to a civilian.
UN Security Council Resolution 1373	2001	Criminalize the provision or collection of funds with intention or knowledge that they are to be used to carry out terrorist acts. Prohibit persons from making funds/resources available for benefit of persons who commit/facilitate/participate in terrorist act.
FATF Special Recommendation II on Terrorist Financing	2001	Criminalize the provision or collection of funds with intention or knowledge that they are to be used to (a) carry out a terrorist act, (b) by a terrorist organization, or (c) by an individual terrorist. Funds do not have be used to carry out/attempt terrorist act or be linked to terrorist act.

Note: Data assembled by author based on UN documents and the FATF interpretive note for Special Recommendation II (following the 2012 revisions, Special Recommendation II is now FATF Recommendation 5).

Alternative Measures of Policy Impact

There are several alternative ways to measure the FATF noncomplier list's effect on terrorist financing policies. A weaker measure of compliance might be to examine whether a country has adopted any law on terrorist financing. This approach could be justified by time trends: most countries did not have laws on terrorist financing prior to 9/11, so perhaps the most significant indicator of policy change is the decision to create any type of stand-alone terrorist financing offense. There are, however, several problems with such a formulation. First, the Convention on the Suppression of the Financing of Terrorism, the UN Security Council, and the FATF all require states to criminalize terrorist financing. For this reason, the simple act of criminalization is unlikely to be a meaningful measure of the FATF's impact on state policy. Second, more than 60 percent of countries had already adopted some kind of law on terrorist financing prior to the FATF's first listing announcement in February 2010, so this dependent variable would severely limit the sample size of the analysis. Finally, as discussed earlier, gaps in terrorist financing legislation are substantively meaningful; all terrorist financing laws are not of equal significance.

Alternatively, a stronger measure of policy change might capture not just legal or regulatory change but also differences in policy implementation. Instead of just considering the date of adoption of new FATF-compliant laws, for example, an empirical analysis could examine indicators of implementation such as the number of law enforcement cases related to terrorist financing, or changes in the number of prosecutions and convictions for this crime. Law enforcement statistics, however, are likely to reflect primarily a country's risk profile and underlying law enforcement capacity rather than its legal implementation. Moreover, countries have different standards for collecting police statistics, which introduces significant noise into the data. As a result, such measures are problematic for a cross-country panel analysis.

The FATF Noncomplier List: Testable Hypotheses

The theory suggests that the FATF noncomplier list stigmatizes states directly and that market pressure intensifies this effect. As a result, being listed should incentivize improved FATF compliance. Gordon Hook, the executive secretary of the Asia/Pacific Group on Money Laundering, described this impact. "The list has had a phenomenal effect on policy makers. If they are listed, they work extremely hard and fast to get off the list. At the government level, we always saw high levels of commitment from the executive, but that would slow down once Parliament was involved. Now countries move at a much faster pace."[56]

> *Hypothesis: Listing and Policy Change*—Countries that are listed by the FATF should adopt FATF-compliant laws on terrorist financing more quickly than nonlisted countries.[57]

Unofficial market enforcement can occur along several pathways. In some cases, banks simply exercise enhanced due diligence, subjecting customers in listed countries to greater scrutiny or longer waiting times. In other cases, banks have refused to allow any transactions from listed countries. In May 2014, for example, banks in the United States, Europe, Germany, and Turkey stopped dealing with certain Afghan commercial banks.[58] By June, the cost of money transfers had gone up 80 percent.[59]

One likely moderator for the effect of the noncomplier list on compliance is a country's integration into international markets. Countries that are more open to transnational financial flows should be particularly responsive to listing. Market integration can be proxied with cross-border bank liabilities, which indicate the amount of money that domestic banks in a particular country owe to international banks. Bank-to-bank transactions are a key part of the global economy, and facilitate trade financing, short-term borrowing, and foreign investment. If the FATF list leads banks to restrict financing to noncompliant countries, countries with higher levels of bank-to-bank lending should have more influential banking sectors that are capable of quickly lobbying the government to undertake necessary policy reforms.

> *Hypothesis: Compliance via Unofficial Market Enforcement*—Listed countries that are highly integrated into global markets should adopt FATF-compliant laws on terrorist financing more quickly than less-integrated listed countries.

The theory presented in chapters 3 and 4 suggests that the FATF has enhanced its focal point power by improving institutional legitimacy, that is, the widespread belief that the FATF has the right to rule. The FATF noncomplier list draws heavily on the FATF's bureaucratic authority, relying on prearticulated criteria and a technocratic monitoring process to make listing decisions. If the FATF's institutional legitimacy is important to its focal point power, then one clear observable implication is that US pressure should have little effect on compliance. This is not to say that US technical assistance or bilateral pressure is unimportant, but rather that the United States' impact is limited because its efforts are more clearly politicized.

> *Hypothesis: Institutional Prominence vs. US Power*—US bilateral pressure, technical assistance, and sanctions should not be associated with significant increases in compliance with FATF standards.

Policy Deepening to Combat Terrorist Financing

These hypotheses are tested with a regression analysis that examines how the noncomplier list affects the length of time that it takes for a country to adopt an FATF-compliant law on terrorist financing. The analysis begins in February 2010 (the start of the current noncomplier list), and the data goes through December 2015.[60] Data is at the country-month level, that is, the data set indicates in a given month whether a country was listed by the FATF and whether it had adopted an FATF-compliant law on terrorist financing. Data on country listing status is hand-coded based on the FATF noncomplier list announcements, which are published online in February, June, and October of every year.

The regressions use a Cox proportional hazards model, which analyzes how variables affect the length of time in months that it takes for a country to criminalize terrorist financing in line with FATF standards. This model is appropriate given the unidirectional nature of the data: once a country has fully criminalized terrorist financing, it is unlikely to repeal its law. Due to this approach, however, countries that criminalized terrorist financing in line with the FATF guidelines prior to February 2010 are excluded from the analysis. Furthermore, once a country has met the FATF standard on the criminalization of terrorist financing, it drops out of the data set. In cases where the proportional hazard assumption does not hold, the analysis follows the advice of Box-Steffensmeier and Zorn (2001), who suggest including a log-time interaction for variables with substantial evidence of nonproportionality.[61]

Selection into listing poses potential challenges for the empirical analysis. If the FATF is more likely to list countries that are also more likely to criminalize terrorist financing, failing to account for the selection process could inflate the findings. Conversely, if the FATF is more likely to list the most reluctant compliers, failing to account for selection could attenuate the results. These concerns are addressed through sample construction and the addition of covariates. A full sample of 132 economies includes all jurisdictions that had not criminalized terrorism in line with the FATF standards as of February 2010. This sample contains forty-six countries that were listed as part of the noncomplier list. As the analysis adds covariates, the sample drops to 120 countries (37 listed) in model 2, 96 countries (32 listed) in model 3, and 87 countries (30 listed) in model 4.[62]

The analysis also uses matching to assemble a second sample of countries likely to be listed. Ho and colleagues (2007) suggest that preprocessing data through matching produces more accurate and less model-dependent causal inferences. The analysis uses nearest-neighbor matching to compare countries with similar probabilities of being listed. This creates a set of twelve listed and twelve nonlisted countries that are similar in terms of diffusion, alliance with the

United States, private-sector credit, capacity, level of democracy, and risk of terrorism. More specifically, the data is subset to the first period of analysis (February 2010) and, drawing on relevant covariates for this period, matching creates a set of twenty-four countries with similar probabilities of being listed as of 2010. Panel data is assembled for these twenty-four countries for the full time period (2010 to 2015), and the analyses are rerun.[63] Matching improves the balance of the sample on the majority of variables included in the model.[64]

A third analysis focuses on all non-FATF member countries that were eligible for listing based on the FATF's criteria in February 2010. When member states set the new listing eligibility threshold of ten failing recommendations in June 2009, the FATF and its regional bodies had already completed close to a hundred evaluations. Most of these countries were members of the FATF's regional bodies, rather than the FATF itself, and as a result, they were not involved in setting the new listing threshold. Instead, these countries found themselves suddenly under consideration for a new listing process, with no ability to change their listing eligibility. The analysis examines how listing affects compliance outcomes within this set of sixty-eight countries, fifteen of which were listed by the FATF.

The unit of observation for all analyses is the country-month. In the simplest model for the full sample, this equates to 7,308 observations and 72 events (instances where a country criminalizes terrorist financing in line with FATF guidelines). In the simplest model in the matched sample, there are 1,104 observations and 17 events. Finally, in the simplest model in the sample of countries eligible for listing, there are 3,420 observations and 36 events.

Dependent Variable: Policy Change on Terrorist Financing

The dependent variable is a dichotomous indicator of whether a country has adopted an FATF-compliant law on terrorist financing in a given month and year. As discussed earlier, this is a clear indication of policy deepening since all countries in the analysis had not adopted FATF-compliant legislation as of February 2009. For a law to be coded as FATF-compliant, it has to extend the terrorist financing offense to any person who willfully provides or collects funds with the intention or knowledge that they are to be used to carry out a terrorist attack, by a terrorist organization, or by an individual terrorist.[65]

Figure 4.2 shows the distribution of this variable over time, separated by whether a country is eventually listed (dashed line) or is never listed (solid line). As of late 2008, most countries had not adopted FATF-compliant laws on terrorist financing. Instead, many countries had partial laws that criminalized terrorist financing but adopted a too-narrow definition of terrorism or criminalized

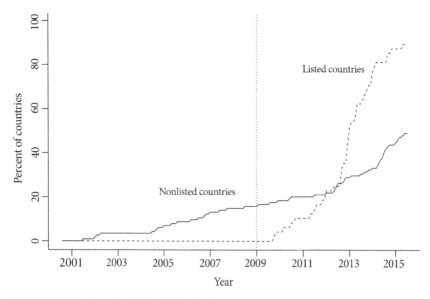

FIGURE 4.2.   Trends in the criminalization of terrorist financing

Note: The figure shows the percentage of never-listed countries (solid line) and countries listed post-2009 (dashed line) that have adopted FATF-compliant laws on terrorist financing. The dotted vertical line indicates the 2009 announcement of the revamped FATF noncomplier list process, which led to the first noncomplier list in February 2010.

financing only when linked to a terrorist act (FATF-GAFI 2015). Such gaps are quite meaningful because terrorists can move money around and often require significant resources to sustain recruitment, propaganda, and legitimation activities (FATF-GAFI 2008).

Since the FATF adopted its new noncomplier list procedures in 2009, countries have been significantly more likely to adopt laws that meet FATF standards. Interestingly, as of 2015, close to 90 percent of listed and formerly listed countries had FATF-compliant laws, whereas only about 50 percent of nonlisted countries had similarly compliant laws. This significant policy deepening by listed countries is the reason that the FATF has removed so many countries from listing. As of October 2018, fifty-five of the sixty-eight listed countries had "graduated" from the noncomplier list following major improvements in their laws.[66]

Explanatory Variables: What Drives Policy Change?

If the noncomplier list incentivizes policy deepening in states, then listed states should be more likely to pass FATF-compliant laws criminalizing terrorist financing. As such, the main explanatory variable is whether, at a given point in time, a country is on the noncomplier list. This variable is operationalized in two ways. The primary operationalization is a dichotomous variable *Listing*, which indicates whether a country is on the noncomplier list at any level (grey, dark grey, or black) in a given month.[67] Operationalizing listing as a dichotomous measure makes sense in part because the nuance of different levels of listing is often lost in media coverage. Ukraine and Argentina, for example, were only on the grey list, yet when Ukraine was removed from the FATF monitoring process, the *Wall Street Journal* headline read "FATF Removes Ukraine from Blacklist, Updates on Argentina" (Rubenfeld 2011). In the dichotomous coding, the variable is equal to 1 if a country is listed at any level and 0 otherwise. In the largest version of the data, approximately 17 percent of observations are coded as 1's.

The effect of listing, however, might also depend on the specific level of listing; therefore, an additional analysis operationalizes the noncomplier list as an ordinal variable. This variable ranges from 0 (no list) to 3 (the blacklist). When the data is differentiated in this way, 12 percent of observations are on the grey list, 1 percent of observations are on the dark grey list, and 4 percent of observations are on the blacklist. The small number of observations in each listing category severely restricts the power of the ordinal analysis; as a result, this test is intended mainly to probe the robustness of the relationship between listing and policy change. The results of this analysis are available in the appendix.

To test the "Compliance via unofficial market enforcement" hypothesis, the analysis includes the variable *Market integration*. This variable is a continuous measure of a country's aggregate cross-border liabilities in 2008, and proxies for a country's level of market integration prior to the FATF's new noncomplier list procedures.[68] Data on cross-border bank-to-bank liabilities come from the Bank for International Settlements (BIS) locational banking statistics. This data set provides information about outstanding claims and liabilities as reported by internationally active banks that are located in the forty-four reporting countries. Because these banks report international cross-border flows, the data cover banking relationships in more than two hundred countries, capturing about 95 percent of all cross-border interbank business. For the countries included in the data set, this variable ranges from USD 7 million for Dominica to USD 1.7 trillion for Germany. The variable is logged to address the skew in the data.

A country's direct ties to the FATF may also affect how quickly it meets FATF standards. The full sample includes the variable *FATF member* to account for whether a country is a member of the FATF in a given year.[69] Countries may also be influenced by the policies of neighbors or regional partners through processes of policy diffusion.[70] Sharman (2008) argues that diffusion has affected the adoption of anti–money laundering policies throughout the developing world. Diffusion can occur through several different mechanisms, as bureaucrats learn about relevant rules and policies, emulate the successes of other governments, adopt best practices in order to compete with other economies, or are coerced into changing their laws.[71] The analysis includes the variable *Diffusion*, which ranges from 0 to 1 and represents the proportion of member states that have adopted FATF-compliant laws on terrorist financing within a country's FATF regional affiliate organization.[72] Germany, for example, is an FATF member, so for Germany, this variable represents the percentage of all FATF countries with compliant laws at a given point in time. Thailand is a member of the Asia/Pacific Group on Money Laundering (APG), an FATF regional body, so for Thailand, diffusion is the percentage of all APG members with compliant laws in a particular month.

Government capacity is also likely to affect the degree to which a country is able to implement the FATF recommendations as well as the time to full compliance. Following previous studies,[73] the analysis controls for capacity using *Gross domestic product (GDP) per capita*.[74] Countries that face a higher threat of terrorism might also be faster to comply with the FATF recommendation on terrorist financing. The analysis includes the variable *Terrorism risk*, which ranges from 0 (lowest risk) to 3 (highest risk).[75] The literature also suggests that a country's political system may affect its ability or willingness to fulfill international commitments.[76] The analysis includes *Democracy*, drawn from Polity IV data.[77]

Per its guidelines, the FATF considers a country's legislative history on terrorist financing when making listing decisions. Prior to 2010, many countries had criminalized terrorist financing, but most of these laws were weak and not in keeping with the FATF standards. The analysis includes the variable *Previous terrorist fin law*, which indicates whether a country had some type of non-FATF-compliant law on terrorist financing as of the end of 2009 (two months before the start of the noncomplier list). Of the 141 countries included in the full sample, ninety-six (68 percent) had adopted some type of non-FATF-compliant law on terrorist financing by the end of 2009.

The FATF builds a pool of potential listed countries based on all countries that receive failing scores on ten or more of the sixteen most important recommendations in their third-round mutual evaluation reports. The analysis includes the variable *Eligible for listing*, which is a dichotomous indicator of whether a country receives ten or more failing ratings on the FATF's key and core recommendations. The FATF and its regional bodies evaluate a country only once per cycle, so for most countries, the number of failing recommendations does not change across the data set.[78]

Another important listing determinant is the size of a country's financial sector (FATF-GAFI 2009). As a proxy for this factor, the analysis includes *Private-sector credit*, which indicates the amount of financial resources that financial corporations provide to the private sector. Such resources may be provided through loans, purchases of nonequity securities, trade credits, or other accounts receivable that establish a claim for repayment. This variable is drawn from the World Bank's "Domestic credit to private sector (% of GDP)" measure and is standardized in 2010 US dollars.

Plausible Alternative: US Power

The most plausible alternative explanation is the possibility that the United States is directly or indirectly responsible for policy change. The FATF's regulatory agenda aligns closely with US foreign policy objectives (see Jakobi 2013, 2018). Scholars have also argued that US economic power has contributed to the diffusion of regulatory standards in other areas of global finance (see Drezner 2007; Posner 2009; Simmons 2001). The US government devotes significant resources to providing technical assistance that promotes the worldwide adoption of financial integrity standards; it also monitors other countries' policies.

The US could affect a country's willingness or ability to criminalize terrorist financing through influence or coercion. The analysis includes the variable *US ally*, which is drawn from the Correlates of War project and indicates whether a country has a defense pact, entente, or neutrality agreement with the United States in a given year (Gibler 2009). To further account for US influence, additional tests rerun the main analysis with four new controls. One model includes the variable *Trade with US*, which is drawn from the IMF and reflects a country's total volume of trade with the United States as a percentage of its GDP. A second model includes *US foreign aid*, which is drawn from USAID and indicates the amount of foreign aid disbursed to a particular country in a given year.

A third model controls for the possibility that the United States might use economic sanctions to pressure countries to change policies. Since 2001, the US secretary of the treasury has had the authority to designate foreign jurisdictions and institutions as "primary money laundering concerns" under section 311 of the USA Patriot Act. US financial institutions and agencies are required to take special measures against designated entities. As of June 2017, the US Treasury had listed twenty banks and five countries under this process. The dichotomous variable *311 sanctions list* indicates whether a country's financial institution or the country itself is on the 311 Special Measures list in a given month. Approximately 2 percent of observations are coded as 1's in the data set.

A final model tests for the effect of bilateral pressure. The US State Department could raise FATF compliance during bilateral meetings or encourage its foreign partners to seek technical assistance. US bilateral pressure is proxied with data from the State Department's annual International Narcotics Control Strategy Report (INCSR), which summarizes money laundering and terrorist financing policies across most countries. It prioritizes countries using a three-tier classification system, where "Jurisdictions of Primary Concern" are major money-laundering countries where financial institutions "engage in transactions involving significant amounts of proceeds from all serious crimes" or where financial institutions are vulnerable because of weak supervisory or enforcement regimes.[79] US pressure is proxied with a continuous variable *US State Dept list* that indicates each country's assigned INCSR tier, where 1 indicates a country is of low concern and 3 indicates a country is categorized as a "Jurisdiction of Primary Concern" in a given year. In the data, approximately 32 percent of observations are coded as 3's.

Results: The Noncomplier List Drives Policy Deepening

The results provide strong support for the hypotheses. Countries on the FATF noncomplier list adopt FATF-compliant laws on terrorist financing more quickly than their nonlisted counterparts, and market integration appears to intensify this effect. Table 4.3 shows the effect of listing on the time it takes for a country to criminalize terrorist financing in line with FATF standards for the full sample. Model 1 serves as a baseline for the effect of listing without controlling for any financial considerations. Model 2 tests the effect of listing and market integration, adding controls for private-sector credit and capacity. Model 3 adds a control for terrorism, while model 4 adds a control for democracy. Across all four models, listing has a positive and statistically significant effect on compliance. In model 4, listed countries are eight times as likely to criminalize terrorist financing in a given period. Policy diffusion also has a strong effect, suggesting that as more states within an organization criminalize terrorist financing, other states are increasingly likely to adopt new laws in line with FATF standards.

Market integration intensifies the effect of listing in a consistently positive and significant manner. In model 4, a 50 percent increase in cross-border liabilities is associated with an 11 percent increase in the probability of criminalizing terrorist financing.[80] While a 50 percent increase in a country's cross-border liabilities may seem like a large change, consider that between 2002 and 2009, at least seven countries in Europe had increases larger than this amount.[81]

Figures 4.3 and 4.4 plot the hazard curves and 95 percent confidence intervals (CIs) for nonlisted and listed countries, based on model 4 in table 4.3. For both figures, the hazard curves represent the probability that a country still has a noncompliant law on terrorist financing over the five-year period after the FATF issues its first noncomplier list announcement in February 2010. Both hazard curves show the probability of noncompliance for non–US ally countries with ten or more failing recommendations. All other variables except listing are set at the means.

TABLE 4.3   Listing, market enforcement, and FATF compliance (full sample)

	DEPENDENT VARIABLE: TIME TO CRIMINALIZATION			
	(1)	(2)	(3)	(4)
Listing	9.029***	8.156***	5.849***	8.429***
	(0.336)	(0.455)	(0.526)	(0.567)
Market integration		1.006	1.003	1.026
		(0.067)	(0.096)	(0.149)
Listing * market integration		1.207**	1.314**	1.345**
		(0.108)	(0.142)	(0.149)
FATF member	1.013	0.623	0.672	0.929
	(0.409)	(0.612)	(0.629)	(0.737)
Previous terrorist fin law	1.370	1.067	0.934	0.877
	(0.286)	(0.357)	(0.402)	(0.448)
Diffusion	1.059***	1.061***	1.073***	1.079***
	(0.013)	(0.017)	(0.020)	(0.021)
Eligible for listing	0.827	1.147	1.103	0.950
	(0.380)	(0.557)	(0.611)	(0.615)
US ally	3.825	1.831	1.942	1.960
	(1.390)	(1.719)	(1.753)	(1.825)
Private-sector credit		1.020	0.935	1.130
		(0.183)	(0.237)	(0.260)
Capacity		1.144	1.174	0.822
		(0.296)	(0.321)	(0.375)
Terrorism			1.071	1.435
			(0.256)	(0.314)
Democracy				0.945
				(0.039)
Observations	7,308	5,850	4,635	4,114
Countries	132	120	96	87
Events	72	52	43	39

* $p < 0.10$; ** $p < 0.05$; *** $p < 0.01$

Note: The table shows the results of Cox proportional hazards models for the full sample, estimating how listing impacts the time it takes for a country to criminalize terrorist financing in line with FATF standards. It displays hazards ratios: values over 1 indicate a positive effect, while values below 1 indicate a negative effect. Standard errors are clustered by country and shown in parentheses. All models include log-time interaction for *US ally*.

Table 4.4 shows the results for the matched sample and the eligible-for-listing sample. Within these samples, listing has an even stronger effect on compliance, and market integration continues to moderate this effect.[82] In the matched sample, listed countries are 13.3 times more likely to criminalize terrorist financing in

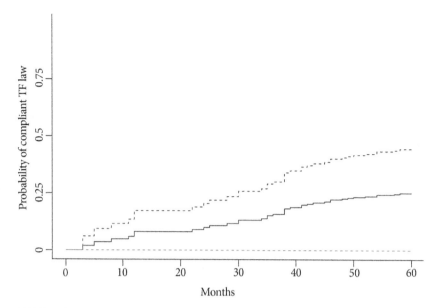

FIGURE 4.3. Compliance improvements in nonlisted countries

Note: The figure shows the probability that a country criminalizes terrorist financing (TF) in a way that complies with FATF standards (solid line) and 95 percent confidence intervals (dotted lines) for model 4 in table 4.3 for nonlisted, non–US ally countries with more than ten failing recommendations.

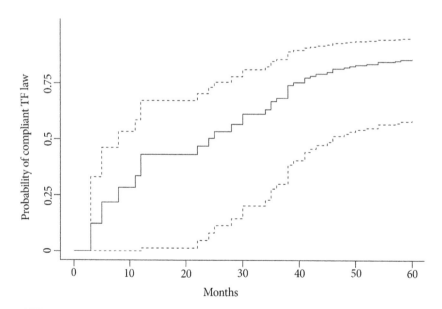

FIGURE 4.4. Compliance improvements in listed countries

Note: The figure shows the probability that a country criminalizes terrorist financing (TF) in a way that complies with FATF standards (solid line) and 95 percent confidence intervals (dotted lines) for model 4 in table 4.3 for listed, non–US ally countries with more than ten failing recommendations.

a given period, while in the sample of eligible-for-listing countries, the estimated effect is even stronger (18.5 in the full model). The sizable increase in the coefficients for listing reflects separation in the data—almost all countries that change their laws are listed by the FATF. In model 1, for example, fifteen of the seventeen countries that comply with FATF standards are listed countries. In model 3, thirty-one of the thirty-six countries that comply with FATF standards are listed

TABLE 4.4   Listing, market enforcement, and FATF compliance (matched sample and eligible-for-listing sample)

	DEPENDENT VARIABLE: TIME TO CRIMINALIZATION			
	MATCHED SAMPLE		ELIGIBLE-FOR-LISTING SAMPLE	
	(1)	(2)	(3)	(4)
Listing	11.467***	13.250*	17.067***	18.491***
	(0.891)	(1.093)	(0.501)	(0.879)
Market integration		1.251		1.011
		(0.281)		(0.218)
Listing * market integration		1.608*		1.589
		(0.396)		(0.287)
Diffusion	1.076	1.144*	1.050***	1.058***
	(0.041)	(0.060)	(0.017)	(0.028)
US ally	0.457	1.010	5.090	0.955
	(4.576)	(5.688)	(1.689)	(2.979)
Private-sector credit		0.390*		1.109
		(0.716)		(0.328)
Capacity		2.713		0.867
		(0.924)		(0.528)
Democracy		0.893		0.933
		(0.078)		(0.056)
Weights	0.001***	0.000**		
	(3.072)	(9.160)		
Observations	1,104	1,018	3,420	1,675
Countries	24	24	66	39
Events	17	16	36	22

* $p < 0.10$; ** $p < 0.05$; *** $p < 0.01$

Note: The table shows hazards ratios for Cox proportional hazards models, estimating how listing impacts the time that it takes for a country to criminalize terrorist financing in line with FATF standards. Values over 1 indicate a positive effect, while values below 1 indicate a negative effect. Standard errors are clustered by country and shown in parentheses. All models include log-time interaction for *US ally*, as well as controls for terrorism risk, previous terrorist fin law, and eligible for listing, none of which are significant.

countries. Such skewed results suggest that the estimates in the full sample are attenuated and underestimate the full effect of listing. An additional possibility is that the FATF listing process is driving countries toward the extremes of compliance—listed countries become more likely than before to change their policies, while nonlisted countries become less likely (since they know that they are temporarily safe from the list).

Examining the Alternative Explanation of US Power

US pressure is the most plausible alternative explanation for why countries criminalize terrorist financing in line with FATF standards. To explore this alternative, the analysis replicates model 4 in table 4.3, adding different indicators to proxy for US power or coercion. Table 4.5 displays these results. Model 1 includes a control for a country's level of trade dependence on the United States. Model 2 adds a control for annual US foreign aid to each country. Model 3 controls for whether a country is on the US Department of the Treasury's 311 sanctions list, which pertains specifically to high-risk money laundering countries. Model 4 controls for US bilateral pressure, proxied with an ordinal indicator of whether the US Department of State considers the country to be a high-risk money laundering jurisdiction in a given year.

FATF listing continues to have a strong, positive effect on compliance, while variables proxying for US pressure have insignificant or negative effects. Both trade dependence and US foreign aid have weak, insignificant effects, while US government listing has a negative effect. Countries included on either the US Department of the Treasury's 311 sanctions list or the US Department of State's list of high-risk money laundering jurisdictions are less likely to comply with FATF standards in a given period. The most likely explanation for this finding is the difference in the type of countries listed. The US government uses the 311 list only against the most reluctant compliers because listing requires market actors to stop all business with a listed country or bank. The State Department list, on the other hand, focuses on countries with high volumes of money laundering, and therefore includes most large financial centers (including the United States). As a result, the list is unlikely to lead to any significant material consequences for identified countries.

To probe the robustness of these results, a placebo test examines whether countries eligible for listing improved their laws in the years immediately prior to the creation of the noncomplier list. Between 2005 and 2007, the FATF evaluated more than sixty countries, fifty-six of which had not criminalized terrorist financing in line with FATF standards. Many of these countries were subsequently eligible for listing after the FATF created its new listing procedures in

TABLE 4.5 Listing, market enforcement, and FATF compliance (US power alternatives)

	DEPENDENT VARIABLE: TIME TO CRIMINALIZATION			
	(1)	(2)	(3)	(4)
Listing	8.372***	8.230***	8.618***	8.462***
	(0.568)	(0.559)	(0.564)	(0.555)
Market integration	1.028	1.022	1.050	0.969
	(0.107)	(0.106)	(0.108)	(0.110)
Listing * market integration	1.339**	1.364***	1.340**	1.306**
	(0.149)	(0.149)	(0.149)	(0.151)
Diffusion	1.078***	1.075***	1.084***	1.074***
	(0.021)	(0.021)	(0.021)	(0.021)
US ally	1.990	1.773	2.204	1.742
	(1.828)	(1.831)	(1.830)	(1.819)
Private-sector credit	1.145	1.179	1.236	1.194
	(0.268)	(0.259)	(0.271)	(0.259)
Capacity	0.821	0.908	0.673	0.755
	(0.378)	(0.385)	(0.414)	(0.377)
Democracy	0.946	0.936	0.942	0.926*
	(0.039)	(0.040)	(0.039)	(0.041)
Trade with US (percent GDP)	0.956			
	(0.196)			
US foreign aid		1.128		
		(0.125)		
US—311 sanctions list			0.301**	
			(1.136)	
US—AML list				0.612*
				(0.312)
Observations	4,103	4,114	4,114	4,090
Countries	88	88	88	88
Events	39	39	39	39

* $p < 0.10$; ** $p < 0.05$; *** $p < 0.01$

Note: The table shows hazards ratios for Cox proportional hazards models, estimating how listing impacts the time that it takes for a country to criminalize terrorist financing in line with FATF standards. Values over 1 indicate a positive effect, while values below 1 indicate a negative effect. Standard errors are clustered by country and shown in parentheses. All models include log-time interaction for *US ally*, as well as controls for FATF member, terrorism risk, previous terrorist fin law, and eligible for listing, none of which are significant.

2009. If the FATF noncomplier list is really driving policy change, then these countries should not improve compliance in the years prior to the list's creation. Descriptive statistics confirm this trend. Of the fifty-six evaluated countries with policy gaps on terrorist financing, only two adopted FATF-compliant laws on terrorist financing prior to 2010.[83]

Conclusion: Listing Transforms the Domestic Politics of Compliance

The evidence in this chapter provides strong support for the hypotheses. When the FATF includes countries on its noncomplier list, these states are quicker to pass legislation to meet FATF standards than nonlisted states with similar policy gaps. While listing is effective at incentivizing widespread policy deepening, listed countries with high levels of market integration are the fastest to improve compliance with FATF standards. The FATF noncomplier list appears to be unique in achieving such effects; there is no evidence that US pressure achieves similar results.

The noncomplier list is an effective driver of policy change because it reconfigures domestic incentives in listed states. Qualitative evidence reveals three main reasons why countries fail to comply with FATF recommendations: weak government capacity, the high costs of policy implementation, and competing political priorities. The FATF's organizational structure and in-depth monitoring and assessment process are effective at addressing the first stumbling block. Plenary meetings encourage familiarity with FATF recommendations, and yearlong country reviews reduce ambiguity and build technical expertise in bureaucracies. But when compliance is costly from an economic or political standpoint, the FATF needs to rely on its noncomplier list to transform domestic politics.

By publicly identifying noncompliant countries, the FATF changes the compliance calculations of governments in listed states. The noncomplier list relies in part on a name-and-shame approach that makes government officials concerned about their country's reputation. But the true power of the list is linked to how it serves as a focal point for global banks. This point is explored in greater detail in the next chapter.

5

UNOFFICIAL MARKET ENFORCEMENT AGAINST LISTED COUNTRIES

Mossack Fonseca was a global operation. Headquartered in Panama, the firm was responsible for managing correspondence and transfers for more than 200,000 companies in forty-two countries. The firm's employees rarely met the owners of these companies; instead, they received instructions through intermediaries. A lawyer or an accountant would call and tell the firm to transfer money from one account to another. Mossack Fonseca would fill out the paperwork and initiate the transfer. Few questions were asked. The operation was confidential and seamless, a perfect way to make money disappear, right up until a massive data leak exposed all of its secrets.

Rich people hiding money in offshore accounts is nothing new, but the "Panama papers" controversy revealed the pervasiveness of the problem. The leak implicated twelve national leaders, including Russia's Vladimir Putin and Pakistan's Nawaz Sharif. In the United Kingdom, six members of the House of Lords, three former members of Parliament, and dozens of donors were revealed to be Mossack Fonseca clients. In China, the families of at least eight current and former members of the Politburo, the supreme ruling body, had hidden offshore accounts.[1] Although Mossack Fonseca responded by denying any wrongdoing and citing its strong due diligence procedures,[2] the firm was forced to close its doors in early 2018. The combination of reputational damage, regulatory action from Panamanian authorities, and media coverage destroyed its ability to operate.[3]

For a country like Panama, firms like Mossack Fonseca have historically been a core part of the economy. Offshore financing is a billion-dollar industry, and Panama is an active player. Acting on its own, the Panamanian government had few incentives to increase financial transparency and prevent money laundering. Indeed, Panama's financial sector was strongly opposed to such changes for many years. Why crack down on policies that attracted foreign money and provided additional revenue? The low-regulation, low-transparency climate benefited both the banking sector and the legal industry because it drew international investors and companies.[4]

The government's attitude shifted quickly, however, when the FATF added Panama to its noncomplier list in June 2014. Newly elected president Juan Carlos Varela promised to make passing new anti–money laundering and terrorist financing legislation a top priority for his administration. The president had strong financial incentives to act quickly. Although the FATF had only included Panama on its "Improving Global AML/CFT Compliance" announcement (the grey list), Panama's banking community could already feel the effects. International banks suspended some correspondent relationships with Panamanian banks, increasing everyday costs.[5] Standard & Poor's commented on the FATF listing and suggested that the government would take steps "to address regulatory shortcomings in the coming year."[6] The Panamanian government responded to such incentives, acting quickly to pass new legislation less than a year after the initial listing. Noting this rapid progress, the FATF removed Panama from its list in February 2016.[7]

Panama's story is typical of many countries that end up on the FATF noncomplier list. While most listed countries make immediate rhetorical commitments to policy change, market pressure drives the actual improvements in compliance. The noncomplier list causes global banks and other financial actors to raise the costs of capital and reallocate resources away from listed countries; listed governments, in turn, have strong incentives to change their policies to align with the FATF standards. This market enforcement process is unofficial—the FATF does not require banks to punish listed countries, and indeed, even when countries are on the blacklist, the FATF only suggests considering the risks of identified policy gaps—but FATF member states understand that it is crucial to the list's success. In an interview, Chip Poncy, the former head of the US delegation to FATF, noted this relationship: "FATF works because it drives market behavior . . . through information, expectations, and consequences associated with risk. It unleashes market forces on actors that are not meeting expectations in terms of meeting global standards for managing illicit financing and associated reputational risks."[8]

Governments in listed countries might want to ignore the FATF standards for political or financial reasons. When the FATF noncomplier list leads to slower and more expensive cross-border banking, however, internal politics shift quickly. Domestic banks and companies cannot afford to be cut off from international financial markets or to wait for days for routine transactions. As a result, these actors become advocates for stronger regulation, pressuring their governments to meet the FATF standards.

Why do international market actors act as unofficial enforcers for the FATF list? For banks, the noncomplier list provides a justifiable way of managing uncertainty. The FATF standards require that banks know who they are doing business with and assess the risk profile of individual clients. If a client seems high risk, banks are supposed to take extra steps to verify identities and understand the nature of business; in some cases, banks may even be obligated to report suspicious transactions. But neither the FATF nor government regulators specify precise guidelines for evaluating client risk. The FATF guidelines suggest that banks and other financial institutions should consider risk factors like the illicit financing risk in a customer's country of residence, but banks must assess such risk independently.

As banks weigh client and country risk against potential profits, they are left searching for a defensible standard of behavior. The FATF noncomplier list is uniquely well suited to fulfill this demand. The FATF is a credible, technocratic body that is well known to banks and has unparalleled insights into each country's anti–money laundering policies. Banks integrate listing information into their anti–money laundering compliance systems in order to demonstrate to shareholders and regulators that they are taking precautions related to illicit financing. In practice, when a bank modifies its compliance system in this way, it is likely to scrutinize closely transactions with clients in listed countries. A bank may pause money transfer requests or shut down correspondent accounts with banks in listed countries, and thus cause delays or higher fees. Individuals and firms in listed countries may struggle to transfer money across borders, gain access to trade financing, and receive remittances from family members abroad.

Unofficial market enforcement via banking also has spillover effects that impact other areas of finance. International investors interested in purchasing sovereign debt may view listed countries as higher risk. Foreign direct investment may decline, particularly if countries stay listed for several years. Even domestic stock markets in listed countries may stumble in response to listing, as local companies anticipate higher costs for doing business. All of these secondary effects intensify market pressure for governments to improve compliance with the FATF standards so that the FATF will remove countries from its list.

This chapter showcases unofficial market enforcement. The analysis focuses on the relationship between listing and cross-border bank-to-bank liabilities, that is, the amount of money that domestic banks in listed countries owe to international banks. The chapter begins with qualitative evidence, drawing from news articles and interviews with financial industry professionals to describe under what conditions the FATF list leads to unofficial market enforcement. It discusses in greater detail why banks need information about a country's illicit financing risk and highlights why it is so challenging for banks to find this information on their own. It also explains why the FATF noncomplier list is useful in addressing such informational gaps and describes how market actors respond to listing.

The next section describes the data and empirical strategy. The analysis employs a linear regression model with country-fixed effects to examine how listing relates to cross-border liabilities. It adds a variable indicating a country's noncomplier list status to a standard economic model of cross-border bank lending. The quantitative analysis finds that the noncomplier list leads to an estimated 13 percent decline in cross-border bank-to-bank liabilities, compared to when a country is not on the noncomplier list. An additional discussion highlights how listing may also generate spillover effects for sovereign spreads and trade financing.

Country Reputation and Global Capital Flows

In today's globalized economy, market actors often require information about foreign governments. Banks build transnational networks so that individuals and companies can send money overseas, import or export goods, and buy foreign stocks and bonds. Investors purchase debt from emerging economies, while companies build transnational supply chains and acquire properties overseas. In all of these cases, market actors base resource allocation decisions in part on foreign government reputations. Because market decision-making is interdependent, market actors must consider not only their own beliefs about a foreign government's policies and practices but also how other market actors are likely to assess the same country. Reputation is thus doubly important for decision-making.

The specific inputs into a country's reputation are likely to vary across time and place. In the early years of the international effort to stop money laundering, banks and financial institutions were largely indifferent to a country's illicit financing risk. But an intellectual shift took place in the late 1990s. FATF member states began to pass laws and issue new regulations on financial transparency. Such efforts increased after the 9/11 terrorist attacks, when the FATF expanded its mandate to include combating terrorist financing. The FATF adopted a more global approach, expanding the task force's membership and creating the Non-Cooperative Countries and Territories (NCCT) process to punish nonmember states that failed to follow FATF guidelines. As discussed in chapter 3, the FATF's NCCT process explicitly drew on market coercion to pressure uncooperative countries. The FATF recommended that financial institutions give special attention to transactions with clients and firms in uncooperative countries (FATF 2000, 12) and even called for member states to employ countermeasures against several listed countries (Gardner 2007). For the first time, banks were forced to take note of which countries were failing to follow the FATF guidelines.

Bank Demand for Information about Illicit Financing Risk

In today's economy, banks have strong incentives to consider a country's illicit financing risk when deciding how to conduct business abroad. Bank profit functions are tied directly into international regulations on combating illicit financing. The FATF recommendations require countries to regulate their banking sectors in order to address the risk of money laundering and terrorist financing. Banks are expected to establish "customer due diligence procedures" in which they screen customers using a risk-based approach. If clients come from riskier countries, a bank should scrutinize their business more closely. Banks typically subject customers from high-risk jurisdictions to longer screening and administrative procedures. In some cases, financial institutions might even opt to forgo all business with certain high-risk countries (Collin et al. 2016). Banks may implement the FATF standards even if governments do not require it: according to Chip Poncy, "In many countries, banks comply with FATF standards in addition to meeting local requirements in order to gain legitimacy in the global financial system."[9]

In addition to international and domestic regulatory incentives, banks face the possibility of government enforcement if they fail to implement regulations on customer due diligence. Since the 2008 financial crisis, government regulators in countries like the United States and the United Kingdom have taken punitive action against banks that failed to implement anti–money laundering policies. While US regulators are responsible for many of the largest fines, such as HSBC's USD 1.256 billion fine in 2012, other countries have increasingly taken punitive action against banks in recent years. Between 2008 and 2018, worldwide regulatory fines against banks totaled approximately USD 26 billion, and fines for a recent fifteen-month period hit USD 10 billion. More

TABLE 5.1 Regulator fines (2008–2018)

REGION	AMOUNT IN US$
North America	23.6 billion
Europe	1.7 billion
Asia/Pacific	609 million
Middle East	9.5 million

Note: The table shows the amounts of fines that regulators have levied against banks for anti–money laundering and sanctions violations by region.

Source: Data comes from Laura Glynn, "2008–2018: Assessing the Impact of Global AML & Sanctions Fines," Fenergo (website), 25 September 2018, https://www.fen ergo.com/blog/2008-2018-assessing-the-impact-of-global-aml-sanctions-fines/.

than 60 percent of this total is linked to enforcement actions outside of the United States.[10] Table 5.1 provides information on the fines that regulators have imposed for anti–money laundering, know-your-customer, and sanctions violations, separated by region.

Banks also have reputation-based incentives to consider a client's illicit financing risk. Reputational damage can lead to financial costs, or at the most extreme, complete collapse. Riggs Bank was once considered the premiere banking institution in Washington, DC; over its 150-year history, it boasted of banking for more than twenty US presidents and numerous foreign embassies.[11] Yet in the early 2000s, when the US government discovered the bank was helping several dictators launder money, the scandal's reputational damage contributed to the bank's complete collapse. Despite the relatively small financial penalties (fines totaling USD 59 million), share prices dropped 20 percent in eight months, equivalent to approximately USD 130 million (Jamieson 2006). Given this stark example, it is perhaps unsurprising that bank officials are concerned about reputational effects. Indeed, damage to reputation is often used as a way to sell risk management systems to financial actors.[12]

Due to regulatory and reputational incentives, banks devote significant resources to assessing a country's risk of money laundering and terrorist financing. In 2017, banks and other financial institutions expected to spend more than USD 8 billion on anti–money laundering and combating terrorist financing compliance software and programs.[13] Large banks have sizable compliance departments that use complex risk algorithms to assess the risk of doing business with banks and customers in other countries. Banks compile their own information, purchase software systems from companies like Thomson Reuters and Accuity, and hire employees to oversee the compliance process. But managing these risk models is an incredibly complex and cumbersome task. Regulators expect banks to have clearly defined methodologies.

National regulation also requires that banks validate their risk models, creating an additional compliance burden.

The FATF noncomplier list is an ideal input into this process. The FATF is a well-known and credible institution; it created the standards that governments and banks seek to follow. The FATF's monitoring and evaluation process provides unparalleled access to information on domestic regulations and enforcement actions—information that would be difficult for banks or even other states to acquire on their own. Banks are also very familiar with the FATF's work and process. The FATF meets with banks and other financial actors on an annual basis through its Private Sector Consultative Forum, which has allowed private actors to provide crucial feedback on the FATF's work (de Oliveira 2018). While FATF monitoring may not have always played a major part in banks' risk decisions, one practitioner noted that in recent years, "as banks have come under greater scrutiny and as the FATF's profile has been raised—now notably contributing to the G-20 agenda—it is hard for a bank to ignore the FATF's decisions."[14]

Banks rely on the list for reasons beyond its informational content. If banks purely wanted information on country risk, they could look to the FATF's mutual evaluation reports, which provide two-hundred-plus pages of details on each country's laws and regulations. The FATF has produced these reports for several decades and makes them publicly available. Yet interviews suggest that bank compliance officials rarely consider mutual evaluation reports. The lengthier evaluations provide more context and details but leave room for considerable interpretational ambiguity. In practice, banks can justify ignoring the reports because of this ambiguity. In contrast, the noncomplier list's precise signal is a clear way of organizing expectations.

The noncomplier list also signals how *other* banks are likely to identify "high risk" countries. Banks want to maximize profit opportunities while minimizing risk exposure. If the FATF includes a country on its noncomplier list, a bank can assume that other banks will subject the country to greater scrutiny. If the bank itself fails to take action, it may struggle to defend its compliance protocols to regulators and shareholders. Indeed, one financial industry official posited that the FATF's value to banks is linked to how the organization is perceived by the United States and its regulators: US regulators expect that banks will adjust their risk models to account for the FATF noncomplier list because of the FATF's authority and credibility in this issue area.[15] For smaller banks, the FATF noncomplier list is even more essential, since these entities rarely have the resources to build compliance departments or purchase comprehensive software systems. Small banks instead rely on the FATF noncomplier list as a defensible way of grouping countries into risk categories.

A final reason why the noncomplier list may be a useful signal to banks is because it operates in the shadow of explicit coercion. Many bank officials remember the FATF's earlier NCCT process and are aware of the FATF's call for countermeasures against North Korea and Iran. Even if the FATF explicitly calls for no coercive action against listed countries, banks understand that the FATF could potentially call for member states to levy countermeasures against listed countries if such countries were continually noncooperative. Moreover, if the FATF moves countries up to its blacklist, it advises its members to "consider the risks arising from the deficiencies associated with each jurisdiction" in doing business with blacklisted countries.[16] Banks may respond to blacklisting with even tougher due diligence procedures, or in some cases, the termination of long-standing business relationships. Given this expectation, banks may change how they do business in response to any level of listing.

How Banks Unofficially Enforce FATF Rules

Banks act as unofficial enforcers for the FATF in ways that lead to significant financial consequences for listed countries. When the FATF includes a country on the noncomplier list, banks integrate this information directly into their risk models; these models, in turn, drive bank procedures for verifying customer identities and monitoring potential anti–money laundering transactions. International banks may subject banks in listed countries to greater scrutiny, particularly through correspondent banking channels. An executive from a private bank in Ethiopia, which was listed in 2010, reported that when the country was on the noncomplier list, "in informal ways, the big correspondent banks would raise the list regularly."[17] Individuals and companies in listed countries often experience delays in transferring money or difficulty conducting business abroad.

If the FATF moves a country up to a higher listing level, foreign banks may decide to conduct enhanced due diligence against customers from the listed country. Under enhanced due diligence procedures, banks must obtain more detailed information and documents from clients about their identities and the nature of their business. This process is costly for banks and therefore worth undertaking primarily for high-value clients. For lower-value clients or firms, banks may opt to forgo business entirely or charge a premium for the additional work.

Turkey's experience on the FATF noncomplier list illustrates how financial actors may undertake enhanced due diligence, even when such actions are not explicitly called for. When the FATF initially placed Turkey on the noncomplier list in June 2011, it took the unusual step of placing the country directly on what would later become known as the blacklist. In its initial listing

announcement, the FATF called on its members to consider "the risks arising from the deficiencies" while doing business with Turkey. The Association
of Certified Anti–Money Laundering Specialists, a transnational network of
financial integrity specialists, advised its members that "undertaking enhanced
due diligence is the only way to mitigate the risk of being used as a conduit for
criminal or terrorist activities" when doing business with Turkey.[18] A Standard
Bank official noted that "foreign banks, less actively involved in Turkey, might
see Turkey's possible position on the FATF blacklist as a reason to limit or
restrict business."[19]

When banks engage in unofficial market enforcement, it can lead to a variety of financial consequences. In some cases, existing customers may not feel
much of an effect, but banks will be reluctant to establish business relationships with new clients or jurisdictions. During Thailand's time on the noncomplier list, Thai financial institutions encountered unexpected difficulties
obtaining permits to open branches in EU countries, and an EU bank even
contemplated scrapping a deal to lend money to Thai banks.[20] In the case of
Bosnia, which was listed in 2015, existing customers also felt the effect of listing: foreign banks closed Bosnian accounts, canceled transactions, and raised
the price for cross-border payments. The EU intensified such effects by placing Bosnia on its own anti–money laundering blacklist, which was based on
the FATF list.[21]

More significantly, listing can lead international banks to terminate correspondent banking relationships with banks in listed countries. Over the last five
years, international banks have increasingly opted to pull out of high-risk financial jurisdictions, sometimes leaving individuals and companies in such countries without access to major currencies. In recent years, this problem, which is
termed de-risking, has drawn increased attention from development-oriented
finance organizations like the World Bank and the International Monetary Fund
because it reduces access to the formal financial system among vulnerable populations.[22] Although not all de-risking behavior is due to the FATF know-your-
customer requirements or its noncomplier list, the FATF noncomplier list can
intensify the problem for high-risk, low-yield countries. In the South Pacific, for
example, de-risking is a huge problem for many small island nations. The chief
operating officer of a bank in Vanuatu (listed in 2016) reported that "with all the
de-risking going on and the grey listing [of Vanuatu] we are more in survival
mode than growth mode."[23]

De-risking may also occur in a domino pattern, as actions affecting one country cause ripple effects across the globe. US banks, for example, have increased
due diligence against Australian banks, which are viewed as higher risk due to
their remittance-heavy relationships with many small island states in the Pacific.[24]

In response to increased US due diligence, Australian banks have had to change their business relationships with other banks in the region. In one case, an Australian bank cut relationships with remittance services across the board (Alwazir et al. 2017). Between January 2014 and April 2015, banks in Australia closed more than seven hundred accounts belonging to remittance businesses. Other banks report carrying out robust due diligence on remitter customers on a case-by-case basis (AUSTRAC 2019, 7).

Although bank enforcement against listed countries could take a variety of forms, the consequences of such action are straightforward: banks and customers in listed countries should find it harder and more expensive to access international capital. Both risk profiling and enhanced due diligence are likely to lead to a decline in international banks lending to banks in listed countries.

> *Hypothesis: Listing and Unofficial Market Enforcement*—International bank loans to banks in listed countries should decline when countries are on the noncomplier list.

If the FATF noncomplier list is unique in how it influences bank financial flows, then other types of information about a country's illicit financing risk should not generate similar aggregate effects. The FATF has produced detailed monitoring reports for three decades; these reports form the basis of most FATF listing decisions. When the FATF revamped its noncomplier list process in 2009, it used mutual evaluation reports to make decisions about which countries to list. The information in these earlier reports, however, is much more ambiguous and difficult for banks to interpret, and therefore less likely to lead to measurable shifts in market behavior.

> *Hypothesis: The Noncomplier List as a Unique Focal Point*—Noncompliant countries that were evaluated by the FATF between 2005 and 2007 should not have experienced declines in cross-border bank-to-bank lending prior to the creation of the noncomplier list.

Measuring Market Enforcement

A regression analysis examines the effect of the FATF noncomplier list on cross-border bank-to-bank liabilities in listed countries for the period of 2010 to 2015. Data is at the country-quarter-year level. Because the cross-border liability data is quarterly and the FATF updates its noncomplier list three times per year (February, June, and October), each observation indicates whether a given country is on the noncomplier list at the end of the quarter (March,

June, September, or December). Data on country listing status is hand-coded from FATF noncomplier list announcements, which are published online. The baseline sample includes eighty-nine countries with available data; this sample is assembled to match the baseline sample in the Cox proportional hazards analysis in chapter 4.

To see whether listing is associated with declines in liabilities, the analysis uses an ordinary least squares regression model with country-fixed effects. This approach examines how international bank lending to banks in a specific country correlates with the country's listing status. One notable downside of this approach is that it effectively discards never-listed countries when estimating the relationship between listing and liabilities; for this reason, the appendix includes a robustness check with two-way fixed effects that control for both country and year. Because qualitative research suggests that financial institutions did not immediately restrict access to financing in response to listing, particularly in the early years of the noncomplier list, all explanatory variables are lagged by one year. This one-year lag also addresses concerns about reverse causality.

One potential concern with a panel regression approach is that the FATF listing process is not random: countries that are listed are likely to be different from those that are not. This nonrandom selection into listing could lead to under- or overestimation of the association between listing and cross-border bank liabilities. If the FATF is more likely to list countries that are, based on preexisting characteristics, more likely to experience a decline in cross-border lending, for example, then the empirical analysis could overstate the relationship between the noncomplier list and cross-border liabilities. Conversely, if the FATF is more likely to list countries with robust financial sectors, the empirical analysis might understate the link. Notably, these concerns are not eliminated by the use of fixed effects, as the subpopulation of listed countries contains less cross-border liability variation than the full set of countries.[25]

Concerns about selection bias are addressed in several ways. The model includes standard control variables, such as inflation and the exchange rate, which are commonly used to model cross-border bank flows between countries. By controlling for factors that are likely to influence cross-border bank-to-bank transfers, the analysis increases the comparability of listed and nonlisted countries and makes it easier to discern the underlying effect of listing.

Control variables, however, cannot fully address concerns that the population of listed countries might be systematically different from the population of nonlisted countries. In addition to the baseline sample, the analysis assembles two comparable groups of countries that are likely to have similar probabilities of being listed. Following the empirical design outlined in chapter 4, one sample is constructed using matching. Preprocessing data by matching produces more accurate and less model-dependent inferences (Ho et al. 2007). The analysis uses nearest-neighbor matching to construct two samples where observations have similar probabilities of being listed based on core economic variables that are commonly included in models of economic flows. The largest version of the matched sample includes eighty-one countries, thirty-four of which were listed by the FATF.[26]

A second sample focuses on the population of countries that were eligible for listing as of February 2010. In June 2009 FATF member states decided that any countries that received failing ratings on ten or more of the FATF's sixteen most important recommendations would automatically become eligible for listing. At the time of this decision, the FATF and its affiliates had already completed compliance evaluations (known as "mutual evaluation reports") for close to a hundred countries and territories. Most of these economies had little to no input into the FATF's new listing criteria but found themselves eligible for the new listing process. The largest version of this sample includes a group of sixty-two states, thirty-three of whom were on the FATF noncomplier list.[27]

Dependent Variable: Cross-Border Liabilities

The theory suggests that listing should be associated with unofficial market enforcement, that is, a redistribution of resources away from noncompliant states. While a number of market actors could serve as would-be enforcers for FATF standards, qualitative research suggests that banks are the most likely actor to change business practices based on FATF information. To examine changes in bank behavior, the empirical analysis examines the link between listing and quarterly cross-border bank-to-bank liabilities, that is, the money that banks in a given country owe to international banks in a particular time period. If international banks charge higher rates or restrict lending to listed countries, then the noncomplier list should be associated with a decline in cross-border liabilities in listed countries.

Data on cross-border liabilities is drawn from the Bank for International Settlements (BIS) locational banking statistics.[28] This data set provides information about outstanding claims and liabilities as reported by internationally active banks located in the forty-four reporting countries. Because these banks report international cross-border flows, the data covers banks in more than two hundred economies. BIS estimates the statistics capture about 95 percent of all cross-border interbank business. The dependent variable is cross-border liabilities—that is, the amount of money that domestic banks in a particular country owe to international banks—for each quarter for the period of 2010 to 2015. This variable ranges from USD 7,000 (Nauru) to

USD 1.26 trillion (Germany). The dependent variable is logged to address its highly skewed distribution.[29]

Explanatory Variables for Cross-Border Lending

The primary independent variable of interest is whether, at a given point in time, a country is on the noncomplier list. Since February 2010, the FATF has issued updates to its noncomplier list three times a year under the auspices of its International Cooperation Review Group process. Regional bodies, cochaired by an FATF member state and a non-FATF member, review states that are eligible for inclusion on the list. After a yearlong process, these bodies determine which states will be publicly identified by the FATF. Once countries are included on the noncomplier list, they must address all identified deficiencies in order to be removed from the list. A dichotomous variable *Listing* indicates whether a country is on the noncomplier list at the end of each quarter of the year.

Global factors like market volatility and country-specific macroeconomic factors are likely to affect bank lending (Herrmann and Mihaljek 2010). Controls for *GDP growth* and *Inflation* account for the fact that faster-growing economies might have a greater demand for credit, while high inflation might limit the credit supply. *Real exchange rate* is used to proxy for how markets view the strength of a country's economy; as exchange rates increase, cross-border liabilities are likely to decline. This data comes from IFS and shows the ratio of the price level abroad and the domestic price level.[30] Finally, the analysis includes *Market volatility*, which is the quarterly average of the Chicago Board Options Exchange 3-Month Volatility Index. This variable is designed to be a constant measure of the three-month implied volatility of the S&P 500 index.

The private sector's preexisting engagement with the global economy is likely to affect how banks weigh the relative risks and benefits of lending to different countries. In particular, the local banking sector's leverage ratio—that is, the relationship between its core capital and total assets—may affect bank-to-bank transfers across borders. Following Bruno and Shin (2015a), the analysis includes the variable *Credit-to-GDP ratio*, which proxies for the leverage of local banks using the ratio of bank assets to capital from the World Bank WDI data set. *Capital account openness*, drawn from the Wang-Jahan capital account openness index, is a continuous variable ranging from 0 to 1 and indicates the degree to which a country maintains an open capital account.[31] This indicator is based on information contained in the IMF's Annual Report on Exchange Arrangements and Exchange Restrictions. Because it is only available through 2013 and changes little within a country from year to year, data is extended through 2015.

Several additional variables are important for explaining cross-border liabilities but unfortunately limit the sample size due to data availability. *Debt-to-GDP ratio* is a commonly used measure of a country's economic health, particularly for emerging economies. Higher levels of external debt should make borrowers more vulnerable, which may reduce an international bank's willingness to lend money (Takats and Avdjiev 2014). *Interest spread* (drawn from the World Bank WDI data set) indicates the difference between the local lending rate and the US Fed Fund rate; spreads may affect the price determinants of local demand for cross-border credit. Finally, *Money supply* (from the World Bank WDI) accounts for the fact that local borrowers may borrow in US dollars and then deposit the local currency proceeds into the domestic banking system, which would lead banking in flows to be associated with increases in M2.[32] Because the inclusion of these variables limits the sample size so extensively, all regressions are run with and without these variables.

Results: Listing and Declines in Bank Lending

The results of the regression analysis indicate that the FATF noncomplier list is associated with declines in bank lending to banks in listed countries. Table 5.2 shows the average effect of the noncomplier list on cross-border liabilities for the country-fixed effects regressions. Models 1 and 2 run the analyses for the baseline sample, models 3 and 4 replicate this approach for the matched sample, and models 5 and 6 analyzes the sample of all countries that were eligible for listing as of February 2010.[33] All models contain country-fixed effects; as a result, the coefficients are estimates of the effect of within-country changes of the key variables.

Listing has a negative effect across all six models. In four of the six specifications (including all three models with complete control variables), the effect is strong and statistically significant. In model 2, listing is associated with approximately a 10.6 percent decrease in liabilities, while in models 4 and 6, listing is associated with between a 12.6 and 12.8 percent decrease.[34] To provide context for these numbers, consider a country like the Philippines, which was listed from 2010 to 2013. In 2010, the Philippines' average cross-border liabilities per quarter were USD 11.5 billion. Based on an estimated 12.8 percent decrease, listing should be associated with a decline of approximately USD 1.5 billion in cross-border liabilities. In this case, the actual decline was actually even larger than predicted by the model—by 2011, the average quarterly cross-border liabilities in the Philippines had dropped to USD 8.7 billion. Bank lending rebounded to prelisting levels only in 2014, after the country's removal from the list.[35]

TABLE 5.2 The noncomplier list and cross-border bank-to-bank lending

	DEPENDENT VARIABLE: CROSS-BORDER LIABILITIES					
	FULL SAMPLE		MATCHED SAMPLE		ELIGIBLE-FOR-LISTING SAMPLE	
	(1)	(2)	(3)	(4)	(5)	(6)
Listed	-0.047	-0.112*	-0.073**	-0.135***	-0.053	-0.137***
	(0.059)	(0.059)	(0.034)	(0.046)	(0.041)	(0.042)
Inflation	0.004	0.009**	0.004	0.008	-0.003	-0.015**
	(0.004)	(0.004)	(0.005)	(0.010)	(0.004)	(0.006)
GDP growth	-0.004	0.006	-0.006	0.002	-0.007**	0.011
	(0.010)	(0.010)	(0.003)	(0.013)	(0.003)	(0.013)
Real exchange rate	-0.003	0.008	-0.010	0.008	-0.009**	0.010**
	(0.007)	(0.007)	(0.007)	(0.006)	(0.004)	(0.004)
Credit-to-GDP ratio	-0.436	2.765	0.711**	5.239	-0.326	4.624***
	(1.953)	(1.953)	(0.329)	(3.641)	(1.024)	(1.614)
Capital account openness	-0.005**	-0.003	-0.004*	-0.011*	-0.003*	-0.001
	(0.002)	(0.002)	(0.002)	(0.006)	(0.002)	(0.003)
Market volatility		-0.007		-0.001		0.002
		(0.010)		(0.013)		(0.003)
Debt-to-GDP ratio		0.004		0.054***		0.038**
		(0.017)		(0.012)		(0.016)
Interest rate spread		0.0004		0.0002		-0.001
		(0.001)		(0.004)		(0.002)
Observations	1579	462	710	176	1098	289
Countries	89	31	81	10	62	21
Listed countries	32	10	34	10	33	10

* $p < 0.10$; ** $p < 0.05$; *** $p < 0.01$

Note: The table shows the results of an OLS model examining the effect of listing on cross-border liabilities across three different samples. The full sample mirrors the sample population in chapter 4: all non-FATF countries that had failed to criminalize terrorist financing in line with FATF standards as of February 2010. The dependent variable is logged. All models include country-fixed effects and a cubic time polynomial. Standard errors are

Cross-border liabilities in Turkey provide additional support for this quantitative estimate. The FATF listed Turkey in February 2010. In February 2011, the FATF moved Turkey up to a higher listing level (its so-called blacklist). Following significant policy change and an on-site visit to verify improvements, the FATF finally removed Turkey from the list in June 2014. During Turkey's time on the noncomplier list, cross-border liabilities declined from USD 28.8 billion to USD 18.3 billion. These numbers reflect a 36 percent decline over Turkey's four years on the list. Figure 5.1 shows this trend.

One notable challenge for this analysis relates to the small sample size. A country-fixed effects approach generates estimates from within-unit variation; as a result, never-listed countries are excluded from the analysis when estimating the effect of listing on liabilities. Furthermore, a complete model of cross-border bank flows requires including additional variables that are missing for many countries. Models 2, 4, and 6 base their listing estimates on variation in ten countries: Indonesia, Kyrgyzstan, Mongolia, Namibia, Nepal, Nigeria, the Philippines, Sri Lanka, Thailand, and Uganda. While these listed countries are similar on average to other listed countries in terms of capital openness, liability flows, and credit-to-GDP ratio, this subgroup is somewhat different in terms

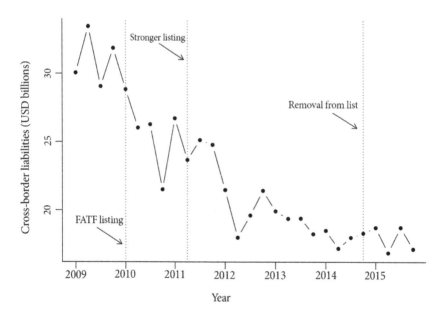

FIGURE 5.1.   Turkey: Cross-border liabilities

Note: The figure shows cross-border bank-to-bank liabilities in Turkey from 2009 to 2015. The FATF added Turkey to the noncomplier list in February 2010 and moved it up to the blacklist in February 2011. Following significant policy change, the FATF removed Turkey from the noncomplier list in June 2014.

of economic development. Listed countries excluded from the analysis include both low-income, underdeveloped economies like Afghanistan and Zimbabwe and high-income economies like Antigua and Barbuda and Kuwait. In contrast, the listed countries included in all models are primarily lower-middle-income countries[36] with growing economies.

While t-tests reveal no statistically significant differences between the two groups based on 2009 data (see appendix for more details), the differences in economic development may be significant for the analysis. The ten primarily lower-middle-income countries may be a prime target for market enforcement, as such countries are often open to global finance but not large enough to attract capital regardless of politics. Indeed, in an interview, one anti–money laundering expert hypothesized that market enforcement might work in this manner, stating, "I think the impact of the ICRG listing falls most heavily on countries that have 'developing' economies that rely on the international financial system, have external borrowings in foreign currencies and are banked by global (as opposed to regional) correspondent banks. They are most vulnerable."[37]

While it is difficult to generalize for the full population of countries based on this subsample, the results have several implications. First, other emerging economies or countries that are highly connected to the financial system are likely to experience similar effects from listing. These countries are newly integrated into global finance and thus more vulnerable to its whims and caprices. Second, similar effects probably play out among low-income and upper-middle-income countries as well, but to lesser degrees. When Afghanistan was on the FATF list, many Western banks already refused to do business with the country because of its weak regulation, and so Afghan banks routed payments through Turkey or China instead. Prolonged listing may not have altered Western bank practices, but it eventually led Turkish banks to close Afghan accounts and Chinese banks to halt dollar transactions; as a result, commodity prices rose 10 percent.[38] Finally, the existence of market enforcement, even among a subset of countries, is likely to influence how governments in all listed countries approach compliance with FATF standards: governments may be driven to avoid financial penalties even if they themselves have yet to experience such consequences.

The Noncomplier List as a Unique Focal Point (Placebo Test)

To analyze whether the FATF noncomplier list has a unique association with cross-border lending as compared to other information about country risk, an additional regression examines whether noncompliant countries experienced declines in cross-border lending in periods prior to the noncomplier list. More specifically, the analysis focuses on the group of thirty-eight countries that the FATF assessed between 2005 and 2007. Of these countries, the FATF subsequently included fourteen on the noncomplier list based on the results of these earlier monitoring reports. A regression analysis probes whether countries that were listed post-2009 but evaluated in the earlier period experienced declines in cross-border lending prior to listing. In effect, this analysis functions as a type of placebo test, evaluating whether the FATF's detailed information about countries' illicit financing vulnerabilities correlates with declines in cross-border lending or if the FATF noncomplier list has unique signaling power. If listing is truly driving the changes in cross-border lending patterns (rather than descriptions of underlying country characteristics) then the noncomplier list should have no effect on cross-border liabilities in previous years.

Model 1 from table 5.2 is replicated for the period of 2007 to 2009, matching each country's listing status in the years 2010 to 2012.[39] Each country's listing status is linked to a period three years earlier (e.g., if a country was listed in 2010, its new placebo listing date is 2007). If banks are responding to underlying information contained in the FATF mutual evaluation reports, rather than the signal of the noncomplier list, listed countries should experience declines in lending. Instead, the placebo analysis indicates that listing actually has a weak positive effect on cross-border liabilities. These results (available in the appendix) provide further support for the argument that the noncomplier list is a unique focal point for banks.

Spillover Effects of Market Enforcement via Banking

The FATF noncomplier list's effect on cross-border banking is powerful not just because it raises the costs of business for the domestic banking sector in listed countries, but also because bank-to-bank enforcement affects other aspects of a country's economy. When banks restrict business based on the noncomplier list, disruptions in financial flows may affect remittances, foreign investment, or trade. This section focuses on two potential economic spillover effects: disruptions to trade financing and decreases in the willingness of international investors to purchase sovereign debt in listed countries. Both processes intensify the noncomplier list's impact.

Disruptions to Trade Financing

About a third of all financing for international trade is done through bank-issued letters of credit (Bank for International Settlements 2014). In this system of payment, an importer might ask a domestic bank to issue a letter of credit on its behalf. This letter of credit will serve as a contractual guarantee that the issuing bank will pay the contract value to the exporter if certain conditions are fulfilled. The letter of credit will be sent to the exporting company, and in most cases, to a local bank in the exporting country to confirm the obligation. The local bank acts as a second-line risk mitigator—if the importing country's bank defaults, the exporter's bank agrees to still pay the exporter.[40]

Bank-authorized letters of credit facilitate trade by providing access to capital for companies to expand business relationships and by helping mitigate the risk of nonpayment. Although firms in many countries rely on trade financing, firms in emerging markets are particularly dependent on bank financing to support trade (Bank for International Settlements 2014). Trade partners tend to view contractual relationships with firms in developing countries as riskier than contracts with firms in wealthier countries and are often only willing to engage in such transactions with some kind of bank guarantee. As a result, trade relationships between countries are dependent in part on the willingness of banks in one country to engage with banks in the other.

The FATF noncomplier list can potentially disrupt these relationships by leading banks in developed countries to view banks in listed countries as higher risk. Banks provide letters of credit as secondary products—trade financing earns relatively low returns, so banks typically offer it when they already have other, more profitable products. When the FATF lists a country, however, international banks often reevaluate the costs and benefits of ongoing relationships with banks in the listed country, with potential spillover effects for trade financing. Listed countries are aware of such concerns. When the FATF threatened to move Nepal from the grey list up to the blacklist, for example, the government feared that blacklisting would lead international banks to disregard letters of credit and payments issued by Nepali traders.[41] Similarly, when the FATF relisted Panama in June 2019, the managing directors of regulatory and risk services firm Alvarez and Marsal noted that "major impacts of this distinction [listing] may be felt in the financial services, trade finance and the shipping industries."[42]

The Noncomplier List and Sovereign Debt

Bank-to-bank enforcement may also affect how some international investors view the potential risks and gains of purchasing government debt from listed countries. If banks begin to restrict foreign transactions with a listed country, key economic inputs such as trade may become more costly. The majority of cross-border flows are conducted in US dollars or euros; when financial institutions close business relationships with domestic banks in a listed country, they cut off access to these key currencies (Durner and Shetret 2015, 19).[43] For this reason, international investors may follow developments related to the FATF noncomplier list. When the FATF removed Panama from the noncomplier list in February 2016, for example, Moody's described the development as "positive for the sovereign credit of Panama and banks because it confirms that the authorities have the capacity to cope with the risks of money laundering" (Moody's 2016). When the FATF relisted Panama in June 2019, a senior analyst at Moody's noted that the relisting was "a negative development for offshore Panamanian banks funded mainly by foreign investors" and that the list would "increase scrutiny from the international financial community and its interactions with Panamanian financial institutions."[44]

The FATF noncomplier list may also affect a country's creditworthiness because listing may be interpreted as a signal about a country's willingness to repay its debt obligations. Listing is a sign that a government is lagging behind in financial regulation and failing to implement best practices. Listing also suggests that government has failed to prioritize its financial reputation. Most listed countries have ample opportunities to avoid being listed. Once the FATF determines that a country is eligible for the noncomplier list, its government has a year to change its policies to prevent being listed. Given the possibility of significant economic consequences from listing, if a government fails to avoid the noncomplier list, this lack of action is a strong signal that the government prioritizes other considerations over its reputation in financial markets. When Ethiopia was on the noncomplier list, the Ethiopian central bank was focused on following international best practices in order to become a destination for foreign investors. The FATF list interfered with this process. One private bank official noted, "For the central bank, Ethiopia was in the process of preparing for an external bond issue—the first-ever euro bond. They didn't want to be blacklisted at the same time as issuing the new bond."[45] The official went on to note that the central bank was crucial for pushing the Ethiopian government to undertake necessary reforms and encouraging private banks to adopt necessary policy changes in order to meet FATF standards.

Conclusion: Focal Point Effects and Unofficial Market Punishment

International banks operate in an uncertain environment. Global regulation requires banks to subject clients from high illicit financing risk countries to greater scrutiny but provides little guidance about how to determine such risk.

The FATF noncomplier list fills this demand. Banks integrate the list into their risk models, raising the costs of doing business for banks and clients in listed countries.

Cross-border banking is a powerful tool of international pressure because it is the lifeline of global finance. Every country in the world depends on ties between banks to send money across borders, but the nature of this relationship varies significantly. Some countries may depend on cross-border banking networks for foreign direct investment or trade financing, while other countries may rely on global banking to send and receive remittances. The FATF noncomplier list has the ability to drive policy improvements across a variety of contexts. The next chapter expands on this point through case studies of Thailand and the Philippines.

6

FIGHTING ILLICIT FINANCING IN SOUTHEAST ASIA

In December 2017, Thai officials cracked open one of the biggest wildlife smuggling operations in the world. The case began with a routine inspection. Customs officers examined suitcases from an incoming flight and searched them for illegal goods. Inside the bags were rhino horns, poached from the world's dwindling and endangered rhino population. The international trade of rhino horns has been illegal since 1977, yet poachers have killed thousands of rhinos in recent years.[1] Despite the illegal cargo, officials appeared to clear the suitcases. The bags traveled through customs where they were later picked up by a Thai government official working in the airport. From Africa to Thailand, two stops in a much larger illicit trafficking operation.[2]

Billions of dollars' worth of illegal wildlife slip across borders every year. Authorities rarely find the cargo and catch the perpetrators. In this case, however, custom officials tipped off the Thai police. Rather than seize the goods, the police employed a method called "controlled delivery," in which authorities allow illegal goods to move through the trade network to locate more participants. Within weeks, Thai authorities had arrested Bach "Boonchai" Mai, a Thai national of Vietnamese origin who was notorious in the illegal wildlife trade. Bach and his brother run the Hydra syndicate, which spans Africa to China and traffics in ivory, rhino horns, tigers, and pangolins.[3] By stopping Bach, the Thai police hoped that they had dealt a significant blow to the Hydra network.

But if Bach's arrest represented a high point for environmental groups, the aftermath showed how difficult it can be to stop organized crime. Bach was released on bail within a week, allowing Hydra to continue its operations. Even more troubling, in January 2019, a Thai court dismissed charges against Bach after the prosecution's key witness changed his testimony.[4] What had once seemed like a major victory for the fight against wildlife trafficking now reflected the many ways that criminals can slip through the justice system.

Stopping organized crime is challenging because there are so many moving pieces. Whether transporting drugs, labor, or animal parts, crime syndicates rely on suppliers, traffickers, and buyers spread out over countries and continents. Most participants have only limited knowledge of the whole operation; as a result, it is difficult for any single law enforcement entity to unravel the network. Investigators run up against government corruption, coercion, and witness tampering at every step of the process.

The international effort to stop money laundering offers a partial workaround to some of these problems. It may not always be possible to send a kingpin to jail, but government officials can seize his assets and make it more difficult for him to use his money. A few years before Thai authorities arrested Bach, the Thai Anti–Money Laundering Office froze USD 37 million in assets belonging to Daoruang Kongpitak, a woman accused of running a large operation that traffics in rosewood and tigers. The Anti–Money Laundering Office's actions show how the Thai government's improved capacity vis-à-vis illicit financing has led to tangible accomplishments. The case also reveals, however, that the fight against bad money can sometimes accomplish what law enforcement officials cannot. While Thai authorities were able to trace the money's criminal origins and implement the asset freeze, the government never brought criminal charges against Kongpitak. To this day, she remains free.[5]

This chapter showcases how the Financial Action Task Force's (FATF) noncomplier list has transformed the ways that Thailand and the Philippines fight illicit financing. On the surface, these countries seem like they should be highly motivated to stop money laundering and terrorist financing. Both Thailand and the Philippines are transit points and final destinations for organized crime. Both governments have also struggled with terrorist insurgencies, portions of which have ties to international terrorist groups like the Islamic State and Al-Qaeda. On the other hand, Thailand and the Philippines also have economic, institutional, and cultural characteristics that favor privacy and financial secrecy. This chapter shows how the FATF noncomplier list has overcome political opposition and shifted cultural norms in ways that promote compliance with FATF standards.

Southeast Asia has more than two decades of experience with combating illicit financing. Countries in the region worked with the United States, Australia, and several other FATF members to found the Asia/Pacific Group on Money Laundering (APG) in 1997. The APG is one of the oldest FATF affiliate bodies. Although Thailand and the Philippines were both founding APG members, they struggled to conform with the FATF standards. In 2000, the FATF listed the Philippines as an "uncooperative country" under its Non-Cooperative Countries and Territories (NCCT) process; the significant market punishment from this listing led the Philippine Congress to adopt its first anti–money laundering law. In 2009, the FATF revamped its process for dealing with noncompliant economies, and in 2010, both countries were placed on the noncomplier list. The two governments largely ignored the list until banking lobbyists began to highlight its financial costs. Listing meant domestic banks were suffering from increased international scrutiny and higher transaction costs. In response to these pressures, legislatures in both countries rushed through bills to appease the FATF. The cases reveal how the FATF noncomplier list's impact on compliance is tied directly to market enforcement.

The FATF's Fight against Illicit Financing in Southeast Asia

In the mid-1990s, the FATF began an effort to improve regional anti–money laundering cooperation in Asia. Following several multilateral meetings, thirteen economies founded the APG in 1997.[6] The APG is an autonomous regional body with its own secretariat, but it is part of the FATF global network and helps member states implement the FATF standards. The APG's five primary functions include evaluating member state compliance, providing technical assistance and training, researching illicit financing methods and trends, engaging with other members of the FATF regional network, and engaging with the private sector.[7]

The creation of the APG was part of a broader effort to widen international action against money laundering. In the late 1990s, the FATF expanded its membership to include new strategically important countries and established several additional regional bodies. It also designed its first blacklist of countries and territories with high levels of financial secrecy: the Non-Cooperative Countries and Territories list. Under the NCCT process, the FATF publicly identified fifteen countries in June 2000 and six additional countries in June 2001.[8] The Philippines was one of six countries in the Asia/Pacific region included on the

NCCT list,[9] and despite an initial round of policy improvements, it remained listed until 2005 (FATF-GAFI 2005).

The FATF officially ended its NCCT process in 2006, and shortly thereafter, it established the International Cooperation Review Group (ICRG) to evaluate economies with illicit financing gaps. The ICRG process initially targeted only a small group of jurisdictions, but in 2008, the FATF decided to redesign it so that FATF members would be able to list a broader set of countries. In June 2009, the FATF adopted new ICRG procedures whereby countries that received failing ratings (partially compliant or noncompliant) on ten or more of the FATF's sixteen most important recommendations would be eligible for listing. Under the new procedures, the FATF would review all eligible jurisdictions and publicly identify those countries and territories that failed to make sufficient progress. An updated version of this process continues today, more than ten years later.

The FATF's listing process separates economies based on the extent of noncompliance and uncooperative behavior. Its primary list, known colloquially as "the grey list," identifies countries and territories with "strategic AML/ CFT deficiencies" that have also committed to action plans to remedy such gaps.[10] If countries fail to make progress, they may be placed on the "dark grey list," which serves as a warning prior to blacklisting. The FATF's third list is what media outlets often term "the blacklist." It includes countries that have more significant problems or have demonstrated little political will to remedy problematic practices. The blacklist is not explicitly coercive; however, the FATF calls on its members to "consider the risks arising from the deficiencies associated with each jurisdiction."[11] Finally, the FATF maintains a countermeasures list, although to date, this list has only ever included Iran and North Korea.[12]

From its inception, the FATF noncomplier list included numerous countries in the Asia/Pacific region. Table 6.1 shows the noncomplier list as of October 2010, when nearly a third of the listed countries were from Asia. This high proportion reflects the region's numerous risk factors, the strategic importance of many regional economies, and the unwillingness of governments to be proactive in adopting new anti–money laundering or combating terrorist financing measures.

The subsequent case studies describe Thailand's and the Philippines' experiences on the noncomplier list. The FATF listed both countries in 2010. After little evidence of policy change, the FATF placed both countries on its dark grey list to amplify pressure. While the Philippines was able to pass new legislation quickly enough to avoid the blacklist, Thailand ended up on the blacklist for nearly a year. The case studies suggest that in both countries, unofficial market

TABLE 6.1 Countries on the FATF noncomplier list (as of October 2010)

COUNTRY	DATE LISTED
Angola	June 2010
Antigua and Barbuda	February 2010
Azerbaijan	February 2010
Bangladesh	October 2010
Bolivia	February 2010
Ecuador	June 2010
Ethiopia	June 2010
Greece	February 2010
Honduras	October 2010
Indonesia	February 2010
Iran	February 2010
Kenya	February 2010
Morocco	February 2010
Myanmar	February 2010
Nepal	February 2010
Nigeria	February 2010
North Korea	February 2010
Pakistan	June 2010
Paraguay	February 2010
Philippines	October 2010
Qatar	February 2010
São Tomé and Príncipe	October 2010
Sri Lanka	February 2010
Sudan	February 2010
Syria	February 2010
Tanzania	October 2010
Thailand	February 2010
Trinidad and Tobago	February 2010
Turkey	February 2010
Turkmenistan	June 2010
Ukraine	February 2010
Venezuela	October 2010
Vietnam	October 2010
Yemen	February 2010

Note: Data coded by author based on FATF public announcements. The FATF listed Iran and North Korea under its old listing process; in these cases, the date listed is the first year of the new noncomplier list procedures. APG member states are shaded in gray.

punishment, particularly through the banking system, was crucial for driving compliance improvements.

The Philippines

FATF pressure has played a decisive role in generating policy change in the Philippines. On multiple occasions, the government has only passed new anti-money laundering legislation under direct pressure from the FATF. In 2001, the FATF called on its members to enhance surveillance of transactions with the Philippines and threatened countermeasures against the country (FATF-GAFI 2001a, 3). The FATF's actions increased banking scrutiny and, under pressure from business interests and overseas workers, the Philippine government eventually adopted new legislation. A similar process played out in 2010 when the FATF identified the Philippines under its new noncomplier list. After the Philippines' earlier experience, the possibility of a second round of market punishment was enough to reconfigure domestic politics in the Philippines and led to the passage of new legislation. While the Philippines improved its overall compliance, however, the government left a notable gap, exempting casinos from any reporting requirements. The Philippines only addressed this gap when the FATF threatened to list the country for a third time.

Background

The Philippines is vulnerable to money laundering for several reasons. Although the country transitioned from authoritarian rule to democracy in 1986, the government has struggled with corruption and rules that favor the governing elite.[13] The country's economy is heavily dependent on remittances from overseas workers,[14] with personal remittances comprising around 10 percent of the country's total gross domestic product.[15] In addition to the risk of criminals sending money through remittance providers, the Philippines' cash-based economy provides many domestic avenues for disguising criminal proceeds. Nearly half of the country's population is "unbanked," meaning that people hold no accounts at financial institutions or mobile money providers.[16] Cash transactions are thus common even for very large purchases. Underlying illicit activities such as tax crimes, smuggling, corruption, drugs, and arms trafficking are also common and increase the risk of money laundering (Asia/Pacific Group on Money Laundering 2019, 20).

The Philippines also faces a high risk of terrorist financing. The country's biggest terrorist threat is the Abu Sayyaf Group, which is an offshoot of Al-Qaeda and includes rogue factions of several separatist groups. The Abu Sayyaf Group has been responsible for numerous terrorist attacks, including assassinations, bombings, kidnappings, and beheadings. Kidnapping and extortion also serve as "systematic and established method[s] of raising funds for their operations" (Asia/Pacific Group on Money Laundering 2019, 43) and thus make the country vulnerable to terrorist financing.

The Philippine government has participated in the global effort to combat illicit financing for several decades. Although the country is not an FATF member, it was a founding member of the APG and served as APG cochair from 1998 to 2000. Despite these international efforts, the Philippines did not criminalize money laundering or take significant steps to meet the FATF standards until the 2000s. As a result, when the FATF began to identify uncooperative countries in 2000, it included the Philippines on its list.

The Philippines as an "Uncooperative Country"

When the FATF added the Philippines to its NCCT list in 2000, the country lacked the basic components of an effective anti–money laundering system.[17] Philippine law did not require financial institutions to identify customers or keep records of transactions, and banks were permitted to operate under high levels of secrecy. The country also lacked any specific legislation criminalizing money laundering (FATF-GAFI 2000b, 9).

Although the FATF threatened financial countermeasures against all NCCT-listed countries that failed to change their laws within a year, the Philippines was slow to react. One year after the initial listing announcement, Philippine president Gloria Arroyo had committed to passing an anti–money laundering law, but the proposed legislation sat in congressional committees. In June 2001, the FATF warned the Philippines that it must pass the legislation by September 30 or it would face countermeasures (FATF-GAFI 2001a, 4). The Philippines had three months—significantly less time than it would normally take the country to pass such a complex piece of legislation—and so the executive branch had to act quickly. The Department of Finance, the Department of Justice, and the central bank (Bangko Sentral ng Pilipinas [BSP]) wrote a draft law and passed it to both congressional chambers.[18] The BSP also became a vocal advocate of the law and warned of the consequences of failure. In an August 2001 briefing for House reporters, a BSP legal counsel warned that the banking industry was already facing delays with transactions. If the FATF levied countermeasures, banks would subject cross-border transactions to additional scrutiny and discourage foreign investment.[19] The Bankers Association of the Philippines joined the BSP in advocating for the law's passage, estimating a loss of up to 34 million pesos (approximately USD 666,000) per day if the FATF imposed sanctions.[20]

Even with this strong advocacy from the banking sector, the Philippine Congress almost failed to pass the legislation by the FATF deadline. Many in the government perceived the NCCT process as unfair and argued that the FATF had no right to dictate domestic law. Immediately after the NCCT list was announced in June 2000, a spokesman for the Philippine president's office described the listing as "grossly unfair and not reflective of the Philippines' broader efforts on combating money laundering and corruption."[21] In the run-up to the September 30 deadline, senators criticized the FATF pressure as impinging on Philippine sovereignty.[22] Such critiques continued throughout the NCCT process as the Philippine government negotiated with the FATF over incremental legal changes but watched other countries be delisted.[23] At a 2002 hearing, a senator on the banking committee argued, "Our criticism of FATF is that what they require from one country should be clear and should not apply exclusively to the Philippines but to others they are monitoring."[24]

The Philippine Congress adopted its first anti–money laundering act at the end of September 2001, just in time to avoid FATF countermeasures. But the FATF soon assessed that the law had several key gaps: it set too high of a financial threshold for reporting suspicious transactions and also required authorities to secure a court order before examining any suspicious accounts.[25] Thus began another contentious process where the executive branch and the banking community urged amendments to the legislation and the Philippine Senate resisted modifications but eventually caved to market pressure.

In addition to pressure from the banking industry, two other market forces were important for incentivizing the Philippine government to change its policies. Because remittances often flow through cross-border banking, advocacy groups representing overseas workers were particularly active in warning about the economic repercussions of countermeasures. In March 2003, for example, eleven business groups and twenty migrant workers' groups submitted a joint petition that warned of more rigorous screening and remittance delays if the Philippines failed to pass legislation.[26] In 2005, when the FATF announced that the Philippines would soon be removed from the list, the Department of Labor and Employment anticipated a surge in remittances from Filipinos working overseas.[27]

The domestic stock market in the Philippines also appears to have followed developments related to the FATF NCCT process. The FATF's threat of countermeasures led to declines in stock prices.[28] When the FATF finally removed the Philippines from the NCCT list in February 2005, the composite index rose to its highest since January 2000. The chairman of local brokerage firm

Westlink Global Equities linked the price increase to the FATF, saying, "Investors cheered the news of the Philippines being removed from the FATF blacklist. This, together with the extended buying momentum, propelled the market higher."[29]

Listed Again: The Noncomplier List

Soon after the FATF revamped its listing process in 2009, the FATF publicly identified the Philippines once again as having serious deficiencies with its anti–money laundering regime. Unlike the NCCT process, where the FATF handpicked countries to review for potential listing, the FATF's new procedures mandated a review of all countries that received failing ratings on ten or more of the FATF's sixteen most important recommendations.[30] In the APG's July 2009 evaluation of the Philippines, assessors found that the Philippines was partially compliant or noncompliant with thirteen of the FATF's sixteen "key and core" recommendations. The Philippines had failed to criminalize terrorist financing or to make crimes like human trafficking and terrorist financing predicate offenses for money laundering.[31] Its regulatory regime also had key gaps, including requiring only low-quality government identification documents that were easy to forge (Asia/Pacific Group on Money Laundering and the World Bank 2009).

The Philippines immediately entered the FATF's new review process, but the government paid little attention to improving the country's anti–money laundering regime; policy makers had other top priorities. In November 2009, a politically motivated massacre left fifty-seven people dead and led to a countrywide scandal.[32] A spring 2010 presidential election brought a new leader, who now had to deal with the FATF's looming threat.

The FATF added the Philippines to its noncomplier list in October 2010. Placing the country on its grey list, the FATF highlighted the same gaps in the country's anti–money laundering and combating terrorist financing regimes that had been highlighted in the 2009 evaluation. The Philippine government had incomplete laws on money laundering and no specific legislation criminalizing the financing of terrorism; the government allowed for financiers to be prosecuted only if the funds were linked to a specific act of terrorism. In the context of international counterterrorism cooperation, such gaps were highly problematic, since individuals could theoretically raise money for global terrorist organizations without facing a risk of prosecution.

The international context for the Philippines' second listing was different from the first. While the old NCCT process targeted only non-FATF members, the new noncomplier listing process followed a bureaucratic threshold approach that applied to all FATF and non-FATF members. Indeed, in its first February 2010 listing announcement, the FATF listed two FATF members (Greece and Turkey). While the NCCT process grouped the Philippines together with all other unco-operative countries, the new FATF process established different levels of listing. The Philippines was on the grey list, which was officially an announcement titled "Improving Global AML/CFT Compliance—Ongoing Progress." Because this list was noncoercive, the FATF included a much broader cross-section of countries. By October 2010, the grey list had already identified problems in thirty-two countries, including fellow emerging market economies Indonesia, Nigeria, and Turkey.

Another striking difference between the FATF's first and second listing pro-cesses is the way that the Philippine government perceived the organization's mission. Whereas politicians in the Philippines complained throughout the NCCT process that the FATF was threatening the Philippines' sovereign right to determine its own policies, such comments were less common while the Philip-pines was on the noncomplier list.[33] Lawmakers still resisted the FATF's attempts to rush the process, particularly when the FATF threatened to bump the Phil-ippines up to its blacklist, but they no longer challenged the legitimacy of the FATF's mission. Instead, they opposed the FATF's attempt to force through legis-lation in a short amount of time.[34]

If the FATF's changes to the listing procedures improved perceived legiti-macy, the creation of a separate grey list also initially muted the list's impact. Whereas the news media in the Philippines immediately covered the FATF's 2000 NCCT listing announcement, it completely ignored the FATF's decision to add the Philippines to the grey list in October 2010. Indeed, the country's top business newspaper, *Business World*, did not report on the new noncom-plier list until March 2012, eighteen months after listing. Media attention increased only after the FATF moved the Philippines from its grey list to its dark grey list and threatened to blacklist the country if it did not pass legisla-tion by May 2012.[35]

Once the FATF raised the possibility of the blacklist, domestic politics shifted to support compliance. Philippine president Benigno S. C. Aquino III pressured the Congress to act quickly in advance of the May deadline, even proposing that the House and Senate hold a special legislative session to amend the Anti–Money Laundering Act and criminalize terrorist financing.[36] The Philippine Congress waited until it returned to session in May, but by this point, financial pressure had increased. On 18 May, APG executive secretary Gordon Hook sent a letter to the BSP governor urging the Philippines to pass legislation before the FATF's plenary session in late June. In the letter, Hook warned that the Philippines could end up on the blacklist and noted how the list had affected fellow APG member

Thailand, which was blacklisted in February 2012. Hook included an article from the *Bangkok Post*, which reported that some Europe-based financial institutions had stopped transactions in Thailand following the listing.[37]

With such a tight time frame, the Philippine Congress raced to pass legislation in advance of the FATF's June 2012 meeting. The Senate and House fast-tracked bills amending the 2001 Anti–Money Laundering Act and criminalizing terrorist financing, skipping the normal bicameral conference committee process. In commenting on the new legislation, a presidential spokesman explicitly tied the laws to the FATF, noting that he hoped the legislation "will be signed before the FATF deadline [and that] FATF would view actions of the Senate and the House as in compliance with requirements."[38]

The Philippines gained a temporary reprieve, as the FATF moved the country back down to the grey list but warned that more changes were needed. The FATF told the Philippine Anti–Money Laundering Council that the government needed to pass new amendments in order to expand the type of institutions subject to regulation, broaden the definition of money laundering, and increase predicate crimes to include offenses like bribery and tax evasion. Less than two weeks after the president had signed the previous amendments, Senator Sergio R. Osmena III, the chairman of the Senate banks committee, warned, "We will have to pass the third bill. Otherwise, I expect we will be downgraded to dark grey then blacklisted."[39]

Once again, the Philippine Congress pushed forward to meet the FATF-imposed time constraints. In September, President Aquino certified a bill to amend the Anti–Money Laundering Act as "urgent" in order to allow Congress to fast-track approval.[40] As the FATF's mid-October plenary approached, APG executive secretary Gordon Hook warned the BSP that, per FATF procedure, a country can only be on the dark grey list once. If the Philippines failed to pass legislation this time, the FATF might be forced to blacklist the country.[41] Despite such pressure, however, the Senate was unable to pass the legislation, in part due to opposition from senators who opposed adding real estate brokers to the list of institutions that must submit suspicious transaction reports to the Anti–Money Laundering Council.[42]

The FATF opted to give the Philippines four more months to pass new legislation. The Anti–Money Laundering Council had argued convincingly that the Philippine government was committed to passing new legislation before the FATF's February 2013 deadline.[43] But while the amendments made it through the House without much trouble, the related bill languished in the Senate. One senator warned that expanding the list of predicate crimes for money laundering would allow whichever party controlled the Philippine executive branch to use the Anti–Money Laundering Council against its political opponents. The bill also faced opposition from jewelers and real estate agents who opposed new reporting requirements.[44] In February, weeks before the FATF was scheduled to meet, the House and Senate finally agreed on legislation that would expand reporting requirements. Real estate, jewelry, and precious metal dealers were all now required to report suspicious transactions to the Anti–Money Laundering Council.[45]

The Philippines' new legislation heralded the start of the FATF's delisting process,[46] but it also contained a key policy gap. During a last-minute bicameral conference, the Congress had removed a provision that would have subjected the casino industry to anti–money laundering reporting requirements. House members and the Philippine Amusement and Gaming Corp (PAGCOR) had lobbied aggressively, arguing that including casinos in the bill would deter investors and potentially stifle the Philippines' growing gambling industry. At the time of the bill's adoption, the Philippines was weeks away from opening a USD 4 billion casino complex in Manila; the country was hoping to rival Macau, Las Vegas, and Singapore as a gaming hub.[47] When the FATF removed the Philippines from the noncomplier list in June, it warned that the government needed to continue to work with the APG to address this gap, as well as the full range of problems identified in the 2009 evaluation.[48] Several years later, this legislative gap would lead to the Philippines' third encounter with the FATF list.

The Role of Market Pressure during the Noncomplier List

Unofficial market enforcement was crucial for driving compliance improvements in the Philippines. The Philippine government passed major legislation on money laundering and terrorist financing because policy makers feared the financial consequences of blacklisting. Technically, the FATF blacklist only calls for member states and financial institutions to "consider the risks" of each country's deficiencies, yet listing creates significant market enforcement. In the Philippines, market enforcement manifested through at least three distinct pathways: cross-national banking, remittance providers, and the Philippine stock market. Each set of actors responded in different ways, but all three types of pressure worked to incentivize government action.

The FATF noncomplier list's most recognizable impact was on cross-border banking. Because of its previous experience with the NCCT process, the Philippine government understood how even the prospect of enhanced scrutiny could lead banks to close correspondent accounts, delay transactions, and charge

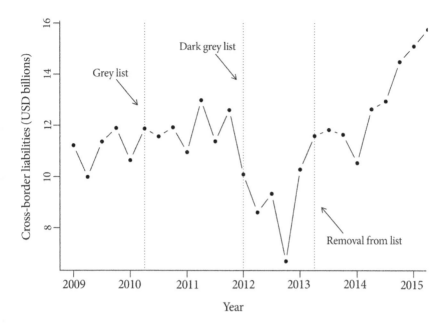

FIGURE 6.1. Listing and cross-border liabilities in the Philippines

Note: The figure shows cross-border liabilities (billions of US dollars) from 2009 to 2015. The FATF listed the Philippines in October 2010 and in February 2012 placed the country on its dark grey list for failing to improve its laws in a timely fashion. The FATF moved the Philippines back to the grey list in June 2012 after the country passed new legislation to remedy some deficiencies but warned that the government needed to make additional improvements to its anti–money laundering regime. Following significant legal changes, the FATF removed the Philippines from the noncomplier list in June 2013.

higher prices for cross-border transfers. Although the FATF does not caution its members to treat grey list countries differently, the Philippine Anti–Money Laundering Council noted that other countries are more cautious in their dealings and transactions with any listed country.[49] Figure 6.1 suggests the Philippines' time on the noncomplier list was associated with a decline in cross-border bank lending.

Once the FATF officially threatened the Philippines with the blacklist, Philippine senators and congressmen repeatedly cited concerns about how listing would affect banking and remittances from overseas foreign workers. In June 2012, when the FATF moved the Philippines from the dark grey list back down to the grey list—an effective upgrade for market purposes—the central bank highlighted how avoidance of the blacklist was positive news for overseas workers and for the economy.[50] When the FATF announced in February 2013 that it would conduct an on-site visit to verify the Philippines' reforms, the chair of the Senate Committee on Accountability of Public Offices and Investigations said that he

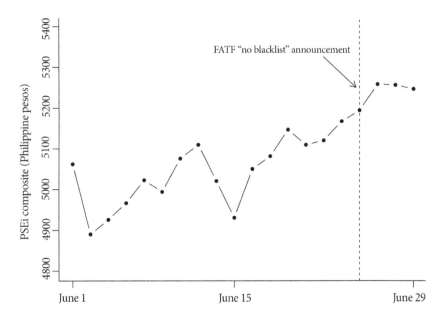

FIGURE 6.2. Philippine stock market reaction to "no blacklist" announcement

Note: The figure shows the closing price of the Philippine Stock Exchange Composite Index (PSEi) for June 2012. On 26 June 2012, the FATF announced it would not put the Philippines on its blacklist—a move heralded by markets as a positive development.

hoped the on-site visit would lead to delisting, which would benefit millions of overseas Filipino workers.

There is also some evidence that the Philippine stock market was responsive to FATF pressure. When the FATF announced that it would not blacklist the Philippines in June 2012, the managing director for First Grade Holdings, Inc., a top brokerage firm in the Philippines, told reporters that the news could have a positive effect on financial markets since it would smooth the flow of cross-border transactions.[51] *Business World* reported that stocks climbed in response to news that the Philippines had averted being blacklisted as a money-laundering haven.[52] Figure 6.2 shows the average price of the Philippine Stock Exchange Composite Index in June 2012.[53] The figure suggests that the price of the index did increase following the FATF's "no blacklist" announcement.

The Third Blacklisting Threat

The FATF removed the Philippines from its noncomplier list in June 2013, but the APG continued to monitor the country's progress even after delisting.

The Philippines' biggest gap was its failure to subject casinos to money laundering reporting requirements. Without the direct threat of the FATF's list, the Philippine legislature stalled in addressing this deficiency. In November 2013, a member of the House of Representatives submitted a bill that would require casinos and other gambling establishments to report all persons who borrow or win large amounts;[54] almost a year later, the House had not passed it.[55] The Philippines had clear business incentives to allow financial secrecy. In October 2014, for example, Caesars Entertainment Corp. announced that it would seek a license to build a casino in the Philippines—the first time that a US company would enter the local casino market.[56] With other Asian gambling locales tightening their anti–money laundering regulations, the Philippines was well positioned to benefit from its lax casino rules.

Momentum began to shift in early 2016 when the Philippines found itself at the center of the biggest bank heist in history. In an elaborate cyber heist, North Korean hackers managed to steal USD 101 million from the Bangladesh central bank. They transferred the majority of the funds to the Philippines, where the money went to casinos and online gambling venues, and then seemingly vanished into thin air. Because of the gap in the law, investigators could not track the money beyond the gambling venues.[57]

Immediately, the media began to link the FATF's call for stronger legislation with the Philippines' casino gap. A *Wall Street Journal* article from March notes, "In 2013, an international anti-money-laundering watchdog warned the Philippines that there was a gaping hole in its defenses against people illegally moving money around its economy: the country's casinos." The article goes on to describe how in light of the recent theft, Filipinos working abroad could face higher charges when they send money home.[58] Senators began to worry that the FATF would put the Philippines back on the noncomplier list,[59] and as a result, many became more vocal about supporting new legislation to close the loophole.[60] By April, the Anti–Money Laundering Council had prepared new legislation to expand anti–money laundering requirements to the casino industry.[61]

The pressure on the Philippines intensified in fall 2016 due to two developments. First, during the APG's September 2016 annual meeting, APG member states gave the Philippines until June 2017 to pass a bill that included casinos or the APG would refer the country again to the FATF's noncomplier list process.[62] Second, the APG scheduled the Philippines' next compliance evaluation for 2018. In an October 2016 budget hearing, the executive director of the Anti–Money Laundering Council warned senators that the country needed to expand the law to include casinos within the next year, or it would be blacklisted by the

FATF.[63] In the run-up to the June 2017 deadline, the Philippine Congress finally passed bills amending the Anti–Money Laundering Act in May 2017.[64] Philippine president Rodrigo Duterte signed the law in July, allowing the country to avoid any adverse FATF action.

The FATF listing process has transformed the policy landscape in the Philippines over the last two decades. When the FATF placed the Philippines on its NCCT list in 2000, the country had no laws criminalizing money laundering or terrorist financing. It lacked even basic anti–money laundering regulations like customer identification and record keeping, and it allowed financial institutions to operate with excessive secrecy (FATF 2001a). By 2009, the Philippines had key components of an anti–money laundering regime, but considerable gaps in its legal framework and no legislation criminalizing terrorist financing (Asia/Pacific Group on Money Laundering and the World Bank 2009). Key parts of the Philippine government, such as the Anti-Money Laundering Council, also struggled to implement the FATF regulations (Asia/Pacific Group on Money Laundering and the World Bank 2009, 10). Ten years later, however, the Philippines has adopted a much more comprehensive framework to combat illicit financing. Although the APG still identified implementation challenges in its 2019 evaluation of the Philippines, the country received compliant or largely compliant ratings on twenty-eight of the FATF's forty recommendations (compared to fourteen of forty-nine in 2009). Overall, the Philippines' legal and regulatory framework on stopping illicit financing has changed significantly since 2000, and the evidence strongly suggests that the FATF is responsible for much of this policy change.

Thailand: Business Associations Driving Policy Prioritization

Thailand's experience on the noncomplier list demonstrates how market pressure via global banking can reconfigure domestic politics. Thailand has a relatively high risk of money laundering and terrorist financing, but the country was compliant with few FATF recommendations when it was listed in February 2010. The Thai government viewed anti–money laundering and combating terrorist financing as low priorities compared to other, more pressing political matters. The FATF noncomplier list's impact on markets caused the banking community and private-sector actors to advocate for compliance improvements. Over the course of listing, Thailand significantly improved its policies and was subsequently removed from the list in 2013. Its most recent compliance assessment suggests the improvements have been long-lasting.

Background

Thailand has numerous characteristics that make it vulnerable to illicit financing. It is situated in the heart of Southeast Asia and has expansive borders that make it vulnerable as both a destination and a transit point for illicit funds (Asia/Pacific Group on Money Laundering 2017). Although Thailand is an important regional economy and attracts significant foreign investment, many of its transactions are cash-based and occur through the informal sector (Asia/Pacific Group on Money Laundering 2017, 25).[65] Thailand has domestic problems with many types of crime, including drug trafficking, human trafficking, illegal logging, and corruption (IMF 2007, 24), but political turmoil over the last fifteen years has made it difficult for the government to craft effective policy responses.[66]

In addition to money laundering, Thailand faces a high risk of terrorist financing. For several decades, the Thai government has confronted an ethnoreligious separatist insurgency from Malay-Muslim rebels. As of January 2019, this insurgency was responsible for the deaths of nearly seven thousand people. Transnational terrorist groups like Al-Qaeda and Jemaah Islamiyah are also a threat, reportedly using Thailand as a transit point and a base for attacks.[67] The country's core risks of terrorist financing come from domestic terrorist groups, transnational groups attempting to target Thailand for financial support or to launder criminal proceeds, and financial vulnerabilities from returning Islamic State foreign fighters, who use Thailand as a transit point (Asia/Pacific Group on Money Laundering 2017, 17).

Thailand has been an active participant in the global effort to stop illicit financing since the mid-1990s. The Thai government began drafting an antimoney laundering bill in 1994 and finally adopted legislation in 1999. In addition to criminalizing money laundering, the 1999 law created the Thai Anti–Money Laundering Office (AMLO), which serves as a financial intelligence unit that collects and investigates suspicious financial transactions. Thailand is also a founding member of the APG and underwent its first APG mutual evaluation to review compliance with FATF standards in 2002 (IMF 2007, 41). It has since completed two more evaluations.

Thailand before the 2010 Noncomplier List

When the International Monetary Fund (IMF) assessed Thailand's compliance with the FATF recommendations in 2007,[68] it rated Thailand as fully compliant with only two of the forty-nine recommendations. Thailand received noncompliant or partially compliant ratings on more than half of the recommendations, including all nine of the recommendations on combating terrorist financing.

The monitoring report highlighted the need for Thailand to amend the Anti–Money Laundering Act to expand the list of predicate offenses, impose anti–money laundering obligations on financial institutions that pose illicit financing risks, strengthen enforcement, and properly criminalize the financing of terrorism (IMF 2007, 10).

At the time of Thailand's 2007 review, the FATF had relatively few tools for pushing compliance improvements. Its listing process required that an FATF member nominate a country and that the FATF membership approve the listing. Only a minority of FATF members were willing to nominate uncooperative states.[69] As a result, the FATF identified only six countries under this process.[70] Thailand faced no real threat of listing, and therefore the government's only incentive to improve compliance was the requirement to submit a follow-up report to the FATF within two years (FATF-GAFI 2009b, 12). Given this weak incentive structure and Thailand's ongoing political challenges, it is not surprising that the government did little to remedy its noncompliance.

Thailand and the Noncomplier List

When the FATF redesigned its listing process in 2009, Thailand automatically became eligible for the new noncomplier list. Thailand was noncompliant or partially compliant with thirteen of the FATF's sixteen most important recommendations. The Thai government failed to address these gaps in the intervening period, and so in February 2010, the FATF added Thailand to the grey list. In its first listing statement, the FATF called on Thailand to criminalize terrorist financing, establish and implement procedures to freeze terrorist assets, and strengthen its supervision of relevant laws.

As in the Philippines, the FATF's decision to put Thailand on the grey list had little impact on domestic politics in the first two years. The FATF's listing process was new and specified no direct financial consequences, and so Thai newspapers paid little attention to listing, even after the FATF bumped Thailand up to the dark grey list in October 2011.[71] The AMLO, however, recognized the potential consequences of listing almost immediately. Shortly after listing, the AMLO launched a big public information campaign to convince the Thai National Assembly to adopt new laws.[72] Yet the response from the rest of the government was sluggish. According to Dr. Twatchai Yongkittikul, the former secretary-general of the Thai Bankers' Association, "explaining to members of Parliament, especially those who were not familiar with financial matters and those from remote provinces, why we needed to comply with the FATF's recommendations was difficult."[73] By the end of 2010, Thailand had approved a national strategy to combat illicit financing and had drafted a proposed law to criminalize terrorist financing (US Department of State 2011), but the country had made no other improvements.

Domestic problems in Thailand also impeded the government's efforts. Political and civil unrest, combined with catastrophic flooding, the dissolution of the National Assembly, and new elections in 2011, all compounded the usual challenges of drafting new laws. While Thailand was unable to adopt new legislation by the end of 2011, it did take steps to strengthen the AMLO by increasing its staff and establishing a clear compliance-monitoring role.[74] The government also worked to train financial institutions, particularly money changers and transfer businesses, about their requirements to report suspicious transactions (US Department of State 2012, 171).

Such changes were not sufficient to satisfy the FATF, which threatened to move Thailand to its blacklist if the government did not address legislative gaps by February 2012. Representatives of the Thai government tried unsuccessfully to explain to the FATF that the delay in legislation was due to circumstances outside of their control.[75] In addition to ongoing domestic turmoil, a series of terrorist bombings occurred in Bangkok in the week prior to the FATF meeting.[76] Nevertheless, the FATF moved Thailand to the blacklist. In its public announcement, the FATF acknowledged that Thailand had "faced external difficulties from 2009 to 2011 which significantly impacted the legislative process" but nonetheless highlighted the need for the country to adequately criminalize terrorist financing, establish a procedure for freezing terrorist assets, and strengthen supervision of its anti–money laundering regime.[77]

The FATF's decision to move Thailand to the blacklist changed the political dynamics surrounding Thailand's anti–money laundering regime. Media attention increased significantly: whereas prior to February 2012, no domestic media outlets had reported on the FATF, numerous articles appeared after blacklisting. The *Nation/Thailand*, one of Thailand's two English-language newspapers, reported on the FATF list for the first time on 15 February 2012. In the two weeks that followed blacklisting, the paper published eight more articles on the subject. *Thai Rath*, a widely read Thai-language language newspaper, published six articles in the week that followed listing, including an article describing how the Thai Chamber of Commerce was concerned that the list would lead foreign investment to go to Singapore and Malaysia instead of Thailand.[78] Within days of Thailand's move to the blacklist, the Thai ruling party had announced its intention to rush through two new laws on terrorist financing and money laundering.[79] The prime minister told the Council of State, the AMLO, and the Finance Ministry to determine how Thailand should modify its laws to address the FATF's concerns.[80]

While the blacklist undoubtedly increased pressure on the Thai government, general confusion among Thai officials and the media may have muted some of its initial impact. Unlike in the Philippines, where the government and media had a shared view of the blacklist, the Thai government seems to have been confused about how to interpret the FATF's February 2012 announcement. In a statement soon after listing, the AMLO argued publicly that the country was not on the blacklist, presumably because it viewed the FATF's countermeasures list (which has only ever been applied to North Korea and Iran) as the true "blacklist."[81] Media coverage in the months following listing was equally confused, as the news outlets referred to the list sometimes as the "dark grey list," sometimes as the "grey list," and other times as the "blacklist." Notably, however, in all of these stories, government and business officials highlighted adverse market consequences due to listing.[82]

By May 2012, the business industry was pushing strongly for the Thai government to adopt new legislation. The Joint Private Standing Committee, a group of the private sector's three most powerful industry organizations,[83] convened a meeting with the prime minister and argued for rushing through measures to stop illicit financing.[84] A day after the meeting, Deputy Prime Minister and Finance Minister Kittiratt Na-Ranong promised an expedited enactment of new legislation before the FATF's deadline of February 2013.[85] In a public statement, Na-Ranong linked anticipated policy change directly to the FATF list.[86]

The Joint Private Standing Committee continued to play an active role in pushing for compliance improvements throughout Thailand's time on the list. In June 2012 Thailand's House of Representatives unanimously passed two bills designed to address the legislative gaps identified by the FATF.[87] But the Joint Private Standing Committee warned that the Parliament had revised and weakened the legislation too much. Payungsak Chartsuthipol, Federation of Thai Industries chairman, cautioned, "If the government continues [to press ahead and] to pass the current revised draft law, Thailand will still have a bad image in tackling money-laundering and preventing support for terrorist activities."[88] Although the Thai Parliament amended the legislation, the bill slowed in the Senate. By October, the Federation of Thai Industries was warning business leaders to be prepared for severe repercussions if the Senate failed to pass the legislation by February 2013.[89] Private-sector organizations urged the government to skip its normal 120-day waiting period and begin implementing the laws immediately on passage so as to prepare for the FATF's February 2013 deadline.[90]

The Thai Parliament eventually adopted final legislation in November 2012. While the bills met with near unanimous support, at least one senator criticized the FATF for forcing Thailand to adopt new laws or face more market pressure. Senator Khamnoon Sithisamarn told the *Bangkok Post*, "The deliberation of the two bills has been limited, with conditions on timing and content. The economy of Thailand has been held hostage."[91] Nevertheless, the king of Thailand certified the new bills in early February 2013 and the FATF moved Thailand back to the grey list.

Thailand officially "graduated" from the noncomplier list in June 2013. During its last four months on the list, Thailand readied itself for the FATF's on-site visit. In April, the Thai minister of justice demonstrated policy implementation by announcing a list of 291 foreign terrorists and terrorist organizations subject to sanctions.[92] To further reassure the FATF that Thailand was also targeting domestic terrorists, the AMLO subsequently released a second list of nine domestic terrorists from the southern provinces.[93] The FATF finally removed Thailand from the public listing process in June 2013. In its explanation for delisting, the FATF noted the country's significant progress in improving its laws and regulations on illicit financing.[94]

The Role of Market Pressure

The Thai government improved its compliance with FATF standards almost exclusively due to realized and anticipated market consequences. While the naming-and-shaming process of the noncomplier list incentivized some policy change early on, it was insufficient motivation for significant compliance improvements. Domestic politics changed when the Thai business community began to experience negative financial consequences from listing; these actors became strong advocates for strengthening Thailand's anti–money laundering regime. Market enforcement against the banking sector, the larger business community, and even Thai diplomats abroad served to motivate the Thai government to improve compliance with the FATF standards.

The Thai business community was the first to understand the noncomplier list's negative financial impact. By 2011, international banks had begun to integrate the FATF list into their cross-border banking strategies and to adjust risk appraisals of listed countries. Even before Thailand was on the blacklist, Thai banks found it more challenging to do business abroad, as foreign banks asked additional questions about anti–money laundering rules and regulations. The Thai business community was particularly concerned about the list because foreign transactions were taking longer and were more costly than before.[95] Prior to the FATF's February 2012 plenary session, the Federation of Thai Industries, the Thai Chamber of Commerce, the Thai Bankers' Association, the Federation of Thai Capital Market Organizations, and the Tourism Council of Thailand wrote a letter to the prime minister, pressing her to make a statement in advance of the FATF's meeting.[96] During this period, the central bank and Thai minister of finance also expressed concern about potential harm of the blacklist.[97]

When the FATF moved Thailand to the blacklist in February 2012, domestic banks highlighted potential negative effects. The CEO of Kasikornbank told reporters that the listing hurt Thailand's image, and that the House needed to pass new legislation quickly or listing would hurt Thailand's economic and social development.[98] A senior executive vice president of KBank, another large Thai bank, argued that banks would now be required to inspect customer transactions more closely, driving up operating costs.[99] Thai banks began to report difficulties obtaining permits to open branches in EU countries, and a bank in the EU even contemplated scrapping a deal to lend money to Thai banks.[100] By May 2012, the Thai Bankers' Association could point to specific problems arising from listing, such as a French bank that denied a Thai firm a loan to purchase machinery because of the FATF list.[101]

Complaints and concerns were not confined to the banking industry. Thai business leaders worried that the blacklist would hurt both trade and foreign direct investment.[102] After the February 2012 blacklisting, the president of the Small and Medium Enterprise Development Bank of Thailand cited concerns that the list could lead new trade partners to inspect more closely financial transactions with Thai manufacturers.[103] In a roundtable organized by the Federation of Thai Industries, business leaders argued that the list's long-term impact could include reduced foreign investment, fewer mergers and acquisitions, weaker international trade, and declining tourism.[104]

While the FATF list had many indirect impacts on the Thai government via the business community, the market enforcement process also affected Thai government officials directly. In October 2012 the justice minister reported that Thai diplomats in Washington, DC, were struggling to cash bank checks and conduct financial transactions due to the list.[105] US banks were refusing to cash checks issued by Thai banks or to allow Thai diplomats to open new accounts in the United States. Faced with such reports, the AMLO admitted that it could do nothing to stop US banks from scrutinizing Thai diplomats except to inform the FATF of Thailand's new laws and hope that the organization would remove Thailand from the list in 2013.[106]

Financial Costs of Listing

Quantifying the full impact of the noncomplier list on Thailand's economy is difficult due to the diverse ways in which the list affected financial flows. There is, however, at least correlational evidence that the noncomplier list affected cross-border liabilities. Figure 6.3 shows cross-border liabilities (money that Thai banks owe to international banks) between 2009 and 2015. When the FATF listed Thailand in February 2010, cross-border liabilities stayed relatively stable; however, after the FATF bumped Thailand up to a higher listing level in February 2012, cross-border liabilities declined significantly. As Thailand started to modify its policies, cross-border flows began to increase again, and this trend continued for a year after Thailand's removal from the list.

There is also correlational evidence that the noncomplier list affected the risk premium for long-term debt. Figure 6.4 shows the yield spread for ten-year bonds sold by the Thai government between 2009 and 2015.[107] In the two years following Thailand's listing, the spread rose from 1.1 to 2.2 as investors viewed Thailand as an increasingly risky investment prospect. While it is true that Thailand experienced a number of challenges during this time, such as massive floods and political unrest, these events do not appear to correlate with bond spreads. For example, in the latter part of 2011, Thailand had major flooding, leading to billions of dollars in economic damages (Quadir 2012), yet the yield spread was already increasing prior to flooding and increased more after the floods ended. During the period of massive political turmoil in late 2013, the yield spread was actually decreasing. While the figure does not provide definitive evidence of a causal link between the noncomplier list and bond yields, it suggests that the noncomplier list and yield spreads are correlated.

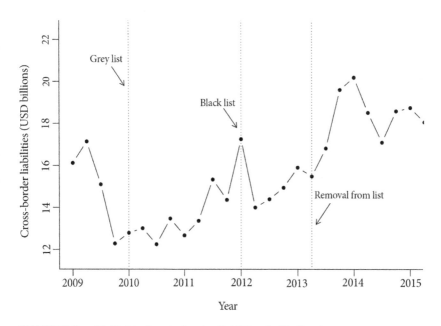

FIGURE 6.3.   Listing and cross-border liabilities in Thailand

Note: The figure shows cross-border liabilities (billions of US dollars) from 2009 to 2015. The FATF listed Thailand in February 2010 and in February 2012 placed Thailand on its blacklist for failing to improve its laws in a timely fashion. Following significant legal changes, the FATF removed Thailand from the noncomplier list in June 2013.

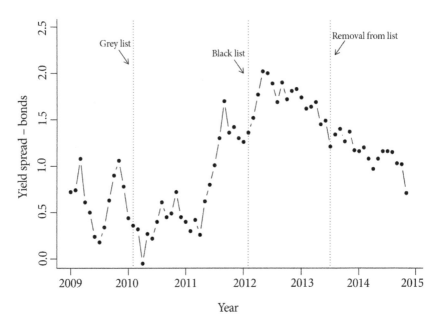

FIGURE 6.4. Listing and sovereign bonds in Thailand

Note: The figure shows the yield spread for Thai long-term debt (ten-year bond, compared to the yield on the US ten-year bond) for the period of January 2009 to December 2014. The FATF listed Thailand in February 2010. In February 2012, the FATF placed Thailand on the blacklist for failing to improve its laws in a timely fashion. Following significant legal changes, the FATF removed Thailand from the noncomplier list in June 2013.

Continued Improvement Even after Listing

The FATF removed Thailand from the noncomplier list in June 2013. Since that time, Thailand has continued to modify its rules and regulations to improve compliance with the FATF standards. The AMLO in particular is much more active in regulating the banking sector, clarifying bank reporting obligations, and promoting information sharing.[108] It has also become an active proponent of new legislation. In August 2014, for example, the AMLO pushed for the government to amend the anti–money laundering laws so as to allow for the automatic seizure of any cash over USD 20,000 that was brought into the country and not declared.[109] In October 2015, the AMLO pushed for legislation to criminalize funding for weapons of mass destruction. Arguing for the measure, the AMLO chief cited concerns about the noncomplier list: "If we are unable to improve our standards as required by the FATF, then there's a risk that Thailand will be blacklisted as a country with high levels of money laundering again, which will seriously affect Thai financial institutions' transactions."[110]

The APG's 2017 evaluation of Thailand highlights the country's continuous progress. The report notes that there is "strong political support for recent AML/CFT reforms" and discusses how "institutional arrangements have developed significantly since the 2007 mutual evaluation report" (Asia/Pacific Group on Money Laundering 2017, 3). In its technical compliance monitoring, the APG found Thailand to be compliant or largely compliant with twenty-five of the task force's forty recommendations. While the evaluation revealed some problems with the effectiveness of preventive measures and financial sanctions, Thailand has improved enough that it avoided even being eligible for the noncomplier list in its latest evaluation.[111]

Conclusion

Many countries fail to adopt stringent laws or regulations to stop illicit financing despite being vulnerable to organized crime, corruption, or terrorism. These states might attract capital from lax oversight, or lack the capacity or political investment necessary to meet international standards. In Thailand, internal instability due to political unrest and catastrophic flooding meant that the government had more important domestic priorities. In the Philippines, a culture of financial secrecy, corruption, and resistance to external pressure made the Congress unwilling to appease international audiences.

While the sources of opposition may vary, the case studies in this chapter illustrate that the FATF noncomplier list is a powerful tool for shifting the politics of compliance. In Thailand, the noncomplier list forced the government to prioritize passing tougher laws on illicit financing. One Thai AMLO official described the list as a "catalyst" for policy change, noting, "I think the ICRG process had a significant effect on Thailand's AML/CFT regime" because the Thai Parliament was able to pass two key legislative acts "in approximate of one year, which is quite an achievement."[112] In the Philippines, the government passed almost every major piece of anti–money laundering legislation while on the FATF list or under direct threat of listing.

In both Thailand and the Philippines, the noncomplier list's impact is best understood through the frame of unofficial market enforcement. The FATF used the economic coercion of the NCCT process to establish the salience of its recommendations, but its reliance on direct market pressure led to widespread resistance and political challenges. The FATF learned from this experience when it designed its new noncomplier list procedures. Rather than directly subjecting countries to financial penalties, the FATF simply provided information that banks could integrate into decision-making. Domestic banks and private industries in listed countries began to advocate strongly for policy improvements, and listed governments had little recourse other than to meet FATF standards. In the Philippines, the FATF's change in tactics led to less resistance and more rapid policy change. Whereas the country lingered on the NCCT list for five years, the Philippines graduated from the noncomplier list in under three. In Thailand, the government took action despite facing numerous internal challenges.

Market enforcement has generated long-term improvements in compliance in Thailand and the Philippines. Both governments now understand that the FATF noncomplier list can negatively impact cross-border lending and bank-to-bank transactions. Over the last decade, these governments have observed market enforcement processes taking place across a variety of listed states, including ones that remain exclusively on the grey list. As a result, they have incentives to work preemptively to improve compliance and avoid the FATF listing threshold. In both cases, governmental officials have adopted new policies in advance of APG monitoring in order to avoid relisting and concomitant market consequences.

If the case studies showcase the power of unofficial market enforcement, they also highlight some of the potential downsides to this approach. When Thailand was on the FATF noncomplier list, its government was confronting a multitude of political threats as well as natural disasters—serious issues that required substantive responses. Yet the FATF forced Thailand to prioritize passing legislation on combating illicit financing and possibly delayed other important policy programs. In the Philippines, market enforcement may have hurt some of the most vulnerable members of society. Thousands of families in the Philippines rely on overseas remittances to afford food, housing, and clothing—if the costs of money transfers increase, these families will receive less. The conclusion weighs these trade-offs, arguing that policy makers should proceed with caution when harnessing the power of market forces against disempowered populations.

Conclusion

THE POWER AND PERIL OF
MARKETS AS ENFORCERS

Trillions of dollars move through the global financial system every year. While the majority of cross-border transfers are legitimate, monetary flows hold everything from family remittances to the ill-gotten gains of crime. In order to detect and prevent criminals and terrorists from sending money across borders, states have made global banks the first line of defense. Banks are expected to screen new clients, mitigate risk in their relationships with other banks, and report suspicious transactions. While data challenges make it difficult to evaluate how these policies have affected aggregate illicit flows, international financial regulations have clearly created barriers to financial access for criminals and noncriminals alike.

How should countries weigh the risk of illicit funds against concerns about financial inclusion? Over the last thirty years, policy makers have leaned toward minimizing risk. For three decades, powerful economies have used the Financial Action Task Force (FATF) to develop guidelines and expertise on how countries should reduce financial secrecy. The FATF designs and implements anti–money laundering and combating terrorist financing recommendations, and then uses its global network to monitor compliance in nearly two hundred countries. Member states complement this international action with domestic action, ensuring that banks are creating risk mitigation systems and taking punitive action against financial institutions that fail to meet international guidelines.

The FATF noncomplier list exploits this underlying incentive structure to harness banks as unofficial enforcers. The unofficial nature of this process is key to its power: FATF member states pay fewer enforcement costs for sending a simple signal to market actors rather than directly coercing policy change. As a result, the FATF has been willing to place a large number of countries on its noncomplier list. Though ostensibly noncoercive, foreign banks move resources away from listed countries and raise the costs of business for domestic firms and clients. This market enforcement process reconfigures domestic politics, creating new incentives for governments to comply with FATF standards.

The FATF's narrative can be told in different ways. This book analyzes the FATF's operations in order to understand international cooperation at large, and underscores how states have found an effective way to diffuse standards worldwide. Through this lens, the FATF's story is a tale of an organization that spent years building up credibility and technical expertise and then leveraged those advantages to drive deep and widespread policy change. The noncomplier list's policy impact has been enormous; it has generated a type of cooperation that is rarely observed in international relations.

The concluding chapter builds on this narrative, summarizing the theory's core argument about focal points, unofficial market enforcement, and compliance. It discusses the book's theoretical and empirical contributions and explores the broader policy implications of the research project. It also, however, considers a competing narrative of the FATF's actions as a normative judgment, by powerful countries, that stopping criminals and terrorists should be prioritized over the goals of financial opportunity and inclusion. The final section considers such trade-offs and explores avenues for future research.

Summary of Theory, Contributions, and Findings

The theory of unofficial market enforcement set forth in this book begins from the premise that information can be a powerful form of influence in a globalized economy. When an international organization (IO) provides information that serves as a focal point—that is, the information establishes a shared expectation about how to behave—the IO can use this signaling power strategically to direct market pressure toward certain countries. The theory identifies three key scope conditions that allow an IO to serve as a focal point for states or nonstate actors: informational advantages, economic coercion, and institutional legitimacy. When an IO has acquired institutional salience among market actors, it can use monitoring and signaling to shift market behavior toward punishing uncooperative countries. For IO member states, this unofficial market enforcement process has key strategic advantages over direct economic coercion. States pay fewer enforcement costs for unofficial market pressure and therefore are willing to use it against a broader set of countries. The unofficial nature also makes it more difficult for targeted countries to lobby against the focal point. Instead, unofficial market enforcement reconfigures domestic politics and incentivizes increased compliance.

Theoretical and Empirical Contributions

This book makes several types of contributions to international relations literature. It highlights the wide-reaching power of the global bank network, which can impose significant costs on countries that fail to meet international standards. Cross-border bank-to-bank transactions are the foundation of many types of economic activity. From remittances to trade financing, individuals and firms depend on access to the banking network to participate in the global economy; if international banks decide to impose costs on a country, this financial impact will be felt across society and will incentivize the government to adjust its policies. While previous scholarship has highlighted the importance of high-level bank advocacy and attitudes toward financial regulation, this book underscores how the day-to-day decision-making of banks about something like illicit financing risk can have a powerful impact on domestic politics.

The Bankers' Blacklist also illustrates why leveraging the power of banks through *unofficial* market enforcement is crucial to understanding the FATF's policy impact. Historically, IOs and states have tried to incentivize countries to change their actions through overt economic coercion. But such measures incur large political and economic enforcement costs, and often struggle to generate deep policy improvements. By using a focal point to influence bank actions, the FATF has overcome many of these challenges. FATF member states have been willing to place their allies, key emerging economies, and other strategically important countries on the noncomplier list because it is technocratic and ostensibly noncoercive. The FATF's expertise and clear bureaucratic procedures make it easier to list countries and also harder to remove them without strong evidence of policy improvements. As a result, listed governments have strong incentives to adopt FATF-compliant laws and reforms.

In addition to highlighting the FATF noncomplier list's signaling power, this book sheds light on an important but underexplored topic in international relations: how does an IO become a focal point? In Thomas Schelling's original account of focal points and cooperation, he writes that focal points are context dependent and rely on salience, prominence, and uniqueness (Schelling 1960, 57–58). Building on Schelling's explanation, this book theorizes that an IO can develop its prominence in an issue area through informational advantages, coercive pressure, and legitimacy enhancements. A prominent IO that sends a unique signal about state behavior is more effective at creating a focal point for outside observers. By theorizing about the scope conditions for prominence and the significance of form (and not just content), the argument contributes to the emerging literature on global performance indicators.

This book also makes several empirical contributions. Time variation in the form and content of FATF monitoring makes it possible to probe the argument's scope conditions, particularly as it relates to how the FATF signals country risk. FATF monitoring had only a minimal impact on global banks when it was delivered in long and complex country reports. In contrast, once the FATF provided a unique, unmistakable signal about country risk, banks were able to integrate this information into their decision-making structures. The unique impact of the noncomplier list is supported by a variety of quantitative and qualitative data. Drawing from legal documents, international organization reports, newspapers, and interviews, the book provides a detailed cross-national analysis of policy change in the realm of terrorist financing. This issue area is considered the cornerstone of international cooperation on combating terrorism, which is one of the most pressing security issues for the world today. By triangulating quantitative evidence with interviews and case studies, the chapters provide a clearer picture of how listing leads banks to direct resources away from targeted countries and why this process leads to compliance improvements.

Findings: How Unofficial Market Enforcement Drives Policy Change

This book provides a detailed analysis of international cooperation to combat illicit financing. Efforts to keep "bad money" out of the financial system date back to the 1980s, but they increased exponentially after the 9/11 terrorist attacks. The 9/11 hijackers used bank-to-bank transfers to support training, buy supplies, and purchase plane tickets for their final flights. Because the attacks led to a sense of collective vulnerability, the United States was able to push aggressive counterterrorism action in the United Nations Security Council and in the FATF. Yet despite strong international rules and widespread political support, governments were slow to meet the FATF standards. Laws criminalizing terrorist financing often penalized people only if they supplied money directly for a terrorist act rather than for a terrorist group or individual writ large.

The FATF noncomplier list transformed this trend. Using large-N statistical analysis, *The Bankers' Blacklist* demonstrates how the FATF noncomplier list leads to meaningful, widespread policy change. Listed countries are eight times more likely to adopt FATF-compliant laws on terrorist financing, compared to nonlisted countries, and this effect is strongest for countries with high levels of market integration. Interviews with officials from formerly listed countries and press reporting highlight the impact of the noncomplier list, as political leaders often link new legislation explicitly to the FATF.

Unofficial market enforcement is the key to understanding why countries change their laws. Quantitative analyses show that the noncomplier list leads to a decline in cross-border bank-to-bank lending to listed countries. Qualitative evidence from interviews and newspapers provides additional support for the idea that market actors view listed countries as higher risk. Bank-to-bank enforcement may even spill over into trade financing and the market for sovereign debt. Case studies of Thailand and the Philippines further illustrate this process, showcasing how the noncomplier list led banks to restrict business and charge higher rates to clients in both countries. In Thailand, banks experienced delays in cross-border banking and the closure of correspondent banking relationships, leading Thai banking, business, and industry groups to lobby aggressively for policy change. In the Philippines, lawmakers responded to similar industry pressure as well as to concerns that prolonged listing would lead to problems for overseas workers. Together, the case studies suggest that the noncomplier list had a transformative effect on domestic politics due to its impact on markets.

The empirical analysis also illustrates how the characteristics of the information provider—in this case, the FATF—matter for the creation of a focal point. Interviews and participant-observation at several FATF global network meetings confirm that the FATF is viewed as a highly technical, mostly apolitical body, and that this reputation enhances the organization's credibility and legitimacy among a wide range of audiences. As the central institution in this issue area, the FATF was already well known to the global banking sector and to some types of investors prior to the creation of the noncomplier list. When the FATF began to issue its new list, these market actors had systems in place to integrate the FATF list into their decision-making processes. In contrast, although the US government produces its own annual list of countries of money laundering concern, there is no evidence that this list leads to equivalent financial repercussions.

Finally, the FATF case highlights that an IO must send an unambiguous signal to be effective at changing behavior. The FATF has maintained robust monitoring procedures for decades, and even before the creation of the noncomplier list, it published detailed reports on noncompliant state behavior. Yet market actors were largely unresponsive to such reports. And while states rushed to change their laws in advance of monitoring, governments made few policy changes after the final reports were published. In contrast, when the FATF includes a country on its noncomplier list, it sends a precise signal to market actors about how others will be evaluating the risks of doing business with a given country. Banks and investors can easily integrate such a signal into their decision-making processes, leading to aggregate market enforcement.

Policy Implications: The Power and Peril of Unofficial Market Enforcement

The arguments in this book have several important policy implications. For FATF member states, the noncomplier list is a clear success. It has transformed the global fight against bad money, and FATF member states have paid relatively few costs for this impact. By working first to establish the FATF as a credible and salient monitoring body, FATF member states have found a way to harness market forces without paying high political or economic enforcement costs. Moreover, because market pressure is unofficial, listed countries have difficulty challenging this form of pressure. Given this success story, it is not surprising that the FATF continues to rely on the noncomplier list to incentivize widespread compliance improvements.

For the broader policy community, the FATF's success highlights how information can be an influential policy tool in the modern era. Governments have relied on economic coercion as a form of pressure for thousands of years, dating back to ancient Greece. But globalization has created opportunities for using market forces in less traditional ways. Large economies can shift market decision-making in ways that support international rules. And once banks or firms consider a country's compliance to be relevant to their profit functions, IOs can leverage their credibility and expertise to provide a focal point that shifts global capital away from uncooperative states. This process of unofficial market enforcement requires more of an upfront investment in an IO, but it also appears to be particularly effective at driving deep and widespread policy change.

The FATF's success story also points to more difficult policy questions. For every criminal who finds it more difficult to launder money, there are tens of thousands of regular people who are paying more for simple transactions. Banks spend billions of dollars each year on systems designed to reduce the risk of illicit funds, and these costs are inevitably passed on to consumers. While clients transferring large sums of money may find higher costs merely a nuisance, poorer members of society often consider such fees to be prohibitively expensive. The FATF noncomplier list intensifies these dynamics, raising the costs of business in ways that disproportionately impact the most vulnerable individuals and countries.

Listing can also have long-term impacts that stretch beyond a country's time on the noncomplier list. Banks increasingly opt to forgo low-profit clients and countries entirely, leaving these groups with limited access to the financial system. Access to useful and affordable financial products and services—what the World Bank defines as "financial inclusion"—is an essential component of development. But when the FATF lists a country for its weak anti–money laundering laws or gaps in its terrorist financing legislation, it can become more difficult for vulnerable individuals in that country to participate in the global economy. Remittances become more costly. Trade financing declines or dries up. Banks may even permanently end correspondent relationships with banks in listed countries.

The noncomplier list's strength is thus also a vulnerability: the FATF does not control market enforcement. Banks make decisions based on profits, and their current profit structure encourages them to shift money away from countries with deficient laws on stopping illicit financing. But this profit structure poses a fundamental challenge for policy makers: if a listed government changes its laws in order to meet the FATF standards but banks still refuse to restart business or lower their rates, who is responsible? Banks have terminated tens of thousands of correspondent relationships over the last decade and begun "de-risking" from high-risk clients and economies. De-risking disproportionately affects the poorest, most vulnerable countries and people because these are the situations where even minor risks outweigh meager profit possibilities. But the policy implications of de-risking are enormous. According to the World Bank, "If the current [de-risking] trend continues, people and organizations in the more volatile areas of the world or in small countries with limited financial markets could be completely cut off from access to regulated financial services."[1]

Policy makers interested in keeping terrorists and criminals out of the financial system must take ownership of these consequences. When the FATF relies on its noncomplier list to incentivize policy change, it is also raising the costs of business for individuals, firms, and banks in listed countries. Market enforcement may be unofficial but power is still at work. The world's largest economies and financial centers are using monitoring and the global banking system to export their rules globally. If the process of diffusion leads to policy change but stagnates growth in the least-developed states, it may be worth asking if the current approach is really a success.

Extensions and Future Scholarship

One of the key contributions of this book is to explore the underlying conditions for an IO to serve as a focal point. A robust literature in international relations examines how IOs organize expectations among states and how international rules serve as guideposts for private actors, yet few scholars have examined the origins of IO focal points. This book illustrates one possible pathway—an IO may enhance its own prominence through informational advantages, economic coercion, and legitimacy—but the empirical support focuses exclusively on one issue area. Future research could test the theory in other contexts or explore other ways that an IO might acquire the power to use information to influence states and nonstate actors. Scholars might also explore whether IO focal points have the same impact if they influence other market processes or other types of nonstate actors.

Another important area of inquiry is how global banking shifts have affected other types of cross-border flows. Bank-to-bank transfers are the foundation for many types of economic activity. To understand remittance flows, it may be useful to look at how financial cooperation has increased the costs of sending money across borders. To explore trade patterns, scholars might consider whether firms have ready access to trade financing. A more holistic approach to the global economy may reveal unexpected relationships and patterns.

Finally, at a broader level, this work has implications for how we understand the nature of power in the modern era. Globalization has narrowed the distance between countries and made war more costly. But even as interdependence reduces overt conflict, it has not erased basic power asymmetries. Instead, power can be hidden behind bureaucracy, rules, and information. In some cases, this form of power might enhance an IO's influence over states and nonstate actors in a way that redistributes authority. But an IO focal point may also reinforce long-standing political dynamics between states. Even expertise is conditioned on specific understandings of problems. In creating standards for what constitutes "acceptable" behavior, an IO makes decisions about which attributes are worthy of condemnation and which are not. Future research might explore the origins of monitoring frameworks with an eye toward these political dynamics. How does bargaining within and across institutions affect an IO's construction of a focal point? Which states gain most from a particular problem conceptualization? Unofficial market enforcement may represent a new pathway to compliance, but it might also perpetuate long-standing power dynamics that have operated for centuries.

APPENDIX

TABLE A.1 FATF-style regional bodies and members (as of September 2020)

REGIONAL ORGANIZATION	MEMBERS
Asia/Pacific Group on Money Laundering (APG) *Founded: 1997*	Afghanistan, Australia, Bangladesh, Bhutan, Brunei Darussalam, Cambodia, Canada, China, Cook Islands, Fiji, Hong Kong, India, Indonesia, Japan, Republic of Korea, Laos, Macao, Malaysia, Maldives, Marshall Islands, Mongolia, Myanmar, Nauru, Nepal, New Zealand, Niue, Pakistan, Palau, Papua New Guinea, Philippines, Samoa, Singapore, Solomon Islands, Sri Lanka, Taiwan, Thailand, Timor-Leste, Tonga, United States, Vanuatu, Vietnam
Caribbean Financial Action Task Force (CFATF) *Founded: 1990*	Anguilla, Antigua and Barbuda, Aruba, The Bahamas, Barbados, Belize, Bermuda, Cayman Islands, Curaçao, Dominica, El Salvador, Grenada, Guyana, Haiti, Jamaica, Montserrat, Saint Kitts and Nevis, Saint Lucia, Saint Vincent and the Grenadines, Sint Maarten, Suriname, Trinidad and Tobago, Turks and Caicos Islands, Venezuela, Virgin Islands
Council of Europe Committee of Experts on the Evaluation of Anti-Money Laundering Measures and the Financing of Terrorism (MONEYVAL) *Founded: 1997*	Albania, Andorra, Armenia, Azerbaijan, Bosnia and Herzegovina, Bulgaria, Croatia, Cyprus, Czech Republic, Estonia, Georgia, Hungary, Latvia, Liechtenstein, Lithuania, North Macedonia, Malta, Republic of Moldova, Monaco, Montenegro, Poland, Romania, Russian Federation, San Marino, Serbia, Slovak Republic, Slovenia, Ukraine
Eastern and Southern Africa Anti–Money Laundering Group (ESAAMLG) *Founded: 1999*	Angola, Botswana, Eswatini, Ethiopia, Kenya, Lesotho, Madagascar, Malawi, Mauritius, Mozambique, Namibia, Rwanda, Seychelles, South Africa, Tanzania, Uganda, Zambia, Zimbabwe
Eurasian Group (EAG) *Founded: 2004*	Belarus, China, India, Kazakhstan, Kyrgyzstan, Russia, Tajikistan, Turkmenistan, and Uzbekistan
Financial Action Task Force of Latin America (GAFILAT, formerly GAFISUD) *Founded: 2000*	Argentina, Bolivia, Brazil, Chile, Colombia, Costa Rica, Cuba, Dominican Republic, Ecuador, Guatemala, Honduras, Mexico, Nicaragua, Panama, Paraguay, Peru, Uruguay
Inter Governmental Action Group against Money Laundering in West Africa (GIABA) *Founded: 2000*	Benin, Burkina Faso, Cape Verde, Côte d'Ivoire, the Gambia, Ghana, Guinea, Guinea-Bissau, Liberia, Mali, Niger, Nigeria, São Tomé and Príncipe, Senegal, Sierra Leone, Togo

(continued)

TABLE A.1 (Continued)

REGIONAL ORGANIZATION	MEMBERS
Middle East and North Africa Financial Action Task Force (MENAFATF) *Founded: 2004*	Algeria, Bahrain, Djibouti, Egypt, Iraq, Jordan, Kuwait, Lebanon, Libya, Mauritania, Morocco, Oman, Palestinian Authority, Qatar, Saudi Arabia, Somalia, Sudan, Syria, Tunisia, United Arab Emirates, Yemen
Task Force on Money Laundering in Central Africa (GABAC)	Cameroon, Central African Republic, Chad, Republic of the Congo, Democratic Republic of the Congo, Equatorial Guinea, Gabon

Note: Data assembled by author based on "FATF Members and Observers," FATF-GAFI.org (website), https://www.fatf-gafi.org/about/membersandobservers/.

TABLE A.2 "Blacklisted" countries (2010–2020)

COUNTRY	YEAR LISTED	YEAR REMOVED	LEVEL OF ECONOMIC PRESSURE
Algeria	October 2013	October 2015	"Consider the risks"
Angola	February 2010	June 2010	"Consider the risks"
Bolivia	June 2011	February 2013	"Consider the risks"
Cuba	June 2011	February 2013	"Consider the risks"
Ecuador	February 2010	June 2010	Threat of countermeasures
	June 2012	June 2015	
Ethiopia	February 2010	June 2010	"Consider the risks"
	June 2011	June 2014	
Ghana	February 2012	October 2012	"Consider the risks"
Indonesia	February 2012	June 2015	"Consider the risks"
Iran	February 2010	N/A	Countermeasures
Kenya	June 2011	February 2014	Threat of countermeasures
Myanmar	June 2011	February 2016	Threat of countermeasures
Nigeria	October 2011	June 2013	"Consider the risks"
North Korea	February 2010	N/A	Countermeasures
Pakistan	February 2010	June 2010	"Consider the risks"
	February 2012	June 2014	
Turkmenistan	February 2010	June 2010	"Consider the risks"
São Tomé and Príncipe	February 2010	October 2010	"Consider the risks"
	October 2011	October 2013	
Sri Lanka	June 2011	February 2013	"Consider the risks"
Syria	June 2011	June 2014	"Consider the risks"
Tanzania	February 2012	February 2014	"Consider the risks"
Thailand	February 2012	February 2013	"Consider the risks"
Turkey	June 2011	June 2014	Threat of countermeasures/ membership expulsion
Vietnam	June 2012	October 2013	"Consider the risks"
Yemen	June 2012	June 2014	"Consider the risks"

Note: Data coded by author based on FATF "Public Statement" announcements, which include the blacklist, where the FATF advises its members to "consider the risks arising from the deficiencies," and the countermeasures list, where the FATF calls on its members and other jurisdictions to apply countermeasures. Since 2010, the FATF has only employed countermeasures against Iran and North Korea.

TABLE A.3 Countries included in survival analysis

		COUNTRIES INCLUDED IN ALL MODELS		
Algeria	Argentina	Austria	Bahrain	Bangladesh
Belarus	Belgium	Bolivia	Botswana	Brazil
Bulgaria	Burkina Faso	Chile	Côte d'Ivoire	Croatia
Cyprus	Czech Republic	Dominican Republic	Ecuador	Egypt
El Salvador	Estonia	Finland	Gambia	Germany
Ghana	Greece	Guatemala	Guyana	Haiti
Honduras	Hungary	India	Indonesia	Iraq
Ireland	Japan	Jordan	Kazakhstan	Kenya
Korea	Kuwait	Latvia	Lebanon	Lithuania
Mali	Mexico	Mongolia	Morocco	Mozambique
Namibia	Netherlands	Nicaragua	Niger	Nigeria
Norway	Oman	Pakistan	Panama	Paraguay
Peru	Philippines	Poland	Portugal	Qatar
Romania	Saudi Arabia	Senegal	Sierra Leone	Slovenia
Spain	Sri Lanka	Sudan	Suriname	Sweden
Switzerland	Tanzania	Thailand	Togo	Tunisia
Turkey	Uganda	United Arab Emirates	Uruguay	Venezuela
Yemen	Zambia			

		COUNTRIES INCLUDED ONLY IN MODELS 1, 2, AND 3		
Bahamas	Brunei Darussalam	Guinea	Guinea-Bissau	Iceland
Liberia	Malta	Serbia	Vietnam	

		COUNTRIES INCLUDED ONLY IN MODELS 1 AND 2		
Afghanistan	Belize	Benin	Cambodia	Cabo Verde
Comoros	Dominica	Fiji	Grenada	Kyrgyzstan
Lao PDR	Lesotho	Macedonia	Maldives	Mauritania
Mauritius	Nepal	Samoa	Seychelles	St. Lucia
St. Vincent	Swaziland	Tajikistan	Tonga	

		COUNTRIES INCLUDED ONLY IN MODEL 1		
Angola	Antigua and Barbuda	Barbados	East Timor	Moldova
Myanmar	Nauru	São Tomé & Príncipe	Syria	Turkmenistan
Vanuatu	Zimbabwe			

Note: The table shows the countries that are included in the survival analysis shown in table 4.3 in chapter 4. Countries drop out of the sample due to the introduction of additional control variables.

TABLE A.4   Imputed data replication of table 4.3

	DEPENDENT VARIABLE: CRIMINALIZATION OF TERRORIST FINANCING			
	(1)	**(2)**	**(3)**	**(4)**
Listing	9.050***	9.833***	9.712***	9.639***
	(0.327)	(0.379)	(0.389)	(0.391)
Market integration		1.037	1.034	1.034
		(0.057)	(0.061)	(0.061)
Listing * market integration		1.184**	1.180**	1.178**
		(0.091)	(0.093)	(0.093)
FATF member	1.137	0.797	0.788	0.757
	(0.409)	(0.491)	(0.497)	(0.521)
Previous terrorist fin law	1.302	1.247	1.240	1.212
	(0.280)	(0.285)	(0.288)	(0.303)
Diffusion	1.056***	1.058***	1.058***	1.059***
	(0.012)	(0.013)	(0.013)	(0.013)
Eligible for listing	0.916	1.000	1.005	1.008
	(0.378)	(0.450)	(0.451)	(0.453)
US ally	3.988	3.530	3.504	3.478
	(1.390)	(1.409)	(1.410)	(1.409)
Private-sector credit		1.044	1.054	1.047
		(0.164)	(0.178)	(0.181)
Capacity		1.062	1.059	1.073
		(0.269)	(0.270)	(0.275)
Terrorism			0.976	0.961
			(0.180)	(0.190)
Democracy				1.007
				(0.027)
Observations	7,617	7,617	7,617	7,617
Countries	137	137	137	137
Events	74	74	74	74

* $p < 0.10$; ** $p < 0.05$; *** $p < 0.01$

Note: Hazards ratios for Cox proportional hazards models, replicates models for table 4.3 with imputed data. Values over 1 indicate a positive effect; values below 1 indicate a negative effect. Standard errors are clustered by country and shown in parentheses. All models include a log-time interaction for *US ally.*

TABLE A.5 Replication of table 4.3 (no log-time interaction for *US ally*)

	DEPENDENT VARIABLE: CRIMINALIZATION OF TERRORIST FINANCING			
	(1)	**(2)**	**(3)**	**(4)**
Listing	8.770***	8.122***	5.816***	8.338***
	(0.331)	(0.454)	(0.523)	(0.565)
Market integration		1.005	1.000	1.020
		(0.067)	(0.097)	(0.160)
Listing * market integration		1.209**	1.319**	1.352**
		(0.108)	(0.144)	(0.150)
FATF member	1.021	0.638	0.696	0.987
	(0.412)	(0.613)	(0.632)	(0.734)
Previous terrorist fin law	1.370	1.056	0.915	0.865
	(0.285)	(0.355)	(0.398)	(0.446)
Diffusion	1.061***	1.061***	1.074***	1.080***
	(0.013)	(0.017)	(0.020)	(0.021)
Eligible for listing	0.864	1.155	1.104	0.963
	(0.375)	(0.554)	(0.606)	(0.611)
US ally	1.046	0.934	0.664	0.642
	(0.294)	(0.343)	(0.382)	(0.428)
Private-sector credit		1.009	0.919	1.106
		(0.181)	(0.236)	(0.257)
Capacity		1.162	1.206	0.850
		(0.293)	(0.319)	(0.372)
Terrorism			1.063	1.430
			(0.255)	(0.314)
Democracy				0.943
				(0.039)
Observations	7,262	5,828	4,613	4,114
Countries	132	120	96	87
Events	72	52	43	39

* $p < 0.10$; ** $p < 0.05$; *** $p < 0.01$

Note: Hazards ratios for Cox proportional hazards models, replicates models for table 4.3 without log-time interaction for *US ally*. Values over 1 indicate a positive effect; values below 1 indicate a negative effect. Standard errors are clustered by country and shown in parentheses.

TABLE A.6   Replication of table 4.3 (with ordinal listing variable)

	DEPENDENT VARIABLE: CRIMINALIZATION OF TERRORIST FINANCING	
	(1)	**(2)**
List level—Linear	6.469***	11.050***
	(0.316)	(0.535)
List level—Quadratic	0.467**	0.737
	(0.384)	(0.563)
List level—Cubic	1.579	1.552
	(0.447)	(0.663)
Market integration		1.025
		(0.139)
List level—Linear * market integration		0.784
		(0.214)
List level—Quadratic * market integration		0.621**
		(0.237)
List level—Cubic * market integration		1.125
		(0.213)
FATF	0.955	1.467
	(0.408)	(0.801)
Previous terrorist fin law	1.530	1.088
	(0.297)	(0.478)
Diffusion	1.059***	1.082***
	(0.013)	(0.022)
Eligible for listing	0.840	0.911
	(0.378)	(0.644)
US ally	3.469	1.144
	(1.390)	(1.898)
Observations	7,308	4,114
Countries	132	87
Events	72	39

* $p < 0.10$; ** $p < 0.05$; *** $p < 0.01$

Note: Hazards ratios for Cox proportional hazards models, replicates models for table 4.3 with ordinal listing variable. Private sector credit, capacity, terrorism, and democracy are included in model 2 but are not significant. Values over 1 indicate a positive effect; values below 1 indicate a negative effect. Standard errors are clustered by country and shown in parentheses.

Details on Matching

To assemble a matched sample, I subset the data to period 1 (February 2010) and assembled a data set of all countries with complete information for model variables. I then used the R package MatchIt and nearest-neighbor matching to build a matched sample based on six covariates that could affect a country's probability

TABLE A.7   Balance improvement

	PRE-PROCESSING			MATCHED		
VARIABLE	MEAN (LISTED)	MEAN (NOT LISTED)	DIFF	MEAN (LISTED)	MEAN (NOT LISTED)	DIFF
Distance	0.280	0.154	0.126	0.280	0.278	0.002
Diffusion	−18.092	−17.854	−0.238	−18.092	−17.259	−0.833
US ally	−0.0598	−0.006	−0.054	−0.060	0.024	−0.083
Private-sector credit	−0.885	−0.335	−0.551	−0.885	−1.626	0.741
Capacity	−0.369	−0.152	−0.218	−0.369	−0.910	0.541
Polity IV	−2.385	−0.843	−1.542	−2.385	−2.302	−0.083
Risk of terrorism	−0.752	0.063	−0.815	−0.752	−0.711	−0.042
Countries	27	41		12	12	

Sources: Diffusion data hand-coded by author. US ally data comes from "The Correlates of War Project," https://correlatesofwar.org/. Private-sector credit comes from the IMF, "Monetary and Financial Statistics," https://data.imf.org/?sk=B83F71E8-61E3-4CF1-8CF3-6D7FE04D0930. Capacity (GDP per capita) data comes from the World Bank, "World Development Indicators," https://databank.worldbank.org/source/world-development-indicators. Polity IV data comes from the Center for Systemic Peace, "The Polity project," http://www.systemicpeace.org/. Risk of terrorism comes from the PRS Group, "International Country Risk Guide (ICRG)," https://www.prsgroup.com/explore-our-products/international-country-risk-guide/.

of being listed. This matched sample includes twelve listed countries and twelve nonlisted countries. I then expanded the analysis to include data for this set of twenty-four countries for the full time period (2010 to 2015).

The table below shows the improvement in balance generated by this matched sample. Specifically, it provides the mean value for all variables included in the matching model, comparing listed and nonlisted countries in the full sample and in the matched value. Variables are centered around zero. Averages are for the year 2010.

Details on Differences in Listed Populations

The regression analysis of the relationship between the noncomplier list and cross-border liabilities (table 5.2) estimates the effect of listing based on a subsample of listed countries. When the regression includes the full set of control variables necessary to model cross-border bank flows (as in models 2, 4, and 6), the subsample is limited to ten listed countries: Indonesia, Kyrgyzstan, Mongolia, Namibia, Nepal, Nigeria, the Philippines, Sri Lanka, Thailand, and Uganda. Compared to the broader set of listed countries, this subpopulation is not statistically different along key economic dimensions.

TABLE A.8   Listed sample comparison for table 5.2

VARIABLE	LISTED SUB-SAMPLE		BROADER LISTED SAMPLE		T-TEST
	MEAN	SD	MEAN	SD	P-VALUE
Cross-border liabilities (USD millions)	5554.163	6141.629	7987.834	18137.52	0.173
Capital account openness	0.446	0.298	0.458	0.330	0.829
Credit-to-GDP ratio	34.760	23.169	35.251	28.293	0.912
Gross domestic product (USD billions)	166.482	231.842	94.301	143.558	0.369
GDP growth	2.921	3.014	2.307	5.678	0.651

Sources: Data on cross-border liabilities comes from the Bank for International Settlement, "Locational Banking Statistics," https://www.bis.org/statistics/bankstats.htm. Data on capital account openness comes from Sarwat Jahan and Daili Wang, 2016 (Dec), "Capital Account Openness in Low-Income Developing Countries: Evidence from a New Database," IMF Working Papers, data available at http://www.imf.org/external/datamapper/LB_data. xlsx. Data on credit-to-GDP ratio, GDP, and GDP growth comes from the World Bank, "World Development Indicators," https://databank.worldbank.org/source/world-development-indicators.

List of Interviews

I conducted numerous interviews with officials from FATF member state governments, listed countries, IOs, and the banking sector. Most of these people declined to be interviewed "on the record" due to the sensitivities of this issue area and, in some cases, specific bureaucratic guidelines that do not allow them to make statements for publication. Where possible, I have relied on quotes from individuals who agreed to be interviewed on the record, or have used direct quotes from interviews without specific attribution. A list of all interviews, both cited and uncited, is provided below.

- Interview with FATF global network official, 6 May 2014
- Interview with UNODC official, 7 May 2014
- Interview with UNODC official, 8 May 2014
- Interview with UNODC official, 8 May 2014
- Interview with executive director of an FATF regional body, 10 December 2014
- Interview with an FATF global network official, 9 January 2015
- Interview with official from an FATF regional body, 27 January 2015
- Interview with Gordon Hook, executive director of the Asia/Pacific Group on Money Laundering, 16 February 2015
- Interview with compliance executive, top-five US bank, 28 August 2015
- Interview with official from compliance company, 22 September 2015
- Interview with official from compliance company, 24 September 2015
- Interview with investment services firm official, 25 September 2015
- Interview with Credit Agricole CIB official, 25 September 2015

Table A.5 Noncompiler list and cross-border bank-to-bank lending (two-way fixed effects)

| | DEPENDENT VARIABLE: CROSS-BORDER LIABILITIES | | | | | |
| | FULL SAMPLE | | MATCHED SAMPLE | | ELIGIBLE-FOR-LISTING SAMPLE | |
	(1)	(2)	(3)	(4)	(5)	(6)
Listed	-0.034	-0.107*	-0.070**	-0.143***	-0.045	-0.156***
	(0.044)	(0.064)	(0.035)	(0.062)	(0.042)	(0.053)
Inflation	0.007*	0.010**	0.005	0.007	-0.001	-0.019**
	(0.004)	(0.005)	(0.007)	(0.013)	(0.005)	(0.006)
GDP growth	-0.004	0.005	-0.006	-0.009	-0.006**	0.010
	(0.003)	(0.010)	(0.004)	(0.015)	(0.003)	(0.013)
Real exchange rate	-0.004	0.008	-0.011	0.009*	-0.010**	0.011**
	(0.004)	(0.007)	(0.007)	(0.005)	(0.005)	(0.004)
Credit-to-GDP ratio	-0.413	3.110	0.758**	5.760	-0.312	5.179***
	(1.081)	(2.096)	(0.328)	(2.993)	(1.028)	(1.580)
Capital account openness	-0.003**	-0.0004	-0.001	-0.006	-0.001	-0.001
	(0.001)	(0.002)	(0.002)	(0.005)	(0.001)	(0.003)
Market volatility		-0.007		-0.001		0.003
		(0.010)		(0.014)		(0.003)
Debt-to-GDP ratio		0.003		0.046***		0.039**
		(0.017)		(0.015)		(0.014)
Interest rate spread		0.0003		0.0002		-0.0003
		(0.002)		(0.003)		(0.003)
Observations	1576	459	706	172	1095	285
Countries	89	31	81	10	62	21
Listed countries	32	10	34	10	33	10

* p < 0.10; ** p < 0.05; *** p < 0.01

Note: The table shows the results of an OLS model examining the effect of listing on cross-border liabilities across three different samples. The full sample mirrors the sample population in chapter 4: all non-FATF countries that had failed to criminalize terrorist financing in line with FATF standards as of February 2010. The dependent variable is logged. All models include country- and year-fixed effects. Standard errors are clustered by country.

Sources: Data on listing hand-coded by author. Data on cross-border liabilities from Bank for International Settlements, "Locational Banking Statistics," https://www.bis.org/statistics/bankstats.htm. Data on inflation and real exchange rate comes from the IMF, "International Financial Statistics," https://data.imf.org/?sk=4C514D48-B6BA-49ED-8AB9-52B0C1A0179B. Data on capital account openness comes from Sarwat Jahan and Daili Wang, 2016 (Dec), "Capital Account Openness in Low-Income Developing Countries: Evidence from a New Database," IMF Working Papers, data available at http://www.imf.org/external/datamapper/LB_data.xlsx. Data on credit-to-GDP ratio, debt-to-GDP ratio, GDP growth, interest spread, and money supply comes from the World Bank, "World Development Indicators," https://databank.worldbank.org/source/world-development-indicators. Data on market volatility comes from "CBOE S&P 500 3-Month Volatility Index (VXVCLS)," FRED Economic Data (website), https://fred.stlouisfed.org/series/VXVCLS.

TABLE A.10   Placebo test for effect of listing on cross-border bank-to-bank liabilities

	DEPENDENT VARIABLE: CROSS-BORDER LIABILITIES	
	(1)	(2)
Listed	0.121	0.140*
	(0.089)	(0.079)
Inflation	0.015	0.015
	(0.017)	(0.017)
GDP growth	0.020	0.020
	(0.048)	(0.048)
Real exchange rate	0.013	0.012
	(0.016)	(0.017)
Credit-to-GDP ratio	0.273	0.288
	(2.101)	(2.105)
Market volatility		0.008***
		(0.002)
Observations	153	152
Countries	28	28
Listed countries	11	11

$* p < 0.10; ** p < 0.05; *** p < 0.01$

Note: Dependent variable is logged cross-border liabilities. OLS regression with country-fixed effects and time polynomial, with standard errors clustered at the country level. Quarterly observations for 2007 to 2009. Listing data is from 2010 to 2012.

Sources: Data on listing hand-coded by author. Data on cross-border liabilities from Bank for International Settlements, "Locational Banking Statistics," https://www.bis.org/statistics/bankstats.htm. Data on inflation and real exchange rate comes from the IMF, "International Financial Statistics," https://data.imf.org/?sk=4C514D48-B6BA-49ED-8AB9-52B0C1A0179B. Data on credit-to-GDP ratio and GDP growth comes from the World Bank, "World Development Indicators," https://databank.worldbank.org/source/world-development-indicators. Data on market volatility comes from "CBOE S&P 500 3-Month Volatility Index (VXVCLS)," FRED Economic Data (website), https://fred.stlouisfed.org/series/VXVCLS.

- Interview with Jeff Solomon, financial and risk sales specialist, Thomson Reuters, 28 September 2015
- Interview with official from Thomson Reuters Country-Check, 29 September 2015
- Interview with investment firm official, 8 February 2016
- Interview with official from formerly listed country, 9 February 2016
- Interview with official from a private bank in Ethiopia, 11 February 2016
- Interview with Thai government official, 14 February 2016
- Interview with international development bank official, 7 April 2016
- Interview with official from an FATF-style regional body, 30 June 2016
- Interview with Gordon Hook, executive director of the Asia/Pacific Group on Money Laundering, 30 June 2016
- Participant-observation of Asia-Pacific Group Plenary, 6–8 September 2016

- Interview with Thai banking official, 9 March 2017
- Interview with former FATF president Antonio Gustavo Rodrigues, 29 March 2017
- Participant-observation of MONEYVAL Plenary, 30 May–1 June 2017
- Interview with Gordon Hook, executive director of the Asia/Pacific Group on Money Laundering, 24 January 2018
- Interview with Chip Poncy, head of US government delegation to FATF (2011–13), senior delegation member (2002–11), 7 February 2018
- Interview with Daniel Glaser, assistant secretary for terrorist financing (2011–17), deputy assistant secretary for terrorist financing (2004–11), US Government, 12 February 2018
- Research assistant interview with Dr. Tawatchai Yongkittikul, former secretary-general of Thai Bankers' Association, 7 December 2018
- Research assistant interview with Thai AMLO official, 19 December 2018
- Interview with Tom Keatinge, director, Centre for Financial Crime and Security Studies at the Royal United Services Institute (RUSI), London, 17 December 2020
- Interview with Chip Poncy, head of US government delegation to FATF (2011–13), senior delegation member (2002–11), 21 December 2020

Notes

INTRODUCTION: CROSS-BORDER BANKING IN A GLOBALIZED ERA

1. Joshua Hammer, "The Billion-Dollar Bank Job," *New York Times Magazine*, 3 May 2018, https://www.nytimes.com/interactive/2018/05/03/magazine/money-issue-bangla desh-billion-dollar-bank-heist.html.

2. Melissa Luz Lopez, "Bangladesh Sues RCBC, Bloomberry Resorts Anew for 2016 Bank Heist," CNN Philippines, 1 June 2020, https://www.cnnphilippines.com/business/2020/6/1/Bangladesh-Bank-new-civil-case-2016-heist.html.

3. SWIFT is the world's leading secure financial messaging service and is used by more than eleven thousand financial institutions in more than two hundred countries and territories. For more information, see https://www.swift.com/about-us/discover-swift/messaging-standards.

4. The Fed's compliance software flagged the transfers purely by chance. The word "Jupiter" formed part of the address of the Philippine bank where hackers attempted to transfer money, and by coincidence, "Jupiter" was part of the name of a shipping company that had been placed on the US government's sanctions list for doing business with Iran. Because of the possibility of sanctions violations, Federal Reserve officials examined the transfer requests more closely and discovered other irregularities. Krishna N. Das and Jonathan Spicer, "How the New York Fed Fumbled over the Bangladesh Bank Cyber-Heist," Reuters, 21 July 2016, https://www.reuters.com/article/us-cyber-heist-federal-special-report-idUSKCN1011AJ.

5. "Appendix D—Fundamentals of the Funds Transfer Process," US Department of the Treasury Financial Crimes Enforcement Network, https://www.fincen.gov/sites/default/files/shared/Appendix_D.pdf.

6. This book uses the term "international organization" to describe the FATF because it is a multilateral organization composed of member states with a standing secretariat and an open-ended mandate. As Vabulas and Snidal (2013) highlight, intergovernmental arrangements exist on a spectrum and range from highly formalized to extremely informal.

7. I use the term "dirty money" as a euphemism for the proceeds of crime, that is, money derived from a criminal enterprise. "Money laundering" is a process in which criminals attempt to disguise the origins of illegally obtained money, usually by passing the money through legitimate businesses or enterprises.

8. Agence France-Presse, "Casinos Exempt from Tougher Anti Money-Laundering Law," Rapler.com, https://r3.rappler.com/nation/21209-ph-casinos-exempt-from-tougher-anti-money-laundering-law.

9. For example, see the FATF's announcement from June 2013: http://www.fatf-gafi.org/countries/ a-c/argentina/documents/compliance-june-2013.html. This statement is also based on the author's participant-observation at the 2016 Asia-Pacific Group plenary meeting in San Diego, California, as well as news coverage describing FATF pressure.

10. Melissa Luz T. Lopez, "PHL Removed from Dirty-Money List," *Business World*, 10 August 2017, https://www.bworldonline.com/phl-removed-dirty-money-list/.

11. See also Putnam (1988), which highlights how international negotiations on issues like trade require policy makers to conduct a type of two-level game where they negotiate with domestic and international actors simultaneously.

12. See, for example, Kapstein 1992, 1994; Oatley and Nabors 1998; Singer 2004, 2007; Simmons 2001b; Drezner 2007; and Büthe and Mattli 2014, among others.

13. Notably, recent research indicates that even large economies involved in setting standards may differ in terms of implementation. See, for example, Quaglia 2019.

14. I borrow the term "passive adopters" from Chey 2014.

15. This is the point made in scholarship on epistemic communities. See, for example, E. Haas 1990, and P. Haas 2009, along with the complete May 2009 special issue of *International Organization* (vol. 46, no. 1).

16. A focal point, as first discussed by Thomas Schelling in his canonical book *The Strategy of Conflict*, occurs when information provides "some clue for coordinating behavior . . . for each person's expectation of what the other expects him to expect to be expected to do" (1960, 57).

17. Brummer (2010, 636) also discusses the possibility of countries adopting international financial regulations but underenforcing the rules.

18. See, for example, Greif 1992, 1993; Milgrom et al. 1990; Simmons 2000a; Keleman and Teo 2014; and Kucik and Pelc 2016, among others.

19. Indeed, some scholars have argued that the FATF framework has been relatively ineffective at curbing money laundering and organized crime (Levi 2002, 2015; Levi and Reuter 2006; Madsen 2009; Zoppei 2015; Gutterman and Roberge 2019). Others argue that little is actually known about money laundering (Reuter and Truman 2004), and what is known is often ignored by law enforcement when designing policy (Naylor 1999; Van Duyne 1998).

20. Pozsar et al. (2010) define shadow banks as "financial intermediaries that conduct maturity, credit, and liquidity transformation without explicit access to central bank liquidity or public sector credit guarantees."

21. On this debate see Chayes and Chayes 1993; Checkel 2001; Cortell and Davis 1996; Dai 2002, 2007; Downs et al. 1996; Fisher 1981; Guzman 2007; Henkin 1979; Martin 2011; Simmons 1998; Young 1979. among others.

22. Author interview with Daniel Glaser, 12 February 2018.

23. See, for example, Keohane and Milner 1996; Simmons 2000a; Mosley 2003a, 2000b; Vogel 1996; Lake 2009b; Jensen 2008; Simmons et al. 2006; Johns and Wellhausen 2016; Farrell and Newman 2016, among many others.

24. A significant body of literature in economics has examined the determinants of cross-border bank flows and the effect of cross-border banking on local financial markets. On this former point, see Cerutti et al. 2015, 2017; Obstfeld 2012; and Bruno and Shin 2015a, 2015b, among many others. On the latter point, see Claessens 2006, which reviews relevant literature and highlights the difficulty of separating the effects of cross-border banking on the local banking system from the underlying determinants of the strength of the local system.

25. China is the second largest recipient of remittances from the United States (after Mexico). In 2017 Chinese migrants sent USD 16.1 billion back to China. For more on remittance flows from the United States to other countries, see "Remittance Flows Worldwide in 2017." 2019. Pew Research Center, 3 April, https://www.pewresearch.org/global/interactives/remittance-flows-by-country/.

26. Argentina, Australia, Brazil, Canada, China, France, Germany, India, Indonesia, Italy, Japan, Korea, Mexico, Russia, Saudi Arabia, South Africa, Turkey, United Kingdom, United States, and the European Union.

27. Brian Monroe, "Fincrime Briefing: AML Fines in 2019 Breach $8 billion, Treasury Official Pleads Guilty to Leaking, 2020 Crypto Compliance Outlook, and More," Association of Certified Financial Crime Specialists, 14 January 2020, https://www.acfcs.org/fincrime-briefing-aml-fines-in-2019-breach-8-billion-treasury-official-pleads-guilty-to-leaking-2020-crypto-compliance-outlook-and-more/.

28. For more on this trend, see "Remittances to Fragile Countries," United States Government Accountability Office, March 2018, https://www.gao.gov/assets/700/690 546.pdf.

29. See, for example, Cohen and Benney 2014; Drezner 2014; German and Schwartz 2014; Norloff 2014. In contrast, Kirshner (2014a, 2014b) argues that while the dollar remains predominant, there are warning signs that its hegemony is eroding.

30. In *After Hegemony*, Keohane (1984, 92) writes, "From the perspective of market-failure theories, the information functions of regimes are the most important of all. . . . Even in games of pure coordination with stable equilibria, this may be a problem. Conventions—commuters meeting under the clock at Grand Central Station, suburban families on a shopping trip 'meeting at the car'—become important."

31. Chinkin (1989) argues that treaties with weak or vague obligations are "legal soft law," but in line with most current scholarship, this book focuses on soft law that comes from nonlegal obligations.

32. In the early 2000s, the FATF used a "blacklisting" process (the Non-Cooperative Countries and Territories Group) to coerce nonmember states to adopt FATF recommendations, but this process explicitly relied on coercive market pressure and is distinct in several ways from unofficial market enforcement. The differences between the two approaches are discussed in greater detail in chapter 3.

33. "Market enforcement" is a specific manifestation of what Hadfield and Weingast (2012, 473) call "decentralized enforcement," which they define as "the imposition of penalties [that result] from individual decisionmaking among ordinary agents acting independently, not the decisionmaking of official legal actors . . . nor the result of express pacts for collective action."

34. Noting the many competing actors and interests that play a role in fighting terrorist financing, De Goede (2017, 127) writes, "Considerable tensions, gaps and disjunctures persist . . . problematizing (too) coherent and powerful renditions of US hegemonic power."

35. Author interview with Daniel Glaser, 12 February 2018.

36. UNSC Resolution 1373 (2001).

37. For more on the costs of know-your-customer requirements, see John Callahan, "Know-Your-Customer Will Be a Great Thing When It Works," *Forbes Technology Council Post*, 10 July 2018.

38. Gavin Finch, "World's Biggest Banks Fined $321 Billion since Financial Crisis," Bloomberg, 1 March 2017, https://www.bloomberg.com/news/articles/2017-03-02/world-s-biggest-banks-fined-321-billion-since-financial-crisis.

39. Notable exceptions include Friman and Andreas 1999; Andreas 2004; Williams 2003; Drezner 2007; Hülsse 2008; Sharman 2006, 2008, 2009, 2011; Tsingou 2010; Jakobi 2013, 2015, 2018; Findley et al. 2014a, 2014b; Nance 2015, 2018a, 2018b; De Goede 2017; Clunan 2006; Biersteker and Eckert 2008; Eckert 2008; Acharya 2009. Scholars have also analyzed global counterterrorism cooperation from other angles. See, for example, Pokalova 2015 and Shor 2017 on the diffusion of counterterrorism law.

40. This book also responds to the post-financial-crisis call for IPE scholars to pay more attention to the international and domestic politics of financial regulation (Mosley and Singer 2009; Helleiner 2011; Katzenstein and Nelson 2013).

1. A PRIMER ON INTERNATIONAL FINANCIAL STANDARDS ON ILLICIT FINANCING

1. This summary is drawn from information contained in "United States Court of Appeals for the Fourth Circuit, United States of America vs. Hinda Osman Dhirane and Muna Osman Jama," 18 July 2018, http://www.ca4.uscourts.gov/Opinions/174205.P.pdf.

2. For example, the United States and the United Kingdom's deregulation of domestic financial markets produced competitive advantages over other states and increased global capital mobility, which in turn benefited these same states (Helleiner 1994).

3. In 2017, banks and other financial actors were expected to spend more than USD 8 billion on anti–money laundering and combating terrorist financing compliance software and programs. Christopher J. Pelaez, "AML Compliance Costs—How Much Is Enough?," Global Radar, August 2016, https://www.globalradar.com/aml-compliance-costs-how-much-is-enough/.

4. On the European Union, see Benink 1993; Molyneux et al. 1996. On US deregulation, see Berger et al. 2000.

5. Literature on cross-border flows often analyzes this concept through a discussion of global liquidity, that is, the ease of funding in global financial markets. For more on this topic, see Cerutti et al. 2015 and Shin 2014, among others.

6. "Leverage" refers to a bank's ratio of debt to capital, which reflects its ability to meet its financial obligations.

7. For a more detailed discussion of correspondent banking, see Bank for International Settlements 2016.

8. Cohen (1986, 27) notes that a small number of international banks take in the majority of all cross-border deposits.

9. The exception to this statement has been banks in countries like North Korea, which is subject to universal sanctions.

10. Scholarship on soft law lacks a consensus definition (Abbott and Snidal 2000; Shaffer and Pollack 2009; Guzman and Meyer 2010; Brummer 2015; Karlsson-Vinkhuyzen and Vihma 2009). This description aligns most closely with Newman and Posner 2018.

11. Drawing a clear distinction between hard law and soft law can be misleading, as both are subject to political interpretation and negotiation between states (Goldsmith and Posner 2006; Hafner-Burton and Tsutsui 2007; Hurd 2017).

12. For a more comprehensive discussion of financial standards, see Walter 2008; Helleiner 2014; Brummer 2015.

13. Helleiner (2014) argues that the G-20's role has been overstated and that ultimately it was the United States, not the G-20, that led economic recovery. In contrast, Kirshner (2014, 7) argues that the 2008 financial crisis accelerated the erosion of US influence and the increased political influence of other states, particularly China, which has led to "a new heterogeneity of thinking" about how to manage international finance.

14. For more information, see http://www.fsb.org/what-we-do/implementation-monitoring/.

15. The G-10 included Belgium, Canada, France, Germany, Italy, Japan, the Netherlands, Sweden, Switzerland, the United Kingdom, and the USA. The committee has since expanded its membership to include forty-five institutions in twenty-eight jurisdictions.

16. Regulatory capital can be thought of as the capital that regulators require a bank to hold as a buffer in case the bank suffers a significant loss. Applicable rules define what counts as capital for this purpose.

17. Liquidity typically refers to cash and other assets that can be made available on a short-term basis to meet bank obligations. As discussed earlier, leverage ratio refers to the ratio of debt to capital, which reflects the ability of a bank to meet its financial obligations.

18. Original FATF members included G-7 countries (Canada, France, Germany, Italy, Japan, the United Kingdom, and the United States), Australia, Austria, Belgium, Italy, Luxembourg, the Netherlands, Spain, Switzerland, and the European Commission.

19. FATF members as of September 2020: Argentina, Australia, Austria, Belgium, Brazil, Canada, China, Denmark, Finland, France, Germany, Greece, Hong Kong, Iceland, India,

Ireland, Israel, Italy, Japan, Korea, Luxembourg, Malaysia, Mexico, the Netherlands, New Zealand, Norway, Portugal, Russia, Saudi Arabia, Singapore, South Africa, Spain, Sweden, Switzerland, Turkey, United Kingdom, and United States; FATF member regional organizations: European Commission and Gulf Cooperation Council.

20. The FATF's nine regional affiliates—known as FATF-style regional bodies—are the Asia/Pacific Group on Money Laundering (APG), the Caribbean Financial Action Task Force (CFATF), the Eurasian Group (EAG), the Eastern and Southern Africa Anti–Money Laundering Group (ESAAMLG), the Task Force on Money Laundering in Central Africa (GABAC), the Financial Action Task Force of Latin America (GAFILAT), the Inter Governmental Action Group against Money Laundering in West Africa (GIABA), the Middle East and North Africa Financial Action Task Force (MENAFATF), and the Council of Europe Committee of Experts on the Evaluation of Anti–Money Laundering Measures and the Financing of Terrorism (MONEYVAL). More information on these groups is available in the appendix.

21. Anti–money laundering (AML) and combating the financing of terrorism (CFT) are the FATF's two primary missions. The FATF recommendations also address other related threats to the integrity of the financial system, such as combating proliferation financing.

22. These obligations are set out primarily in FATF Recommendation 5 on customer due diligence and record keeping. Financial institutions are also required to take steps to identify the beneficial owner of accounts where the legal title belongs to one person while property rights belong to someone different.

23. For more on this recommendation and its specific requirements, see FATF (2016).

24. The United States is compliant with most FATF standards; however, it has notably lagged behind other countries on implementing FATF Recommendations on beneficial ownership and know-your-customer requirements for designated nonfinancial businesses and professions. See FATF's 2016 *Mutual Evaluation Report on the United States* for more detail, available at http://www.fatf-gafi.org/media/fatf/documents/reports/mer4/MER-United-States-2016.pdf.

25. See European Commission, "Anti–Money Laundering and Counter Terrorist Financing," https://ec.europa.eu/info/policies/justice-and-fundamental-rights/criminal-justice/anti-money-laundering-and-counter-terrorist-financing_en.

26. Over the past ten years, regulators have imposed USD 26 billion in fines on banks for anti–money laundering violations. See "Global Financial Institutions Fined 26 Billion for AML, Sanctions and KYC Non-Compliance," Fenergo, 26 September 2018, https://www.fenergo.com/press-releases/global-financial-institutions-fined-26-billion-for-aml-sanctions-kyc-non-compliance/. While US regulators are responsible for largest fines, Europe and certain Asia-Pacific countries have also levied significant penalties.

27. "Reputation Damage: The Price Riggs Paid," 2006, https://www.world-check.com/media/d/content_whitepaper_reference/whitepaper-3.pdf.

28. Author interview with Jeff Solomon, financial and risk sales specialist with Thomson Reuters, 28 September 2015.

29. Federal Financial Institutions Advisory Council, "Customer Due Diligence—Overview," 5 May 2018, https://www.ffiec.gov/press/pdf/Customer%20Due%20Diligence%20-%20Overview%20and%20Exam%20Procedures-FINAL.pdf.

30. The FATF Interpretive Note for Recommendation 10 (Customer Due Diligence) specifies that countries identified by FATF assessments as having "effective AML/CFT systems" and "low level of corruption or other criminal activity" may pose less of a threat (FATF 2018, 64).

31. See work by Allen et al. 2012; Yan et al. 2012; Angelini et al. 2015; and Wilf 2016, among others.

32. The original estimate provided by International Chamber of Commerce (2017) was that costs have increased from 15,000 euros to 75,000 euros. I have converted these numbers to dollars based on the average 2017 exchange rate.

33. "Derisking and the Demise of Correspondent Banking Relationships," Accuity (website), https://accuity.com/resources/derisking-demise-correspondent-banking-rela tionships-research-report-accuity/.

34. See graph 2 in Bank for International Settlements (2016, 15).

35. "Sanctions: History Lessons," *Economist*, 19 October 2016, https://www.economist. com/international/2006/10/19/history-lessons.

2. A THEORY OF UNOFFICIAL MARKET ENFORCEMENT

1. Jorge Valero, "Member States Reject Commission's Blacklist of Money Launderers," Euractiv, 7 March 2019, https://www.euractiv.com/section/justice-home-affairs/news/ member-states-reject-commissions-blacklist-of-money-launderers/.

2. The Council is composed of government ministers from all EU countries; listed states could therefore lobby countries directly to vote against the Commission.

3. "Money Laundering and Terrorist Financing: Council Returns Draft List of High Risk Countries to the Commission," Council of the EU press release, 7 March 2019, https:// www.consilium.europa.eu/en/press/press-releases/2019/03/07/money-laundering-and-terrorist-financing-council-returns-draft-list-of-high-risk-countries-to-the-commission/.

4. Panama's Chamber of Commerce, Industry, and Agriculture and its Banking Association criticized the FATF's listing decision, but incoming finance minister Hector Alexander promised to work on a "road map . . . and adopt the pertinent actions to improve the country's international image and leave the list." As quoted in "Incoming Govt Pledges to Get Panama Off 'Grey List,'" BNamericas, 26 June 2019, https://www.bnamericas.com/ en/news/incoming-govt-pledges-to-get-panama-off-grey-list.

5. The Commission's new proposed list included a subset of countries that were on the FATF's February 2020 "Increased Monitoring" list: the Bahamas, Barbados, Botswana, Cambodia, Ghana, Jamaica, Mauritius, Mongolia, Myanmar, Nicaragua, Pakistan, Panama, Syria, Uganda, Yemen, and Zimbabwe. It also included four countries that were already delisted by FATF—Afghanistan, Iraq, Trinidad and Tobago, and Vanuatu—with the caveat that the Commission was still assessing these countries' status. Notably, it excluded the two FATF-listed countries: Albania and Iceland.

6. This book uses the term "international organization" to denote any intergovernmental body with three or more member states. Following Martin and Simmons 2012, it distinguishes an "international organization" from an "international institution," which denotes the set of formal and informal rules that govern international behavior.

7. The European Commission's delegated regulation 2016/1675 (amended by 2020/855) requires financial institutions to apply enhanced due diligence measures when doing business with clients in listed high-risk third countries. Notably, this regulation was adopted after the period of analysis in this book (2010–15) and was not implemented until quite recently.

8. Schelling (1960, 57) writes that some situations need "some clue for coordinating behavior, some focal point for each person's expectation of what the other expects him to expect to be expected to do."

9. A large body of work highlights how enforcement may flow from market actors rather than official sources. On this point, see Greif 1992, 1993; Greif et al. 1994; Milgrom et al. 1990; Simmons 2000a; and Keleman and Tao 2014, among others.

10. Guzman and Meyer (2010) note that many "soft law" issue areas are characterized by coordination problems, where once states agree on a particular set of rules or regulations, these agreements become essentially self-enforcing.

11. A notable exception to the influence of focal points on outcomes occurs when respondents have asymmetric payoffs. In such contexts, focal points may be much less effective at producing coordination (Crawford et al. 2008).

12. International courts may even influence the normative beliefs of states not party to the ruling. On this point, see Helfer and Voeten 2014; Jacob 2014; Vinuales 2008.

13. Allyn Fisher-Ilan, "Israel's Netanyahu Vows Long Fight against U.N. Report," Reuters, 17 October 2009, https://www.reuters.com/article/us-israel-palestinians-un/israels-netan yahu-vows-long-fight-against-u-n-report-idUSTRE59G0YU20091017.

14. Information provision can facilitate reciprocity among states (Keohane 1984; Morrow 2007) and transform how states understand their own interests (Finnemore 1993, 1996; Adler 1997).

15. Dai (2007) highlights the relevance of these two factors for explaining when states are most likely to create a robust IO monitoring scheme. She argues that IO monitoring is most likely when states suffer some cost from other states' noncompliance and when nonstate actors lack the requisite access and expertise to monitor behavior.

16. In the environmental politics realm, for example, NGOs and other nonstate actors have played integral roles in treaty implementation and have expanded their own authority through private rule setting and monitoring (Green 2013).

17. Hurd (1999, 285) notes that "each application of coercion involves an expenditure of limited social capital. . . . For this reason, few complex social orders are primarily based on coercion."

18. On the "logic of appropriateness," see March and Olsen 1998, 2011.

19. "United Nations Introductory Note," United Nations (website), https://www.un.org/en/sections/un-charter/introductory-note/index.html.

20. On norm entrepreneurs and global norm shifts, see Finnemore and Sikkink 1998.

21. For more details, see "First Report of the Analytical Support and Sanctions Monitoring Team Appointed Pursuant to Resolution 1526 (2004) Concerning Al-Qaida and the Taliban and Associated Individuals and Entities," United Nations Security Council S/2004/679, 2004, 9.

22. In contrast, McKeen-Edwards and Porter (2013) and Young (2012) suggest these arguments may overstate the influence of market actors on international standards.

23. On the strategic benefits of ambiguity, see Bernheim and Whinston (1998) and recent work by Carnegie and Carson (2018a, 2018b, 2020).

24. For a comprehensive discussion of this problem, see Healy and Palepu 2001.

25. This point was first made by John Maynard Keynes, who equated financial market decision-making to a newspaper beauty contest where readers are asked to evaluate which five of the hundred photos are most likely to be selected by other readers as "the most beautiful." See Keynes 1936.

26. See, for example, Gollier 2011; Easley and O'Hara 2009; Snow 2011; and Berger et al. 2013, among many others.

27. On this point, see Baumol 1989; Kahneman 2003; Amato et al. 2002; Morris and Shin 2002; Crawford et al. 2008; and Fehr et al. 2018, among others.

28. First-order beliefs reflect an actor's observations about another actor's characteristics or behavioral tendencies. Second-order beliefs are an actor's beliefs about what a larger group of observers believes. O'Neill (1999, 195) terms this latter type of reputation "prestige," which he defines in layman's terms as "everyone knows that everyone knows."

29. Notably, some scholarship suggests that GPIs have no significant impact on policy (Lee and Matanock 2020) or that their impact is mitigated by other factors (Lall 2020).

30. Garrett and Weingast (1993, 176) point out that in the context of multiple paths to cooperation, focal points will not emerge "without conscious efforts on the part of interested actors."

31. Bhuta (2015) illustrates this phenomenon in her study of the state fragility index. Jerven (2013) highlights how such processes can be particularly problematic for the poorest countries because data is often unreliable but nonetheless is used by development agencies to make significant resource allocation decisions.

32. Notably, over the last two decades, the US government has used this process to list only five countries for any period of time: Burma, North Korea, Iran, Nauru, and Ukraine.

33. Cooley and Snider (2015, 32) note that ratings diplomacy may be strategic, but "such interactions also facilitate new dialogues, knowledge transfer, and networking that are more akin to norm diffusion within transnational linkages."

34. See Stephen 2015 for a deeper discussion of the role of indirect speech in international affairs.

35. Sharman (2006, 115–16) adopts a similar view with respect to blacklisting, describing this form of monitoring as containing "assertive declarations": statements that "bring about some alteration in the status or condition of the referred to object" (Sharman, quoting from Searle 1979, 17). This book contends that IO monitoring can function as both indirect speech, giving the IO plausible deniability, and as an assertive declaration if audiences interact with monitoring in such a manner.

36. See also the 2014 *Review of International Political Economy* special issue on the international currency system.

37. Governments may also opt to "cherry-pick" certain best practices without embracing the entire agreement (Brummer 2010, 636).

38. See, for example, Hafner-Burton 2008; Davis et al. 2012; Cooley and Snyder 2015; Kelley and Simmons 2015, among others.

3. THE FATF'S FIGHT AGAINST ILLICIT FINANCING

1. "Sinaloa Cartel," InSight Crime, 29 March 2019, https://www.insightcrime.org/mexico-organized-crime-news/sinaloa-cartel-profile/.

2. El Chapo was originally arrested in 2014, but he escaped and was rearrested in 2016. In 2017, Mexico extradited him to the United States, where he was convicted in 2019.

3. "Global Conflict Tracker: Criminal Violence in Mexico," Council on Foreign Relations, 2 October 2019, https://www.cfr.org/interactive/global-conflict-tracker/conflict/criminal-violence-mexico.

4. Aruna Viswanatha and Brett Wolf, "HSBC to Pay $1.9 Billion U.S. Fine in Money-Laundering Case," Reuters, 10 December 2012.

5. Ibid.

6. Unless otherwise stated, all references to "banks" and "global banking" refer to private-sector banks, not central banks.

7. Martin Arnold, "HSBC Hopes to Leave Era of Scandals Behind," *Financial Times*, 18 February 2018, https://www.ft.com/content/303a4296-12a2-11e8-940e-08320fc2a277.

8. See FATF, "The Banking Sector: Guidance for a Risk-Based Approach," updated October 2014, https://www.fatf-gafi.org/media/fatf/documents/reports/Risk-Based-Approach-Banking-Sector.pdf.

9. This book uses the term "compliance" to denote the degree to which a country's policies conform to international standards.

10. Money Laundering Control Act of 1986.

11. The FATF created a working group on proliferation financing in October 2008 and subsequently developed specific recommendations on how countries should combat

proliferation financing. For more information on these early efforts, see FATF, "Combating Proliferation Financing: A Status Report on Policy Development and Consultation," February 2010, retrieved from https://www.fatf-gafi.org/media/fatf/documents/reports/Status-report-proliferation-financing.pdf. See Nance and Cottrell 2014 for a broader discussion of international cooperation to combat proliferation financing.

12. A wide variety of crimes fall into this category, including illegal arms sales, smuggling, drug trafficking, prostitution rings, embezzlement, insider trading, bribery, and computer fraud. For more on money laundering, see http://www.fatf-gafi.org/faq/moneylaundering/.

13. Clunan (2006, 571) suggests that international cooperation to combat terrorist financing "essentially requires re-conceptualizing the public good of open financial systems as having negative security externalities that must be collectively managed."

14. "Money laundering" was originally focused on the proceeds of drugs and organized crime, but the list of predicate offenses has expanded to include bribery, fraud, prostitution, and many others. FATF guidelines state that "countries should apply the crime of money laundering to all serious offences, with a view to including the widest range of predicate offences" (Financial Action Task Force, 40 Recommendations, updated June 2019, 32, https://www.fatf-gafi.org/media/fatf/documents/recommendations/pdfs/FATF%20Recommendations%202012.pdf).

15. See Volgy et al. 2008 for a discussion of formal IOs, and Vabulas and Snidal (2013, 2020) for a discussion of informal IOs.

16. "Financial Action Task Force: Mandate," Financial Action Task Force, 12 April 2019, https://www.fatf-gafi.org/media/fatf/content/images/FATF-Ministerial-Declaration-Mandate.pdf.

17. Although the FATF includes several economies that are not countries (such as Hong Kong and Macao), this book uses the term "FATF member states" to represent all governments involved in FATF decision-making.

18. See, for example, FATF-GAFI 1998.

19. The FATF's forty recommendations were last updated in October 2020.

20. Interview with Gordon Hook, executive secretary of Asia/Pacific Group on Money Laundering, 16 February 2015.

21. Nance (2018a) argues that the FATF is best described as a "transnational public policy network" rather than as an international organization. Jakobi (2018) similarly emphasizes how the FATF network allows experts to exchange information and shape discourse.

22. The FATF's forty standards are set forth in a 134-page document that provides detailed guidance on required legislative policies and regulatory practices. Standards are typically updated about once per decade. The most recent version of the FATF standards was updated in October 2018 and is available at www.fatf-gafi.org/publications/fatfrecommendations.

23. Participant-observation of the Asia-Pacific Group Plenary Session, September 2016.

24. This accords with Hafner-Burton et al. (2009, 563), who suggest that the strength of a network tie depends on the magnitude and frequency of interaction between the two parties.

25. Participant-observation of the Asia-Pacific Group Plenary Session, September 2016.

26. This statement is based on the author's participant-observation of the Asia-Pacific Group on Money Laundering plenary (September 2016) and the MONEYVAL plenary (May 2017).

27. Author interview with Chip Poncy, 7 February 2018.

28. Ibid.

29. Author interview with Antonio Gustavo Rodrigues, 29 March 2017.

30. This statement is based on participant-observation by the author.

31. Author interview with Gordon Hook, 24 January 2018.

32. This case is described in greater detail in chapter 6.

33. Additional criteria included weak commercial requirements about identifying beneficial owners and registering businesses and obstacles to international cooperation. For more information, see FATF-GAFI 2000a, 2000b.

34. The FATF monitored forty-five countries for potential regulatory weaknesses but only placed some countries on the NCCT list. Masciandaro (2005, 18) writes that these forty-five countries represented about 8 percent of total GDP and 25 percent of foreign bank deposits in the world.

35. FATF Recommendation 21 in FATF's second round of mutual evaluations.

36. See Van Fossen 2003 for a detailed discussion of this issue.

37. Author interview with Daniel Glaser, 12 February 2018.

38. Ibid.

39. Gardner (2007) and Leong (2007) argue that the change in US administrations from Clinton to Bush, combined with the 9/11 terrorist attacks, weakened US support for the NCCT process, which was focused exclusively on stopping money laundering.

40. "Address by Michel Camdessus, Managing Director of the IMF, at the FATF Plenary Meeting on 10 February 1998," in FATF-GAFI 1998.

41. Author interview with Tom Keatinge, director, Centre for Financial Crime and Security Studies, Royal United Services Institute for Defence and Security Studies, 21 December 2020.

42. For a more in-depth discussion of how FATF's membership expansion has improved its legitimacy, see Hülsse 2008.

43. "UN Security Council Resolution 1617," United Nations Security Council, 2005, http://unscr.com/en/resolutions/1617.

44. In the current version of the FATF recommendations, Recommendation 7 requires countries to implement proliferation financing-related targeted sanctions from the Security Council, and Recommendation 2 requires countries to cooperate and coordinate on combating the financing of weapons of mass destruction. For more information, see "FATF Guidance on Counter Proliferation—Financing," Financial Action Task Force, February 2018, http://www.fatf-gafi.org/media/fatf/documents/reports/Guidance-Countering-Proliferation-Financing.pdf.

45. The methodology document describes essential criteria for compliance with each individual recommendation and lays out specific steps that countries should take in order to meet the FATF standards.

46. Between 2008 and 2009, the FATF issued a series of statements highlighting risks in only six countries: Uzbekistan, Iran, Pakistan, Turkmenistan, São Tomé and Príncipe, and Northern Cyprus.

47. Glaser interview.

48. Author interview with Gordon Hook, APG executive director, 30 June 2016. This view was echoed by former FATF president Antonio Gustavo Rodrigues in the 29 March 2017 interview.

49. Of course, as Ernst Haas (1980) points out, even scientific notions are rarely free from ideological elements.

50. The FATF has listed only two of its members under the current noncomplier list process—Greece and Turkey—but it has threatened listing against several others.

51. Glaser interview.

52. Ibid.

53. As of February 2020, the "Improving Global AML/CFT Compliance" list is now titled "Jurisdictions under Increased Monitoring."

54. As of February 2020, the FATF Public Statement is now called "High-Risk Jurisdictions Subject to a Call for Action."

55. In contrast, the former NCCT process explicitly required financial institutions to give special attention to transactions with listed countries.

56. Chapter 4 provides more detailed information on the different FATF noncomplier lists.

57. During the FATF's third round of evaluations, countries that received failing ratings on ten or more of the sixteen most important recommendations were eligible for listing (FATF-GAFI 2009b). In the current round of evaluations, the FATF has a threshold that considers both technical compliance and effectiveness.

58. See FATF Recommendation 10 in "International Standards on Combating Money Laundering and the Financing of Terrorism and Proliferation: The FATF Recommendations," Financial Action Task Force, October 2018, https://www.fatf-gafi.org/media/fatf/documents/recommendations/pdfs/fatf%20recommendations%202012.pdf.

59. This statement is based on interviews with both financial industry professionals and government officials in listed countries.

60. Interview with Gordon Hook, executive director of APG, 16 September 2015.

61. Notably, a substantial body of scholarship has shown that rating agencies often fail to provide complete information about the true quality of an investment, due to conflicts of interest between rating agencies and investors (Krugman 2010), rating-contingent regulation (Opp et al. 2013), and an unwillingness of rating agencies to frequently update ratings (Loffler 2005).

62. Email from investment services firm executive, 15 December 2020.

63. Poncy interview, 7 February 2018.

64. Author interview with Chip Poncy, 21 December 2020.

65. Daniel Dombey, "Turkey under International Pressure over Anti-terrorist Financing Laws," Financial Times, 22 October 2012, https://www.ft.com/content/b05eae86-de0d-3dbb-8b38-c94daa7db320.

66. Statement by Lester Bird, leader of the Antigua Labour Party, in February 2010 after the FATF listed Antigua and Barbuda, as reported in Antigua Observer, 24 February 2010, https://www.antiguaobserver.com/bird-denounces-country%E2%80%99s-inclusion-on-financial-task-force-blacklist/.

67. "Bosnian Banks Face Difficulties after EU Puts Country on Blacklist," Intellinews, 22 November 2016, http://www.intellinews.com/bosnian-banks-face-difficulties-after-eu-puts-country-on-blacklist-110716/.

68. Emily Flitter, "Standard Chartered Fined $1.1 Billion for Violating Sanctions and Anti–Money Laundering Laws," New York Times, 9 April 2019, https://www.nytimes.com/2019/04/09/business/standard-chartered-sanctions-violations.html.

69. In September 2016, the news media began reporting that Wells Fargo bank employees had opened or applied for more than two million bank accounts or credit cards without customers' knowledge. Six months later, the bank was still experiencing a significant decline in credit-card applications and requests for new checking accounts. Laura J. Keller, "Wells Fargo Card Requests Drop by Most since Scandal Erupted," Bloomberg, March 2017, https://www.bloomberg.com/news/articles/2017-03-20/wells-fargo-card-applications-drop-by-most-since-scandal-erupted.

70. Interview with investment services official, 25 September 2015.

71. For more on these cases, see chapter 6.

72. "Caribbean Bankers Urge Guyana to Pass Anti–Money Laundering Laws," Kaieteur News, 7 October 2014, https://www.kaieteurnewsonline.com/2014/10/07/caribbean-bankers-urge-guyana-to-pass-anti-money-laundering-laws/.

73. Author interview with executive of private bank in Ethiopia, 11 February 2016.

74. Mohiuddin Aazim, "Money Laundering, Forex Firms and Remittances," *Dawn* (online), 19 May 2018, https://www.dawn.com/news/1396113.

75. By "sanctions," Ople was referring to the potential market effects of the FATF non-complier list. The FATF does not have the authority to impose sanctions on countries; however, it can call on its members to require financial institutions to exercise enhanced due diligence in doing business with high-risk countries. It can also call on financial institutions to impose countermeasures on countries, although since 2001, this measure has only been used against Iran and North Korea. "Ople: Potential FATF Sanctions Would Hit OFW Remittances," Philippine Association of Service Exporters, 4 March 2016, https://www.pasei.com/ople-potential-fatf-sanctions-hit-ofw-remittances/.

76. "Offshore Investing in the Bahamas May No Longer Be a Viable Option," Thorn Law Group, 29 June 2018, http://www.boston-tax-lawyer.com/blog/offshore-investing-in-the-bahamas-may-no-longer-be-a-viable-option/.

77. Author interview with financial intelligence unit official of formerly listed country, 9 February 2016.

78. Sharman (2009) describes this "pre-emptive compliance" effect during the FATF's earlier NCCT process.

79. Author interview, 27 January 2015.

80. See, for example, Ikenberry and Kupchan 1990; Lake 1993; Simmons 2001a; Drezner 2007; Helleiner 2008; and McNamara 2008, among others.

81. See "Anti–Money Laundering and Counter-Terrorist Financing Measures: United States," Financial Action Task Force, December 2016, http://www.fatf-gafi.org/media/fatf/documents/reports/mer4/MER-United-States-2016.pdf.

82. Collective defense pacts: Albania, Argentina, Bahamas, Bolivia, Greece, Honduras, Panama, Paraguay, the Philippines, Thailand, Trinidad and Tobago, Turkey, Venezuela; other major non-NATO allies: Afghanistan, Bangladesh, Morocco, Pakistan, Tunisia.

83. Glaser interview.

84. The FATF's primary reasons for not listing an eligible country are the small size of its financial sector or its ability to address deficiencies prior to listing.

4. HOW THE NONCOMPLIER LIST DRIVES FATF COMPLIANCE

1. Ozge Ozbilgin and Jonathon Burch, "Turkey Scrambles to Avoid International Financial Blacklist," Reuters, January 2013.

2. Nigerian president Goodluck Jonathan's letter to the Senate, as reported in Uchenna Awom, "Jonathan Raises Alarm over Anti-terrorism Bill," *Leadership* (Abuja), 22 June 2010.

3. "Ecuador and Financial Crime: The Andean Laundry," *Economist*, 25 March 2010, https://www.economist.com/the-americas/2010/03/25/the-andean-laundry.

4. Author interview with Gordon Hook, executive director of the Asia/Pacific Group on Money Laundering (APG), 16 February 2015.

5. This description is based on the interpretive note for FATF Recommendation 26 (FATF-GAFI 2012).

6. Participant-observation, APG Plenary, September 2016.

7. Hook interview.

8. This threshold has subsequently been raised to 15,000 USD/EUR.

9. "Restrictive Laws: How the FATF Is Used to Justify Laws That Harm Civil Society, Freedom of Association and Expression," Charity and Security Network, 13 May 2013, https://charityandsecurity.org/analysis/restrictive_laws_how_fatf_used_to_justify_laws_that_harm_civil_society/.

10. Participant-observation, September 2016.

11. This observation is based on comments made by an evaluation team during the September 2016 APG plenary meeting.

12. In the current round of mutual evaluations, the FATF has partially remedied this problem by instituting a mandatory five-year follow-up report for all countries.

13. In the words of Daniel Glaser, former US assistant secretary for terrorist financing and financial crimes, the goal of the redesigned noncomplier list process was to "establish a system that had automaticity baked into it" (author interview, 12 February 2018).

14. The FATF considers a rating of "noncompliant" or "partially compliant" to be a failing score.

15. This book focuses on the FATF's procedures for its third round of mutual evaluations, in which the FATF relied on a ten failing recommendation threshold for listing eligibility. In the FATF's fourth round of mutual evaluations, the FATF listing criteria are (1) twenty or more failing ratings for technical compliance; or (2) three or more failing ratings for technical compliance on Recs 3, 5, 6, 10, 11, and 20; or (3) low or moderate level of effectiveness for nine or more of the eleven Immediate Outcomes (min: two lows); or (4) low effectiveness for six or more of the eleven Immediate Outcomes.

16. Author interview with Antonio Gustavo Rodrigues, 29 March 2017.

17. Tom Keatinge, email interview with author, 21 December 2020. MER stands for mutual evaluation report. FSRB stands for FATF-style regional body (one of the FATF regional affiliate organizations).

18. "Topic: High-Risk and Other Monitored Jurisdictions," Financial Action Task Force, 2020, http://www.fatf-gafi.org/publications/high-riskandnon-cooperativejurisdictions/?h f=10&b=0&s=desc(fatf_releasedate).

19. Smaller countries that are above the threshold may avoid listing because they are too poor, but they remain in an evergreen pool of eligible jurisdictions; theoretically, they could be listed any time.

20. A FATF-style regional body official noted that the FATF negotiates a very tight time frame for expected policy change with eligible countries, and for most countries, it is nearly impossible to get legislation through in the necessary time (author interview of Gordon Hook, executive director of APG, 30 June 2016).

21. ICRG stands for the International Cooperation Review Group, the official name of the FATF noncomplier list process. Tom Keatinge email interview.

22. Common services include wire transfers, business transactions, and accepting deposits.

23. This report has not been made publicly available, but a summary of its findings are available at http://www.worldbank.org/en/topic/financialmarketintegrity/publication/world-bank-group-surveys-probe-derisking-practices.

24. This statement is based on the author's participant-observation at the two FATF-style regional bodies: APG and MONEYVAL.

25. The one exception to this trend seems to be in the Caribbean, where many small countries were listed as part of the NCCT process in 2000 and 2001. Because of the NCCT initiative's strong effect on the region, news stories suggest political leaders in this region were much more attuned to the possible negative impact of listing. For example, in his statement on Trinidad and Tobago's removal from the noncomplier list, the prime minister explicitly referenced the "devastating economic and reputational consequences" for the Bahamas, the Cayman Islands, Saint Kitts and Nevis, and Saint Vincent and the Grenadines, tied to appearing on the FATF's NCCT list in 2000 (Bissessar 2012).

26. Clarissa Castillo, "Panama out of FATF Gray List, but There Is Still the OECD." Panama America, 19 February 2016, https://www.panamaamerica.com.pa/economia/panama-out-fatf-gray-list-there-still-oecd-1014476.

27. Comments by John Rolle in "Governor Targeting 'Caribbean Lead' in Financial Crime Fight," *Tribune* (Nassau), 14 December 2017, http://www.tribune242.com/news/2017/dec/14/governor-targeting-caribbean-lead-finance-crime-fi/. The FATF subsequently listed the Bahamas in October 2018 after determining that the government had not gone far enough in addressing regulatory gaps.

28. "Philippines: House Pushes for Inclusion of Casinos in AMLA Coverage," TendersInfo—News, 2 February 2017.

29. Guyana has a resource-driven economy where citizen income is supplemented significantly by remittances sent from abroad. Its primary risk of money laundering comes from its geography: much of its unpopulated land borders Venezuela, Brazil, and Suriname, making it an ideal transit route for drug traffickers and smugglers (CFATF-GAFIC 2011, 17).

30. "GBTI CEO Relieved AML Bill Passed Says Banks Guidelines Were Drawn from Amended Act," *Guyana Chronicle*, 1 July 2015, http://guyanachronicle.com/2015/07/01/gbti-ceo-relieved-aml-bill-passed-says-banks-guidelines-were-drawn-from-amended-act.

31. "Guyana's expediency in passing the AML/CFT Bill will not only benefit its own economy and growth but strengthen our regional financial network and its reputation worldwide." Quoted from "Guyana Again Urged—Pass That Anti–Money Laundering Bill," Freedom FM, October 2014.

32. For more information on why Guyana failed to pass legislation in advance of listing, see "Why Has Guyana Failed to Pass an Anti–Money Laundering Bill?," Dialogue, 2014, available at https://www.cfatf-gafic.org/index.php/member-countries/d-m/guyana/101-why-has-guyana-failed-to-pass-an-anti-money-laundering-bill.

33. "GBTI CEO Relieved."

34. Sovereign debt helps a country develop a credit market and provides collateral for secure financial transactions; the yield on sovereign debt also serves as a baseline for pricing other debt instruments in the same market (Vajs 2014).

35. Many governments cultivate central bank independence in order to enhance the credibility of commitments (Rogo 1985; Keefer and Stasavage 2003). Under this condition, central banks have the authority to adopt best practices or implement preferred policies without direct permission from governments.

36. For a detailed discussion of how derisking has affected macroeconomic sectors in the Caribbean, see Williams 2016.

37. "Pakistan's Inclusion on 'Grey List' Is Credit Negative for Banks—Moody's," Reuters, 26 February 2020, https://fr.reuters.com/article/fatf-pakistan-moodys-idUK L3N2AR1TM.

38. The FATF evaluation cycle is ten years. Some countries are evaluated soon after the FATF revises its standards, while others are evaluated much later in the cycle.

39. Hook interview, 30 June 2016.

40. This statement is based on the FATF's 2017 mutual evaluation report on Thailand (see C.4 and C.5, pp. 8–9).

41. This group includes Azerbaijan, Greece, Honduras, Qatar, and Ukraine.

42. When the FATF lists a country, they identify a set of deficiencies to be remedied prior to removal from the list. Most countries have three or four deficiencies; Argentina's initial listing announcement included eight areas of needed improvement.

43. Author interview, 9 February 2016.

44. The FATF has four levels of listing, which are discussed in greater detail in chapter 3.

45. As of February 2020, the FATF's Public Statement is now called "High-Risk Jurisdictions Subject to a Call for Action."

46. As of February 2020, the FATF's "Improving Global AML/CFT Compliance" announcement is now called "Jurisdictions under Increased Monitoring."

47. "MASAK: Activity Report," Financial Crimes Investigation Board (MASAK), July 2012, https://ms.hmb.gov.tr/uploads/sites/2/2019/04/2012-Activity-Report.pdf.

48. Turkey was removed from the FATF list in October 2014.

49. See the appendix for a list of all countries that have appeared on the FATF blacklist since 2010.

50. Author interview, 27 January 2015.

51. For more on these data challenges, see "Expert Meeting on Statistical Methodologies for Measuring Illicit Flows: Concept Note," United Nations Office on Drugs and Crime, 2018, https://unctad.org/meeting/expert-meeting-statistical-methodologies-mea suring-illicit-financial-flows.

52. In focusing on policy deepening, this analysis follows the advice of Downs et al. (1996) and also addresses concerns that observed compliance may be simply due to selection bias, rather than an independent effect of the institution on state behavior (Downs et al. 1996; Von Stein 2005).

53. The FATF originally formulated its recommendations on terrorist financing as separate "Special Recommendations." In 2012, the FATF revised its standards and integrated recommendations on terrorist financing and money laundering. Special Recommendation II is now FATF Recommendation 5.

54. In cases where the date of adoption is not available, the analysis uses the month and year that legislation entered into force.

55. The Convention for the Suppression of Unlawful Seizure of Aircraft (1970), the Convention for the Suppression of Unlawful Acts against the Safety of Civil Aviation (1971), the Convention on the Prevention and Punishment of Crimes against Internationally Protected Persons, including Diplomatic Agents (1973), the International Convention against the Taking of Hostages (1979), the Convention on the Physical Protection of Nuclear Material (1979), the Protocol for the Suppression of Unlawful Acts of Violence at Airports Serving International Civil Aviation (1988), the Convention for the Suppression of Unlawful Acts against the Safety of Maritime Navigation (1988), the Protocol for the Suppression of Unlawful Acts against the Safety of Fixed Platforms located on the Continental Shelf (1988), and the International Convention for the Suppression of Terrorist Bombings (1997).

56. Hook interview, 30 June 2016.

57. This hypothesis corresponds to hypothesis 1 in chapter 3.

58. Jessica Donati, "Exclusive: Afghanistan Suffers Trade Blow as China Halts Dollar Deals with Its Banks," Reuters, 22 May 2014, https://www.reuters.com/article/us-afghan istan-banking/ china-halts-dollar-transactions-with-most-afghan-banks-central-bank-idUSBREA4L0MZ20140522.

59. Sean Carberry, "Afghans Must Pass Anti–Money Laundering Law or Face Blacklist," National Public Radio, 5 June 2014, https://www.npr.org/2014/06/05/319030334/afghans-must-pass-anti-money-laundering-law-or-face-blacklist.

60. The analysis ends in December 2015 because in mid-2015, the FATF began their second Terrorist Financing Fact Finding Initiative, which queried FATF global network countries about the status of their laws on terrorist financing. The FATF's initiative placed additional pressure on nonlisted countries to improve laws and complicates the empirical analysis after the report's publication in February 2016.

61. The analysis includes a log-time interaction for the variable US ally, although results are robust to not including this interaction term. See appendix, which replicates table 4.3 without the log-time interaction term.

62. This reduction in the sample is primarily a result of the addition of the variable *Risk of terrorism*, which comes from the International Country Risk Guide and is available for only a subset of countries. The appendix lists the countries that are included in each model. The results are robust to imputing missing data (see appendix).

63. A standard matching approach would use the entire data set to assemble a matched sample; however, because the analysis uses a hazard model, countries drop out of the sample as they criminalize terrorist financing in line with FATF standards. For this reason, matching requires assembling a group of comparable countries based only on 2010 values, and then expanding the sample to include data on this select group of countries from the complete time period.

64. See the appendix for more details.

65. This language is in line with section 2 of the FATF Interpretive Note to Recommendation 5 (Terrorist Financing Offence). See "Methodology for Assessing Technical Compliance with the FATF Recommendations and the Effectiveness of AML/CFT Systems," Financial Action Task Force, updated February 2019, https://www.fatf-gafi.org/publica tions/mutualevaluations/documents/fatf-methodology.html.

66. The appendix provides a list of all countries listed as part of the noncomplier list, listing dates, and graduation dates (where applicable).

67. The FATF has called for countermeasures against only two countries: Iran and North Korea. These countries are excluded from the analysis because there is no available information about terrorist financing laws in these countries during this time period. The US government and the UN Security Council also had significant sanctions in place against both countries during this time period; as a result, it might be difficult to discern an independent effect of the FATF noncomplier list.

68. This earlier time period is used to indicate market integration because it is prior to the creation of the noncomplier list, which helps mitigate concerns about endogeneity. The analysis estimates the conditional marginal effect of listing moderated by market enforcement through an interaction term, following guidelines set forth in Brambor et al. 2006 and Hainmueller et al. 2019.

69. This variable is excluded from the matched sample analysis and the eligible country analysis because these samples include no FATF members.

70. See Elkins et al. 2006; Gleditsch and Ward 2006; Simmons and Elkins 2004.

71. This summary is based on the description of diffusion offered in Simmons et al. 2006, in which the authors offer four explanations for diffusion: learning, emulation, coercion, and competition.

72. For comparability across institutions, the variable is scaled by rounding to nearest 0.1 value in the regression.

73. See Guzman and Simmons 2005; Horn et al. 1999.

74. This variable is drawn from the World Bank World Development Indicators, and is standardized in 2010 US dollars. Due to the skewed distribution and for ease of interpretability, the variable is transformed by adding 1 and taking the log.

75. Drawn from the International Country Risk Guide. Variable scales from 1 (highest risk) to 4 (lowest risk). For ease of interpretability, the variable is inverted and set to a minimum value of 0.

76. See Helfer and Slaughter 1997; Martin 2000; Mansfield et al. 2002; and Raustiala and Victor 1998, among others.

77. Polity IV codes a country's political system on a scale of -10 to 10, where higher values equate to more democratic countries. These data are supplemented with data from Gleditsch 2013. Given data availability issues for smaller countries, the analysis omits this variable from the matched sample and the eligible-for-listing sample analyses.

78. This variable is omitted from the analysis of the eligible-for-listing sample since the sample includes only countries that had ten or more failing recommendations.

79. "Major Money Laundering Countries," US Department of State, 2016, https://www.state.gov/j/inl/rls/nrcrpt/2016/vol2/253367.htm.

80. Data on cross-border liabilities are logged and therefore the coefficient cannot be interpreted directly. The following formula is used to calculate this estimate: $e^{(\ln(1:3)\,\ln(1:5)}$.

81. These countries are the United Kingdom, Denmark, the Netherlands, Norway, Sweden, Finland, and Ireland. See Allen et al. 2011.

82. Although the interaction term in model 4 of table 2 is not significant, it has a p value of 0.11.

83. Based on the author's original data set, these two countries are Liechtenstein and Georgia.

5. UNOFFICIAL MARKET ENFORCEMENT AGAINST LISTED COUNTRIES

1. "The Panama Papers: How the World's Rich and Famous Hide Their Money Offshore," *Guardian*, 3 April 2016, https://www.theguardian.com/news/2016/apr/03/the-panama-papers-how-the-worlds-rich-and-famous-hide-their-money-offshore.

2. "Mossack Fonseca's Response to the Panama Papers," *Guardian*, 2 April 2016, https://www.theguardian.com/news/2016/apr/03/mossack-fonsecas-response-to-the-panama-papers.

3. Will Fitzgibbon, "Panama Papers Law Firm Mossack Fonseca Closes Its Doors," International Consortium of Investigative Journalists, 14 March 2018, https://www.icij.org/investigations/panama-papers/panama-papers-law-firm-mossack-fonseca-closes-doors/.

4. Eric Lipton and Julie Creswell, "Panama Papers Show How Rich United States Clients Hid Millions Abroad," *New York Times*, 5 June 2016, https://www.nytimes.com/2016/06/06/us/panama-papers.html.

5. "Jitters Ahead of FATF 'Grey List' Announcement," Economist Intelligence Unit, 20 June 2019, http://country.eiu.com/article.aspx?articleid=408138824.

6. Standard & Poor's, "Panama's BBB Rating Affirmed by S&P," *Latin America Herald Tribune*, n.d., last accessed 16 April 2021, http://www.laht.com/article.asp?ArticleId=2355125&CategoryId=23558.

7. The FATF relisted Panama in June 2019, eighteen months after the completion of the country's fourth-round mutual evaluation. In the three years prior to relisting, a political stalemate between the executive and legislative branches made it difficult for the government to adopt key legislation on topics such as tax fraud and to build up the capacity for supervision of the nonfinancial sector. For more on Panama's relisting, see "Why Is Panama Back on the FATF's 'Gray List'?," Dialogue, 17 July 2019, https://www.thedialogue.org/analysis/why-is-panama-back-on-the-fatfs-gray-list/.

8. Author interview with Chip Poncy, 7 February 2018.

9. Ibid.

10. "Anti-Money Laundering and Sanctions Enforcement and Compliance in 2020 and Beyond," Gibson Dunn, 24 June 2020, https://www.gibsondunn.com/wp-content/uploads/2020/06/WebcastSlides-BSA-AML-and-Sanctions-Enforcement-and-Compliance-in-2020-and-Beyond-24-JUNE-2020.pdf.

11. Elliot Carter, "Riggs Bank Was 'The Bank of Presidents,'" 4 September 2016, Architect of the Capital (website), https://architectofthecapital.org/posts/2016/8/27/riggs-bank.

12. Author interview with Jeff Soloman, Thomson Reuters World-Check official, 28 September 2015.

13. Christopher J. Pelaez, "AML Compliance Costs—How Much Is Enough?," Global Radar, 25 August 2016, https://www.globalradar.com/aml-compliance-costs-how-much-is-enough/.

14. Author interview with Tom Keatinge, director, Centre for Financial Crime and Security Studies, Royal United Services Institute for Defence and Security Studies, 21 December 2020.

15. Author interview with investment services firm official, 25 September 2015.

16. Since the FATF removed Myanmar from the blacklist in February 2016, it has not included any new countries on the blacklist, although it continues to add countries to the lower listing levels.

17. Author interview with executive of private bank in Ethiopia, 11 February 2016.

18. Jennifer Hanley-Giersch, "Enhanced Due Diligence Is a Must to Mitigate AML Exposure in Turkey," *ACAMS Today*, 13 September 2012, https://www.acamstoday.org/enhanced-due-diligence-a-must-to-aml-exposure-in-turkey/.

19. Daniel Dombey, "Turkey's Banking Blacklist Risk," *Financial Times*, 16 October 2012, https://www.ft.com/content/bbfe16f0-01c8-357e-84d4-4cce12d1e6b4.

20. Author interview with Thai government official, 14 February 2016.

21. "Bosnian Banks Face Difficulties after EU Puts Country on Blacklist," *Intellinews—Bosnia and Herzegovina Today*, 22 November 2016.

22. See, for example, "De-risking in the Financial Sector," World Bank, 7 October 2016, https://www.worldbank.org/en/topic/financialsector/brief/de-risking-in-the-financial-sector; Adriano (2017).

23. Chief operating officer of Port Vila–based Pacific Private Bank Audrius Bernota, as quoted in "Pacific Islands—Derisking—Pacific Lenders Battle Choppy Waters," *Banker*, 1 February 2017.

24. Anti–money laundering professionals generally view the remittance sector as posing a high risk of money laundering or terrorist financing (Alwazir et al. 2017).

25. See Mummolo and Peterson 2018 for a complete discussion of how to interpret fixed effects regression results.

26. Additional details on matching are available in the appendix.

27. The number of countries in the eligible-for-listing sample is limited by the availability of data for key control variables like credit-to-GDP ratio.

28. BIS is an international financial organization owned by sixty member state central banks. Together, these countries represent about 95 percent of world GDP.

29. Multiple regression assumes that the distribution of the data approximates a normal distribution, but this assumption is clearly violated when the dependent variable is highly skewed. By transforming the variable through logging, the relationship between the independent and dependent variable becomes more linear, producing a regression equation that more closely meets the requisite conditions for accurate statistical inference.

30. Foreign price level is converted into domestic currency units using the nominal exchange rate. Bruno and Shin (2015b) link bank leverage and monetary policy, finding that a contradictory shock to US monetary policy leads to a decrease in the cross-border capital flows of the banking sector.

31. A country's capital account records all transactions made between entities in the country and entities in the rest of the world. Countries with higher levels of capital account openness are typically more integrated in the global economy because it is easier for capital to flow in and out.

32. For a more detailed explanation of this link, see Bruno and Shin 2015a, 21.

33. Results for the full sample are available in the appendix.

34. Because the dependent variable is logged, the analysis calculates the size of the effect using the following formula: $e(coef)-1 * 100$.

35. This case is discussed in greater detail in chapter 6.

36. This categorization is based on the World Bank's 2009 World Development Report.

37. Keatinge interview, 21 December 2020.

38. Praveen Menon and Jessica Donati, "Afghanistan Economy under the Gun as Bank Blacklist Looms," Reuters, 11 June 2014, https://www.reuters.com/article/us-afghan istan-banking/afghanistan-economy-under-the-gun-as-bank-blacklist-looms-idUKK BN0EM14R20140611.

39. Model 2 cannot be replicated due to data limitations (the number of observations drops to thirty-four and the number of countries drops to five).

40. For a more detailed discussion of trade financing and letters of credit, see Niep-mann and Schmidt-Eisenlohr 2017.

41. "Progress Nil, Nepal Risks FATF Blacklisting," *My Republica*, 2012.

42. "Why Is Panama Back on the FATF's 'Grey List'?," Dialogue (website), 17 July 2012, https://www.thedialogue.org/analysis/why-is-panama-back-on-the-fatfs-gray-list/.

43. In trade-dependent regions like the Caribbean, this "de-risking" process has had a major impact on the macroeconomic health of countries (Williams 2016).

44. "Why Is Panama Back on the FATF's 'Grey List'?"

45. Interview with executive from private bank in Ethiopia, 11 February 2016.

6. FIGHTING ILLICIT FINANCING IN SOUTHEAST ASIA

1. Rachael Bael, "More than 1,000 Rhinos Killed by Poachers in South Africa Last Year," *National Geographic*, 25 January 2018, https://www.nationalgeographic.com/news/2018/01/wildlife-watch-rhino-poaching-crisis-continues-south-africa/.

2. "Thai Police Arrest Notorious Wildlife Trafficking Suspect," *Guardian*, 20 January 2018, https://www.theguardian.com/environment/2018/jan/20/thai-police-arrest-notori ous-wildlife-trafficking-suspect.

3. Rachel Nuwer, "Leader of Wildlife Trafficking Ring 'Hydra' Arrested in Thailand," *Sierra Club*, 3 February 2018, https://www.sierraclub.org/sierra/leader-wildlife-trafficking-ring-hydra-arrested-thailand.

4. "Case against Wildlife Trafficking 'Kingpin' Dismissed," *Bangkok Post,* 30 January 2019.

5. "Cat and Mouse: Accused Tiger Trafficker Slips Authorities' Net," *Bangkok Post*, 26 June 2016, https://www.bangkokpost.com/thailand/special-reports/1020221/cat-and-mouse-accused-tiger-trafficker-slips-authorities-net.

6. Founding members of the APG: Australia, Bangladesh, China, Hong Kong (China), Japan, New Zealand, the Philippines, Singapore, Sri Lanka, Taiwan, Thailand, the United States, and Vanuatu.

7. For more on the APG and its missions, see "APG History and Background," Asia/Pacific Group on Money Laundering (website), 2019, http://www.apgml.org/about-us/page.aspx?p=91ce25ec-db8a-424c-9018-8bd1f6869162.

8. For more details on the NCCT process, see chapter 4.

9. Other NCCT countries in the Asia/Pacific region included Indonesia, the Marshall Islands, Myanmar, Nauru, and Niue (FATF-GAFI 2001a).

10. "AML/CFT" stands for anti–money laundering and combating the financing of ter-rorism. Government and financial actors frequently use this term to refer to policies and procedures that are designed to reduce illicit financing; however, for ease of readership, the manuscript relies on synonyms whenever possible.

11. "FATF Public Statement—February 2010," Financial Action Task Force, 18 Febru-ary 2010, http://www.fatf-gafi.org/publications/high-risk-and-other-monitored-jurisdic tions/documents/fatfpublicstatement-february2010.html.

12. For a more detailed description of the FATF's listing process and the noncomplier list's levels, see chapter 3.

13. Since the 2016 election of the Philippines' current president, Rodrigo Duterte, democratic norms have eroded as the president has been engaged in a violent "war on drugs" that has resulted in thousands of extrajudicial killings and damaged rule-of-law norms. Sheila Coronel, Mariel Padilla, David Mora, and the Stabile Center for Investigative Journalism, "The Uncounted Dead of Duterte's Drug War," *Atlantic*, 19 August 2019, https://www.theatlantic.com/international/archive/2019/08/philippines-dead-rodrigo-duterte-drug-war/595978/.

14. Remittance schemes are vulnerable to money laundering because they offer a wide range of products, a variety of distribution channels, and high transfer speed, and they are often cash-intensive businesses (FATF-GAFI 2010, 8).

15. See "Personal Remittances, Received (Percent of GDP)," World Bank, 2019, https://data.worldbank.org/indicator/BX.TRF.PWKR.DT.GD.ZS.

16. See the World Bank's Global Findex data, last updated in 2017, for more information: https://globalfindex.worldbank.org.

17. The FATF did not expand its mission to include combating the financing of terrorism until October 2001.

18. For a more detailed discussion of the passage of the 2001 Anti–Money Laundering Act, see Brillo 2010a, 2010b.

19. Cathy Rose A. Garcia, Jennee Grace U. Rubrico, and Earl Warren B. Castillo, "Anti–Money Laundering Bill to Miss Set Deadline (Senate Refuses to Toe FATF Line)." *Business World*, 14 August 2001.

20. "Philippines BAP Estimates 34 mln Pesos Daily Losses If FATF Orders Sanctions," *AFX—Asia*, 13 September 2001.

21. "Philippines Govt Sees Stricter Money-Laundering Laws Following FATF Report," *AFX—Asia*, 23 June 2000.

22. See, for example, Garcia et al., "Anti–Money Laundering Bill."

23. See, for example, Stephen Temple, "Dirty Dozen Continue to Oppose Changes to Philippines Anti–Money Laundering Legislation," *HIS Global Insight*, 24 February 2003.

24. Senator Francis Pangilinan, quoted in Norman P. Aquino, "Solons Want Assurance Paris-Based FATF Not Singling Out Philippines," *Business World*, 30 August 2002.

25. Daxim L. Lucas, Cathy Rose A. Garcia, Jennee Grace U. Rubrico, and Dymphna R. Calica, "Changes Planned as FATF Rejects Law vs Dirty Money," *Business World*, 1 March 2002.

26. Cecille E. Yap and Jeffrey O. Valisno, "No Compromise on Amendments (FATF Insists on Changes to Dirty Money Law)," *Business World*, 4 March 2003.

27. "Philippines Sees Boost in Worker Remittances after FATF Delisting," AFX Asia, 17 February 2005.

28. Stephen Temple, "Yet More Revisions to Money-Laundering Law Approved as Philippines Battles to Escape Sanctions," *HIS Global Insight*, 7 March 2003.

29. "Manila Shares Close Up on Philippines Removal from FATF Blacklist UPDATE," AFX Asia, 14 February 2005.

30. In 2008 the FATF identified sixteen of its then forty-nine recommendations as "key and core" to the fight against illicit financing. These sixteen recommendations include the criminalization of money laundering and terrorist financing, customer identification and record keeping, and the filing of suspicious transaction reports. A complete list is available in the appendix.

31. A predicate offense is a crime that provides the resources for another crime. Because the crime of money laundering is a crime whereby an individual takes money acquired

from illegal means and passes it through the financial system to disguise its true origins, money laundering statutes always specify predicate offenses.

32. In November 2009 a large force of gunmen intercepted an election convoy traveling to file papers for a regional governorship election and massacred fifty-seven people. The attack, one of the worst ever episodes of election violence in the Philippines, was eventually tied to a former provincial governor and close ally of then Philippine president Gloria Arroyo. See Alastair McIndoe, "Behind the Philippines Maguindanao Massacre," *Time*, 27 November 2009, http://content.time.com/time/world/article/0,8599,194 3191,00.html.

33. Notably, in some cases, lawmakers still downplayed the FATF's influence by noting that proposed amendments were not solely due to the desire to avoid the FATF blacklist. One senator who publicly called for new legislation noted that the FATF cannot force the Philippines to do anything but argued the Philippines should nonetheless pass legislation to fulfill its international commitments against money laundering and terrorism. "Philippines: Guingona Calls for Swift Passage of AMLA Amendment," Thai News Service, 8 May 2012.

34. For example, in October 2012, Senate president Juan Ponce Enrile told reporters, "As a member of the convention, we will have to comply but they [FATF] must not tell us, 'You do this on this given time, otherwise we will blacklist you. Otherwise, we are no longer a sovereign country, we [would be] under the control of a task force over whom we have no say." Quoted in Norman Bordadora, "JPE: PH Ready to Amend 'Laundering Laws Sans Threat," *Philippines Daily Inquirer*, 20 October 2012.

35. This statement is based on a search of articles from *Business World* available through Nexis-Uni. The first article to appear on this subject after February 2010 (the start of the new listing process) is "Country Faces FATF Blacklist (Anti–Money Laundering, Terrorist Financing Bills OK Needed by May," *Business World*, 8 March 2012.

36. Johanna Paola D. Poblete, "Palace in Talks over Special Session for AMLA," *Business World*, 13 March 2012.

37. "FATF Blacklisting Unavoidable Sans Bills OK," *Business World*, 25 May 2012.

38. Antonio Siegfrid O. Alegado, Noemi M. Gonzales, Kathleen A. Martin, and Monica Joy O. Cantilero, "'Dirty' Money Fight Boosted (Hopes Up 'Substantial Compliance' Would Avert FATF Blacklisting)," *Business World*, 7 June 2012.

39. Antonio Siegfrid O. Alegado and Noemi M. Gonzales, "AMLA Changes on Agenda (Following Reprieve from Blacklisting)," *Business World*, 25 June 2012.

40. Kathryn Mae P. Tubadeza, "AMLA Amendments Certified," *Business World*, 20 September 2012.

41. Kathryn Mae P. Tubadeza and Monica Joy O. Cantilero, "Congress to Rush Approval of AMLA Changes (to Avoid Blacklisting by International Watchdog)," *Business World*, 11 October 2012.

42. Kathryn Mae P. Tubadeza, "AMLA Amendments Not Certain," *Business World*, 23 October 2012.

43. Ibid.

44. Cathy Yamsuan and Norman Bordadora, "Senate Will Pass Vital Bills, Assures Sotto," *Philippines Daily Inquirer*, 2 January 2013.

45. Matikas Santos, "Bicam OKs Amendments to Anti-Money Laundering Act," *Philippines Daily Inquirer*, 5 February 2013.

46. Before delisting a country, the FATF conducts an on-site visit to verify policy change. In February 2013, the FATF announced its intention to visit the Philippines in order to confirm that the process of implementing the required reforms and actions is under way. Quoted from "Improving Global AML/CFT Compliance: On-Going Process,"

Financial Action Task Force, 22 February 2013, https://www.fatf-gafi.org/publications/high-risk-and-other-monitored-jurisdictions/documents/improvingglobalamlcftcompli anceon-goingprocess-22february2013.html.

47. "Casinos Get a Pass in Philippines Laundering Law," Agence France-Presse—English, 6 February 2013.

48. "Improving Global AML/CFT Compliance: On-Going Process—21 June 2013," Financial Action Task Force, 21 June 2013, https://www.fatf-gafi.org/publications/high-risk-and-other-monitored-jurisdictions/documents/compliance-june-2013.html.

49. "Country Faces FATF Blacklist (Anti–Money Laundering, Terrorist Financing Bills OK Needed by May)," *Business World*, 8 March 2012.

50. "Philippines: Philippines FATF Upgrade Good for OFWs, Economy BSP," Thai News Service, 26 June 2012.

51. "Trading Seen Sideways with Upward Tilt," *Business World*, 25 June 2012.

52. Cli Harvey C. Venzon, "Good News Fuels Stocks to Climb Further," *Business World*, 26 June 2012.

53. Data from https://www.investing.com/indices/psei-composite-historical-data, accessed 16 September 2019.

54. Sammy F. Martin, "Party List Solon Urges Congress to Pass Bill Seeking to Amend Country's Anti–Money Laundering Laws," Philippine News Agency, 20 November 2013.

55. Marvyn N. Benaning, "Lawmaker Seeks to Widen Scope of Anti–Money Laundering Law," *Business Mirror*, 1 September 2014.

56. Maria Eloisa I. Calderon and Daphne J. Magturo, "Philippines Reeling in Gaming Titans," *Business World*, 31 October 2014.

57. Joshua Hammer, "The Billion-Dollar Bank Job," *New York Times Magazine*, 3 May 2018, https://www.nytimes.com/interactive/2018/05/03/magazine/money-issue-bangladesh-billion-dollar-bank-heist.html.

58. Cris Larano, "A Hole in the Global Money Laundering Defense: Philippine Casinos," *Wall Street Journal*, 18 March 2016, https://www.wsj.com/articles/quest-for-stolen-bangladeshi-funds-leads-to-philippine-casinos-1458324994.

59. John Chalmers and Karen Lema, "For Bank Heist Hackers, the Philippines Was a Handy Black Hole," Reuters, 20 March 2016, https://www.reuters.com/article/us-usa-fed-bangladesh-philippines/for-bank-heist-hackers-the-philippines-was-a-handy-black-hole-idUSKCN0WM13B.

60. "Senators Call for Immediate Inclusion of Casinos in AMLA," Philippines News Agency, 16 March 2016.

61. Imee Charlee C. Delavin, "Fresh Amendments to AMLA Readied," *Business World*, 1 April 2016.

62. "Bill Including Casinos in Ambit of Amla OK'd," *Business Mirror*, 30 May 2017.

63. "PH Faces Blacklist If Law Won't Include Casinos in AMLA Coverage," *Inquirer*, 3 October 2016.

64. "Bill Including Casinos in Ambit of Amla OK'd."

65. Data from Medina and Schneider 2018 estimates the size of Thailand's "shadow economy"—its hidden or informal economy—at around 50 percent of gross domestic product, although much of this activity may be informal rather than illegal.

66. A military coup in 2006 was followed by large-scale protests in 2008, 2009, and 2010. In 2011, a new prime minister was elected and civilian government was restored. Following widespread antigovernment protests in 2013, the Constitutional Court removed the prime minister from office, and in May 2014, the military staged another coup against the government. The military junta has ruled the government since that time.

67. For more on terrorism in Thailand, see "Thailand: Extremism and Counter-Extremism," Counter-Extremism Project, 2019, https://www.counterextremism.com/countries/thailand.

68. The IMF and the World Bank often assist with evaluating FATF compliance for developing countries as part of the IMF's Financial Section Assessment Program.

69. Author interview with Daniel Glaser, deputy assistant secretary for terrorist financing and financial crimes (2004–11), assistant secretary for terrorist financing and financial crimes (2011–17), US Department of the Treasury, 12 February 2018.

70. In 2008 and 2009, the FATF identified Uzbekistan, Turkmenistan, Pakistan, São Tomé and Príncipe, Northern Cyprus, and Iran as noncompliant.

71. This statement is based on a search of both Thai language newspapers and Nexis-Uni.

72. Author interview with Thai government official, 14 February 2016.

73. Research assistant interview with Dr. Tawatchai Yongkittikul, former secretary-general of Thai Bankers' Association, 7 December 2018.

74. Although the Anti–Money Laundering Office was created in 1999, there are indications that it was not functioning as intended. The office launched an investigation into journalists that were critical of the government in 2002, and a court later ruled it has overstepped its jurisdiction. It also failed to launch several investigations into several government corruption cases. "Enforce the Law or Join Pariahs on the Blacklist," *Nation/Thailand*, 14 February 2012, https://www.nationthailand.com/perspective/30175862.

75. "Thailand: Thailand Risks Watch-List Downgrade," Thai News Service, 14 February 2012.

76. Thomas Fuller and Rick Gladstone, "Blasts in Bangkok Add to Suspicions about Iran," *New York Times*, 14 February 2012, https://www.nytimes.com/2012/02/15/world/asia/explosions-in-bangkok-injures-suspected-iranian-national.html.

77. "FATF Public Statement—16 February 2012," Financial Action Task Force, 16 February 2012, http://www.fatf-gafi.org/publications/high-risk-and-other-monitored-jurisdictions/documents/fatfpublicstatement-16february2012.html.

78. "The Thai Chamber of Commerce Points Out the Impact on the Blacklist Pushing AEC Funding to Singapore and Malaysia," *Thai Rath*, 21 February 2012, https://www.thairath.co.th/content/240145.

79. "Two Laws on Laundering to Be Rushed," *Nation/Thailand*, 20 February 2012.

80. "Thailand: Cabinet Assigns AMLO to Discuss Anti-terrorism Measures with Agencies," Thai News Service, 27 February 2012.

81. "Thailand: AMLO Insists Thailand Not on Money Laundering Blacklist," Thai News Service, 21 February 2012.

82. See, for example, "Govt Pushed for Laws," *Nation/Thailand*, 5 May 2012, and "With the Asean Economic Community (AEC) Looming in the Background, Thai Banks Have Significant Hurdles . . . ," *Nation/Thailand*, 18 April 2012.

83. The Joint Private Standing Committee includes the Federation of Thai Industries, the Board of Trade of Thailand, and the Thai Bankers' Association.

84. "Thailand: Prime Minister Urged by Business Groups to Support Revision of Anti–Money Laundering Law," Thai News Service, 10 May 2012.

85. "Thailand: Govt Pledges to Expedite Laws against Money Laundering," Thai News Service, 11 May 2012.

86. Jon Fernquest, "Anti-Money Laundering Blacklist Spells Trouble," *Bangkok Post*, 22 May 2012, https://www.bangkokpost.com/learning/learning-news/294602/anti-money-laundering-blacklist-spells-trouble.

87. "Thailand: House of Representatives Approves in Principle Two Anti–Money Laundering Bills," Thai News Service, 14 June 2012.

88. "Thailand: Joint Private Standing Committee Concerned over Weakening of Draft of Anti-Money-Laundering Law," Thai News Service, 3 July 2012.

89. "Thailand: Threat of Blacklist Looms Large," Thai News Service, 2 October 2012.

90. Tinnakorn Chaowachuen and Petchanet Pratruangkrai, "Anti–Money Laundering Fast Implementation of New Act Urged Way to Ensure Country's Exit from 'Dark Grey List,' Says Private Sector," Nation/Thailand, 26 October 2012.

91. "Senate Accepts Two Anti-terrorism Bills in First Reading," Bangkok Post, 6 November 2012, https://www.bangkokpost.com/thailand/politics/319835/senate-accepts-two-anti-terrorism-bills-in-first-reading.

92. "Terror Groups Hit with Thai Finance Ban," Bangkok Post, 23 April 2012.

93. "Thailand Off Global Money Watch List," Bangkok Post, 23 June 2012.

94. "Improving Global AML/CFT Compliance: On-Going Process—21 June 2013."

95. Author interview with Thai government official, 14 February 2016.

96. "Money Laundering—Terrorism before Being Downgraded," Thai Rath, 16 February 2012, https://www.thairath.co.th/content/238988.

97. "Thailand: Bank of Thailand Worries Possible Blacklisting of Thailand by FATF May Affect Financial Industry Significantly," Thai News Service, 16 February 2012; "Thailand: Finance Minister Fears FATF Blacklist Could Harm Thailand," Thai News Service, 17 February 2012.

98. Sucheera Pinijparakarn and Piyanuch Thamnukasetchai, "Blacklist May Push Up Local Bank Costs," Nation/Thailand, 21 February 2012.

99. Ibid.

100. Author interview with Thai government official, 14 February 2016.

101. "Thailand: Prime Minister Urged."

102. "Financial 'Risk' Status Could Deter FDI," Nation/Thailand, 22 February 2012.

103. "Thailand: SME Bank Worried about Thailand's Financial Credibility after Being Included on Money Laundering Blacklist," Thai News Service, 22 February 2012.

104. "Firms Fear Blacklist," Bangkok Post, 29 March 2012, https://www.bangkokpost.com/business/286467/firms-fear-blacklist.

105. "Thailand/United States: US Banks Refuse to Cash Cheques for Thai Officials," Thai News Service, 5 October 2012.

106. Piyanuch Thamnukasetchai, "AMLO 'Helpless' about Foreign Banks Refusing Transactions," Nation/Thailand, 28 October 2012.

107. The yield spread is calculated by comparing the interest rate on the Thai ten-year bond to the interest rate on the US ten-year bond.

108. In 2015, the Thai government transferred supervisory functions related to anti–money laundering and combating the financing of terrorism from the Bank of Thailand, the Securities and Exchange Commission, and the Office of Insurance Commission to the AMLO. According to the APG, "these changes have resulted in a significant improvement of Thailand's AML/CFT supervision structural framework" (Asia/Pacific Group on Money Laundering 2017, 9).

109. Piyanuch Thamnukasetchai, "AMLO Wants Law on Money Smuggling Made Tougher," Nation/Thailand, 13 August 2014.

110. AMLO chief Pol Colonel Sihanart Prayoonrat quoted in "New Briefs Head; AMLO Seeks Law to Block Funding for Weapons of Mass Destruction," Nation/Thailand, 9 October 2015.

111. The FATF eligibility criteria for the noncomplier list in this current ongoing round of evaluations are: a country with twenty or more failing ratings for technical compliance; a rating of noncompliant or partially compliant on three or more of the following recommendations: 3, 5, 6, 10, 11, 20; a low or moderate level of effectiveness on nine or more of the eleven immediate outcomes (minimum of two lows); or a low effectiveness

rating on six or more of the eleven immediate outcomes. Thailand had failing scores on fifteen of the technical ratings, ratings of noncompliant or partially compliant on only one of the six ratings, low/moderate effectiveness on six ratings, and low effectiveness on only three ratings.

112. Dr. Tawatchai Yongkittikul interview.

CONCLUSION: THE POWER AND PERIL OF MARKETS AS ENFORCERS

1. "De-risking in the Financial Sector," World Bank, 7 October 2016, https://www.worldbank.org/en/topic/financialsector/brief/de-risking-in-the-financial-sector.

References

Abbott, Kenneth W., and Duncan Snidal. 2000. "Hard and Soft Law in International Governance." *International Organization* 54(3): 421–56.

Abdelal, Rawi, and Mark Blyth. 2015. "Just Who Put You in Charge? We Did: CRAs and the Politics of Ratings." In *Ranking the World: Grading States as a Tool of Global Governance*, edited by Alexander Cooley and Jack Snyder. New York: Cambridge University Press.

Acharya, Arabinda. 2009. *Targeting Terrorist Financing: International Cooperation and New Regimes.* New York: Routledge.

Adler, Emanuel. 1997. "Seizing the Middle Ground: Constructivism in World Politics." *European Journal of International Relations* 3(3): 319–63.

Adriano, Andreas. 2017. "When Money Can No Longer Travel." *Finance and Development* 54(2). https://www.imf.org/external/pubs/ft/fandd/2017/06/adriano1.htm.

Allee, Todd L., and Paul K. Huth. 2006. "Legitimizing Dispute Settlement: International Legal Rulings as Domestic Political Cover." *American Political Science Review* 100(2): 219–34.

Allee, Todd, and Clint Peinhardt. 2011. "Contingent Credibility: The Impact of Investment Treaty Violations on Foreign Direct Investment." *International Organization* 65(3): 401–32.

Allen, Bill, Ka Kei Chan, Alistair Milne, and Steve Thomas. 2012. "Basel III: Is the Cure Worse Than the Disease?" *International Review of Financial Analysis* 25:159–66.

Allen, Franklin, Thorsten Beck, Elena Carletti, Philip R. Lane, Dirk Schoenmaker, and Wolf Wagner. 2011. *Cross-Border Banking in Europe: Implications for Financial Stability and Macroeconomic Policies.* London: Centre for Economic Policy Research.

Alwazir, Jihad, Fazurin Jamaludin, Dongyeol Lee, Niamh Sheridan, and Patrizia Tumbarello. 2017. "Challenges in Correspondent Banking in the Small States of the Pacific." IMF Working Paper, 1–29. https://www.imf.org/en/Publications/WP/Issues/2017/04/07/Challenges-in-Correspondent-Banking-in-the-Small-States-of-the-Pacific-44809.

Amato, Jeffery D., Stephen Morris, and Hyun Song Shin. 2002. "Communication and Monetary Policy." *Oxford Review of Economic Policy* 18(4): 495–503.

Andonova, Liliana B., and Ioana A. Tuta. 2014. "Transnational Networks and Paths to EU Environmental Compliance: Evidence from New Member States." *JCMS: Journal of Common Market Studies* 52(4): 775–93.

Andreas, Peter. 2004. "Illicit International Political Economy: The Clandestine Side of Globalization." *Review of International Political Economy* 11(3): 641–52.

Andrews, David M. 1994. "Capital Mobility and State Autonomy: Toward a Structural Theory of International Monetary Relations." *International Studies Quarterly* 38(2): 193–218.

Angelini, Paolo, Laurent Clerc, Vasco Curidia, Leonardo Gambacorta, Andrea Gerali, Alberto Locarno, Roberto Motto, Werner Roeger, Skander Van den Heuvel, and

Jan Vlcek. 2015. "Basel III: Long-Term Impact on Economic Performance and Fluctuations." *Manchester School* 83(2): 217–51.

Arner, Douglas W., and Michael W. Taylor. 2009. "The Global Financial Crisis and the Financial Stability Board: Hardening the Soft Law of International Financial Regulation." *University of New South Wales Law Journal* 32(2): 488–513.

Arslanalp, Serkan, and Takahiro Tsuda. 2014. "Tracking Global Demand for Emerging Market Sovereign Debt." IMF Working Paper, 1–50. https://www.imf.org/en/Publications/WP/Issues/2016/12/31/Tracking-Global-Demand-for-Emerging-Market-Sovereign-Debt-41399.

Asia/Pacific Group on Money Laundering. 2017. *Anti–Money Laundering and Counter-Terrorist Financing Measures: Thailand (Mutual Evaluation Report)*. Sydney: Asia/Pacific Group on Money Laundering.

Asia/Pacific Group on Money Laundering. 2019. *Anti–Money Laundering and Counter-Terrorist Financing Measures: The Philippines (Mutual Evaluation Report)*. Sydney: Asia/Pacific Group on Money Laundering.

Asia/Pacific Group on Money Laundering and the World Bank. 2009. *Mutual Evaluation Report: Anti–Money Laundering and Combating the Financing of Terrorism (Republic of the Philippines)*. Sydney: Asia/Pacific Group on Money Laundering.

AUSTRAC. 2019. "Bank De-risking of Remittance Businesses." *Australian Government Strategic Analysis Brief*. https://www.austrac.gov.au/sites/default/files/2019-07/sa-brief-bank-derisking-remittance-businesses_WEB.pdf.

Baker, Andrew. 2010. "Restraining Regulatory Capture? Anglo-America, Crisis Politics and Trajectories of Change in Global Financial Governance." *International Affairs* 86(3): 647–63.

Ballaran, Jhoanna. 2017 (July 19). "Amended Anti–Money Laundering Law Saves PH from FATF Blacklist—Chiz." Inquirer.net (website).

Ballard-Rosa, Cameron, Layna Mosley, and Rachel Wellhausen. 2019. "Contingent Advantage? Sovereign Borrowing, Democratic Institutions, and Global Capital Cycles." *British Journal of Political Science* 51(1): 1–21. https://globalnation.inquirer.net/158876/amended-anti-money-laundering-law-saves-ph-fatf-blacklist-chiz.

Bank for International Settlements. 2014. "Trade Finance: Developments and Issues." *CGFS Papers* 50:1–67.

Bank for International Settlements. 2016. "Correspondent Banking—Final Report." Basel: Bank for International Settlements. https://www.bis.org/cpmi/publ/d147.htm.

Barnett, Michael N., and Martha Finnemore. 1999. "The Politics, Power, and Pathologies of International Organizations." *International Organization* 53(4): 699–732.

Baumol, William. 1989. "Chaos: Significance, Mechanism and Economic Applications." *Journal of Economic Perspective* 3(2): 77–105.

Beaulieu, Emily, Gary W. Cox, and Sebastian Saiegh. 2012. "Sovereign Debt and Regime Type: Reconsidering the Democratic Advantage." *International Organization* 66(4): 709–38.

Bechtel, Michael M., and Gerald Schneider. 2010. "Eliciting Substance from 'Hot Air': Financial Market Responses to EU Summit Decision on European Defense." *International Organization* 64(2): 199–223.

Benink, Harald A. 1993. *Financial Integration in Europe*. Dordrecht: Kluwer.

Berger, Allen N., Robert Deyoung, Hesna Genay, and Gregory F. Udell. 2000. "Globalization of Financial Institutions: Evidence from Cross-Border Banking Performance." Brookings-Wharton Papers on Financial Services. https://muse.jhu.edu/article/26611/pdf.

Berger, Loic, Han Bleichrodt, and Louis Eeckhoudt. 2013. "Treatment Decisions under Ambiguity." *Journal of Health Economics* 32(3): 559–69.

Bernheim, B. Douglas, and Michael D. Whinston. 1998. "Incomplete Contracts and Strategic Ambiguity." *American Economic Review* 88(4): 902–32.

Bernstein, Steven, and Benjamin Cashore. 2007. "Can Non-state Global Governance Be Legitimate? An Analytical Framework." *Regulation and Governance* 1:347–71.

Best, Jacqueline. 2005. *The Limits of Transparency: Ambiguity and the History of International Finance.* Ithaca, NY: Cornell University Press.

Best, Jacqueline. 2012. "Ambiguity and Uncertainty in International Organizations: A History of Debating IMF Conditionality." *International Studies Quarterly* 56(4): 674–88.

Bhuta, Nehal. 2015. "Measuring Stateness, Ranking Political Orders: Indices of State Fragility and State Failure." In *Ranking the World: Grading States as a Tool of Global Governance,* edited by Alexander Cooley and Jack Snyder. New York: Cambridge University Press.

Biersteker, Thomas J., and Sue E. Eckert. 2008. *Countering the Financing of Terrorism.* New York: Routledge.

Biglaiser, Glen, and Joseph L. Staats. 2012. "Finding the 'Democratic Advantage' in Sovereign Bond Ratings: The Importance of Strong Courts, Property Rights Protection, and the Rule of Law." *International Organization* 66(3): 515–35.

Bisbee, James H., James R. Hollyer, B. Peter Rosendorff, and James Raymond Vreeland. 2019. "The Millennium Development Goals and Education: Accountability and Substitution in Global Assessment." *International Organization* 73(3): 547–78.

Bissessar, Kamla Persad. 2012 (October). Statement by Trinidad and Tobago PM, the Hon Kamla Persad Bissessar, on the Removal of Trinidad and Tobago from FATF List of Countries with Strategic AML/CFT Deficiencies. https://sflcn.com/statement-by-trinidad-and-tobago-pm-the-hon-kamla-persad-bissessar-on-the-removal-of-trinidad-and-tobago-from-fatf-list-of-countries-with-strategic-amlcft-deficiencies/.

Bonneuil, Christophe, and Les Levidow. 2011. "How Does the World Trade Organization Know? The Mobilization and Staging of Scientific Expertise in the GMO Trade Dispute." *Social Studies in Science* 42(1): 75–100.

Borio, C., and P. Disyatat. 2011. "Global Imbalances and the Financial Crisis: Link or No Link?" BIS Working Paper No. 346. http://www.bis.org/publ/work346.pdf.

Box-Steffensmeier, Janet M., and Christopher J. W. Zorn. 2001. "Duration Models and Proportional Hazards in Political Science." *American Journal of Political Science* 45(4): 972–88.

Boyle, Alan E. 1999. "Some Reflections on the Relationship of Treaties and Soft Law." *International and Comparative Law Quarterly* 48(4): 901–13.

Brambor, Thomas, William Roberts Clark, and Matt Golder. 2006. "Understanding Interaction Models: Improving Empirical Analyses." *Political Analysis* 14(1): 63–82.

Brillo, Bing Baltazar C. 2010a. "Power Politics in Policymaking: The Anti–Money Laundering Act of the Philippines." *Arts and Social Sciences Journal* 9:1–14.

Brillo, Bing Baltazar C. 2010b. "The Politics of the Anti–Money Laundering Act of the Philippines: An Assessment of the Republic Act 9160 and 9194." *Asian Social Science* 6(8): 109–25.

Brooks, Sarah M. 2004. "Explaining Capital Account Liberalization in Latin America: A Transitional Cost Approach." *World Politics* 56(3): 389–430.

Brooks, Sarah M., Raphael Cunha, and Layna Mosley. 2015. "Categories, Creditworthiness, and Contagion: How Investors' Shortcuts Affect Sovereign Debt Markets." *International Studies Quarterly* 59(3): 587–601.

Brummer, Chris. 2010. "Why Soft Law Dominates International Finance and Not Trade." *Journal of International Economic Law* 13(3): 623–43.

Brummer, Chris. 2015. *Soft Law and the Global Financial System: Rule Making in the 21st Century*. 2nd ed. Cambridge: Cambridge University Press.

Bruno, Valentina, and Hyun Song Shin. 2015a. "Cross-Border Banking and Global Liquidity." *Review of Economic Studies* 82(2): 535–64.

Bruno, Valentina, and Hyun Song Shin. 2015b. "Capital Flows and the Risk-Taking Channel of Monetary Policy." *Journal of Monetary Economics* 71:119–32.

Brutger, Ryan, and Julia C. Morse. 2015. "Balancing Law and Politics: Judicial Incentives in WTO Dispute Settlement." *Review of International Organizations* 10(2): 179–205.

Buchanan, Allen, and Robert O. Keohane. 2006. "The Legitimacy of Global Governance Institutions." *Ethics and International Affairs* 20(4): 405–37.

Bueno de Mesquita, Bruce, Alastair Smith, Randolph M. Siverson, and James D. Morrow. 2003. *The Logic of Political Survival*. Cambridge, MA: MIT Press.

Busch, Marc L. 2007. "Overlapping Institutions, Forum Shopping, and Dispute Settlement in International Trade." *International Organization* 61(4): 735–61.

Büthe, Tim, and Walter Mattli. 2011. *The New Global Rulers: The Privatization of Regulation in the World Economy*. Princeton, NJ: Princeton University Press.

Büthe, Tim, and Helen V. Milner. 2008. "The Politics of Foreign Direct Investment into Developing Countries: Increasing FDI through International Trade Agreements?" *American Journal of Political Science* 52(4): 741–62.

Cai, Hongbin, and Daniel Treisman. 2005. "Does Competition for Capital Discipline Governments? Decentralization, Globalization, and Public Policy." *American Economic Review* 95(3): 817–30.

Caribbean Financial Action Task Force (CFATF-GAFIC). 2011 (July). *Mutual Evaluation Report: Anti–Money Laundering and Combating the Financing of Terrorism (Guyana)*.

Carnegie, Allison, and Austin Carson. 2018a. "The Disclosure Dilemma: Nuclear Intelligence and International Organization." *American Journal of Political Science* 63(2): 269–85.

Carnegie, Allison, and Austin Carson. 2018b. "The Spotlight's Harsh Glare: Rethinking Publicity and International Order." *International Organization* 72(3): 627–57.

Carnegie, Allison, and Austin Carson. 2020. *Secrets in Global Governance: Disclosure Dilemmas and the Challenge of International Cooperation*. New York: Cambridge University Press.

Cerny, Philip G. 1990. *The Changing Architecture of Politics: Structure, Agency and the Future of the State*. London: SAGE.

Cerny, Philip G. 2010. *Rethinking World Politics: A Theory of Transnational Neopluralism*. Oxford: Oxford University Press.

Cerutti, Eugenio, Stijn Claessens, and Lev Ratnovski. 2015. "Global Liquidity and the Drivers of Cross-Border Bank Flows." IMF Working Papers 14/69.

Cerutti, Eugenio, Stijn Claessens, and Lev Ratnovski. 2017. "Global Liquidity and Cross-Border Bank Flows." *Economic Policy* 32(89): 81–125.

Cerutti, Eugenio, Giovanni Dell'Ariccia, and Maria Soledad Martinez Peria. 2005. "How Banks Go Abroad: Branches or Subsidiaries?" World Bank Group Policy Research Working Paper.

Chaudoin, Stephen. 2016. "How Contestation Moderates the Effects of International Institutions: The International Criminal Court and Kenya." *Journal of Politics* 78(2): 557–71.

Chaudoin, Stephen, Helen V. Milner, and Xun Pang. 2015. "International Systems and Domestic Politics: Linking Complex Interactions with Empirical Models in International Relations." *International Organization* 69(2): 275–309.

Chayes, Abram, and Antonia Handler Chayes. 1993. "On Compliance." *International Organization* 47(2): 175–205.

Checkel, Jeffrey T. 2001. "Why Comply? Social Learning and European Identity Change." *International Organization* 55(3): 553–88.

Chey, Hyoung-kyu. 2014. *International Harmonization of Financial Regulation? The Politics of Global Diffusion of the Basel Capital Accord.* New York: Routledge.

Chinkin, Christine M. 1989. "The Challenge of Soft Law: Development and Change in International Law." *International and Comparative Law Quarterly* 38(4): 850–66.

Chwieroth, Jeffrey. 2007. "Neoliberal Economists and Capital Account Liberalization in Emerging Markets." *International Organization* 61(2): 443–63.

Claessens, Stijn. 2006. "Competitive Implications of Cross-Border Banking." Policy Research Working Papers, World Bank. https://elibrary.worldbank.org/doi/abs/10.1596/1813-9450-3854.

Clunan, Anne L. 2006. "The Fight against Terrorist Financing." *Political Science Quarterly* 121(4): 569–96.

Coen, David, and Mark Thatcher. 2008. "Network Governance and Multi-Level Delegation: European Networks of Regulatory Agencies." *Journal of Public Policy* 28(1): 49–71.

Cohen, Benjamin J. 1986. *In Whose Interest? International Banking and American Foreign Policy.* Binghamton, NY: Council on Foreign Relations.

Cohen, Benjamin J. 1998. *The Geography of Money.* Ithaca, NY: Cornell University Press.

Cohen, Benjamin J. 2011. *The Future of Global Currency: The Euro versus the Dollar.* New York: Routledge.

Cohen, Benjamin J., and Tabitha M. Benney. 2014. "What Does the International Currency System Really Look Like?" *Review of International Political Economy* 21(5): 1017–41.

Collin, Matthew, Samantha Cook, and Kimmo Soramaki. 2016. "The Impact of Anti–Money Laundering Regulation on Payment Flows: Evidence from SWIFT Data." Tech. Rept. 445. https://www.cgdev.org/impact-anti-money-laundering-SWIFT-data.

Committee on Payments and Market Infrastructures. 2016. "Correspondent Banking." Bank for International Settlements. https://www.bis.org/cpmi/publ/d147.htm.

Cook, Colleen W. 2007. "Mexico's Drug Cartels." Congressional Research Service Report for Congress, RL34215.

Cooley, Alexander, and Jack Snyder. 2015. *Ranking the World: Grading States as a Tool of Global Governance.* New York: Cambridge University Press.

Cooter, Robert. 1998. "Expressive Law and Economics." *Journal of Legal Studies* 27:585–608.

Cortell, Andrew P., and James W. Davis. 1996. "How Do International Institutions Matter? The Domestic Impact of International Rules and Norms." *International Studies Quarterly* 40(4): 451–78.

Crawford, Vincent P., Uri Gneezy, and Yuval Rottenstreich. 2008. "The Power of Focal Points Is Limited: Even Minute Payoff Asymmetry May Yield Large Coordination Failures." *American Economic Review* 98(4): 1443–58.

Curley, Shawn P., J. Frank Yates, and Richard A. Abrams. 1986. "Psychological Sources of Ambiguity Avoidance." *Organizational Behavior and Human Decision Processes* 38:230–56.

Dafoe, Allan, Jonathan Renshon, and Paul Huth. 2014. "Reputation and Status as Motives for War." *Annual Review of Political Science* 17(1): 371–93.

Dai, Xinyuan. 2002. "Information Systems of Treaty Regimes." *World Politics* 54(4): 405–36.

Dai, Xinyuan. 2007. *International Institutions and National Policies*. Cambridge: Cambridge University Press.

Davis, Christina L. 2004. "International Institutions and Issue Linkage: Building Support for Agricultural Trade Liberalization." *American Political Science Review* 98(1): 153–69.

Davis, Christina L., and Yuki Shirato. 2007. "Firms, Governments, and WTO Adjudication: Japan's Selection of WTO Disputes." *World Politics* 59(2): 274–313.

Davis, Kevin, Angelina Fisher, Benedict Kingsbury, and Sally Engle Merry. 2012. *Governance by Indicators: Global Power through Quantification and Rankings*. Oxford: Oxford University Press.

Deeg, Richard, and Mary A. O'Sullivan. 2009. "Review: The Political Economy of Global Finance Capital." *World Politics* 61(4): 731–63.

Dehousse, Renaud. 1997. "Regulation by Networks in the European Community: The Role of European Agencies." *Journal of European Public Policy* 4(2): 246–61.

Denecker, Olivier, Florent Istace, Pavan K. Masanam, and Marc Niederkorn. 2016. "Rethinking Correspondent Banking." *McKinsey on Payments* 9(23): 1–9.

De Goede, Marieke. 2005. *Virtue, Fortune, and Faith*. Minneapolis: University of Minnesota Press.

De Goede, Marieke. 2007. "Underground Money." *Cultural Critique* 65:140–63.

De Goede, Marieke. 2012. *Speculative Security: The Politics of Pursuing Terrorist Monies*. Minneapolis: University of Minnesota Press.

De Goede, Marieke. 2017. "Banks in the Frontline: Assembling Space/Time in Financial Warfare." In *Money and Finance after the Crisis: Critical Thinking for Uncertain Times*, edited by B. Christophers, A. Leyshon, and G. Mann. Hoboken, NJ: John Wiley & Sons.

de Oliveira, Inês Sofia. 2018. "The Governance of the Financial Action Task Force: An Analysis of Power and Influence throughout the Years." *Crime, Law, and Social Change* 69:153–72.

Dolan, Lindsay. 2020. "Labeling Laggards and Leaders: International Organizations and the Politics of Defining Development." Working paper, available at https://lindsayrdolan.com/research.

Downs, George W., and David M. Rocke. 1995. *Optimal Imperfection? Domestic Uncertainty and Institutions in International Relations*. Princeton, NJ: Princeton University Press.

Downs, George W., David M. Rocke, and Peter N. Barsoom. 1996. "Is the Good News about Compliance Good News about Cooperation?" *International Organization* 50(3): 379–406.

Doyle, T. 2002. "Cleaning Up Anti–Money Laundering Strategies: Current FATF Tactics Needlessly Violate International Law." *Houston Journal of International Law* 24(2): 279–313.

Drezner, Daniel W. 2005. "Globalization, Harmonization, and Competition: The Different Pathways to Policy Convergence." *Journal of European Public Policy* 12(5): 841–59.

Drezner, Daniel W. 2007. *All Politics Is Global: Explaining International Regulatory Regimes*. Princeton, NJ: Princeton University Press.

Drezner, Daniel. 2014. *The System Worked: How the World Stopped Another Great Depression*. Oxford: Oxford University Press.

Durner, Tracey, and Liat Shetret. 2015 (November). "Understanding Bank De-risking and Its Effects on Financial Inclusion." Global Center on Cooperative Security. https://www-cdn.oxfam.org/s3fs-public/file_attachments/rr-bank-de-risking-181115-en_0.pdf.

Easley, David, and Maureen O'Hara. 2009. "Ambiguity and Nonparticipation: The Role of Regulation." *Review of Financial Studies* 22(5): 1817–43.

Eberlein, Burkard, and Abraham L. Newman. 2008. "Escaping the International Governance Dilemma? Incorporated Transgovernmental Networks in the European Union." *Governance: An International Journal of Policy, Administration, and Institutions* 21(1): 25–52.

Eckersley, Robyn. 2007. "Ambushed: The Kyoto Protocol, the Bush Administration's Climate Policy and the Erosion of Legitimacy." *International Politics* 44:306–24.

Eckert, Sue E. 2008. "The US Regulatory Approach to Terrorist Financing." In *Countering the Financing of Terrorism*, edited by Thomas J. Biersteker and Sue E. Eckert. New York: Routledge.

Elkins, Zachary, Andrew T. Guzman, and Beth A. Simmons. 2006. "Competing for Capital: The Diffusion of Bilateral Investment Treaties, 1960–2000." *International Organization* 60(4): 811–46.

Ellsberg, Daniel. 1961. "Risk, Ambiguity and the Savage Axioms." *Journal of Economics* 75(4): 643–69.

El Taraboulsi-McCarthy, Sherine. 2018. "The Challenge of Informality: Counter-terrorism, Bank De-risking and Financial Access for Humanitarian Organisations in Somalia." HPG Working Paper. https://odi.org/en/publications/the-challenge-of-informality-counter-terrorism-bank-de-risking-and-financial-access-for-humanitarian-organisations-in-somalia/.

Erb, Claude B., Campbell R. Harvey, and Tadas E. Viskanta. 1999. "New Perspectives on Emerging Market Bonds." *Journal of Portfolio Management* 25(2): 83–92.

Erbenova, Michaela, Yan Liu, Nadim Kryiakos-Saad, Alejandro Lopez-Mejia, Giancarlo Gasha, Emmanuel Mathias, Mohamed Norat, Francisca Fernando, and Yasmin Almedia. 2016 (June). "The Withdrawal of Correspondent Banking Relationships: A Case for Policy Action." IMF SDN/16/06. https://www.imf.org/external/pubs/ft/sdn/2016/sdn1606.pdf.

Espeland, Wendy Nelson, and Michael Sauder. 2007. "Rankings and Reactivity: How Public Measures Recreate Social Worlds." *American Journal of Sociology* 113(1): 1–40.

Farrell, Henry, and Abraham Newman. 2015. "The New Politics of Interdependence: Cross-National Layering in Trans-Atlantic Regulatory Disputes." *Comparative Political Studies* 48(4): 497–526.

Farrell, Henry, and Abraham Newman. 2016. "The New Interdependence Approach: Theoretical Development and Empirical Demonstration." *Review of International Political Economy* 23(5): 713–36.

Farrell, Henry, and Abraham Newman. 2019. "Weaponized Interdependence: How Global Economic Networks Shape State Coercion." *International Security* 44(1): 42–79.

FATF-GAFI. 1990. *The Forty Recommendations of the Financial Action Task Force on Money Laundering*. Paris: FATF/OECD.

FATF-GAFI. 1992. *Annual Report: 1991–1992*. Paris: FATF/OECD.

FATF-GAFI. 1993. *Annual Report: 1992–1993*. Paris: FATF/OECD.
FATF-GAFI. 1996. *Annual Report: 1995–1996*. Paris: FATF/OECD.
FATF-GAFI. 1998. *Annual Report: 1997–1998*. Paris: FATF/OECD.
FATF-GAFI. 1999. *Annual Report: 1998–1999*. Paris: FATF/OECD.
FATF-GAFI. 2000a. *Annual Report: 1999–2000*. Paris: FATF/OECD.
FATF-GAFI. 2000b. *Review to Identify Non-cooperative Countries or Territories: Increasing the Worldwide Effectiveness of Anti–Money Laundering Measures.* Paris: FATF/OECD.
FATF-GAFI. 2001a. *Review to Identify Non-cooperative Countries or Territories: Increasing the Worldwide Effectiveness of Anti–Money Laundering Measures.* Paris: FATF/OECD.
FATF-GAFI. 2001b. *Financial Action Task Force on Money Laundering Annual Report: 2000–2001.* Paris: FATF/OECD.
FATF-GAFI. 2004. *Annual Report: 2003–2004*. Paris: FATF/OECD.
FATF-GAFI. 2005. *Annual and Overall Review of Non-cooperative Countries and Territories.* Paris: FATF/OECD.
FATF-GAFI. 2008. *Terrorist Financing*. Paris: FATF/OECD.
FATF-GAFI. 2009a. *ICRG Co-Chairs' Report*. Paris: FATF/OECD.
FATF-GAFI. 2009b. *Third Round of AML/CFT Mutual Evaluations: Process and Procedures.* Paris: FATF/OECD.
FATF-GAFI. 2010. *Money Laundering through Money Remittance and Currency Exchange Providers.* Paris: FATF/OECD and MONEYVAL.
FATF-GAFI. 2012. *International Standards on Combating Money Laundering and the Financing of Terrorism and Proliferation.* Paris: FATF/OECD.
FATF-GAFI. 2014 (27 January). *International Cooperation Review Group—Taking Account of the New FATF Standards in the ICRG Process: Issues for Discussion (FATF/ICRG(2013)16/REV2).* Paris: FATF/OECD.
FATF-GAFI. 2015. *Results of the Terrorist Financing Fact-Finding Initiative—FATF Members.* Paris: FATF/OECD.
FATF-GAFI. 2016. *International Standards on Combating Money Laundering and the Financing of Terrorism and Proliferation.* Paris: FATF-OECD.
FATF-GAFI. 2018. *International Standards on Combating Money Laundering and the Financing of Terrorism and Proliferation.* 2018 Update. Paris: FATF/OECD.
FATF-GAFI. 2019. *International Standards on Combating Money Laundering and the Financing of Terrorism and Proliferation: FATF Recommendations.* Updated June 2019. Paris: FATF/OECD.
Fearon, James D. 1998. "Bargaining, Enforcement, and International Cooperation." *International Organization* 52(2): 269–305.
Federal Financial Institutions Examination Council. 2018 (May). "Customer Due Diligence—Overview." *FFIEC BSA/AML Examination Manual*. https://www.ffiec.gov/press/pdf/Customer%20Due%20Diligence%20-%20Overview%20and%20Exam%20Procedures-FINAL.pdf.
Fehr, Dietmar, Frank Heinemann, and Aniol Llorente-Saguer. 2018 (August). "The Power of Sunspots: An Experimental Analysis." *Journal of Monetary Economics*: 1–32.
Findley, Michael G., Daniel L. Nielson, and J. C. Sharman. 2014a. "Causes of Noncompliance with International Law: A Field Experiment on Anonymous Incorporation." *American Journal of Political Science* 59(1): 146–61.
Findley, Michael G., Daniel L. Nielson, and J. C. Sharman. 2014b. *Global Shell Games: Experiments in Transnational Relations, Crime, and Terrorism.* New York: Cambridge University Press.

Finnemore, Martha. 1993. "International Organizations as Teachers of Norms: The United Nations Educational, Scientific, and Cultural Organization and Science Policy." *International Organization* 47(4): 565–97.

Finnemore, Martha. 1996. *National Interests in International Society.* Ithaca, NY: Cornell University Press.

Finnemore, Martha, and Kathryn Sikkink. 1998. "International Norm Dynamics and Political Change." *International Organization* 52(4): 887–917.

Fisher, Roger. 1981. *Improving Compliance with International Law.* Charlottesville: University Press of Virginia.

Friman, H. Richard, and Peter Andreas, eds. 1999. *The Illicit Global Economy and State Power.* Lanham, MD: Rowman & Littlefield.

Gadinis, Stavros. 2012. "The Financial Stability Board: The New Politics of International Financial Regulation." *Texas International Law Journal* 48:157–76.

Gardner, Kathryn L. 2007. "Fighting Terrorism the FATF Way." *Global Governance* 13:325–45.

Garrett, Geoffrey. 1998. "Shrinking States? Globalization and National Autonomy in the OECD." *Oxford Development Studies* 26(1): 71–97.

Garrett, Geoffrey, and Barry R. Weingast. 1993. "Ideas, Interests and Institutions: Constructing the EC Internal Market." In *Ideas and Foreign Policy: Beliefs, Institutions, and Political Change*, edited by Judith Goldstein and Barry R. Weingast. Ithaca, NY: Cornell University Press.

Germain, Randall, and Herman Schwartz. 2014. "The Political Economy of Failure: The Euro as an International Currency." *Review of International Political Economy* 21(5): 1095–1122.

Gibler, D. M. 2009. *International Military Alliances, 1648–2008.* Washington, DC: CQ Press.

Gill, Stephen R., and David Law. 1989. "Global Hegemony and the Structural Power of Capital." *International Studies Quarterly* 33(4): 475–99.

Ginsburg, Tom, and Richard H. McAdams. 2004. "Adjudicating in Anarchy: An Expressive Theory of International Dispute Resolution." *William and Mary Law Review* 45(4): 1229–1339.

Gleditsch, Kristian S. 2013. "Modified Polity P4 and P4D Data, Version 4.0." http://www.ksgleditsch.com/polity.html.

Gleditsch, Kristian S., and Michael D. Ward. 2006. "Diffusion and the International Context of Democratization." *International Organization* 60(4): 911–33.

Goldsmith, Jack L., and Eric A. Posner. 2005. *The Limits of International Law.* New York: Oxford University Press.

Gollier, Christian. 2011. "Portfolio Choices and Asset Prices: The Comparative Statics of Ambiguity Aversion." *Review of Economic Studies* 78(4): 1329–44.

Goodman, John B., and Louis W. Pauly. 1993. "The Obsolescence of Capital Controls? Economic Management in an Age of Global Markets." *World Politics* 46(1): 50–82.

Gordon, Richard K. 2010. "The International Monetary Fund and the Regulation of Offshore Centers." In *Offshore Financial Centers and Regulatory Competition*, edited by Andrew P. Morriss. Lanham, MD: Rowman & Littlefield.

Gourevitch, Peter. 1978. "The Second Image Reversed: The International Sources of Domestic Politics." *International Organization* 32:881–912.

Gourinchas, Pierre-Olivier, and Maurice Obstfeld. 2012. "Stories of the Twentieth Century for the Twenty-First." *American Economic Journal: Macroeconomics* 4(1): 226–65.

Government of the Philippines. 2017. *The Philippines Second National Risk Assessment on Money Laundering and Terrorist Financing*. Manila: Philippine Anti-Money Laundering Council.

Gray, Julia. 2013. *The Company States Keep: International Economic Organizations and Investor Perceptions*. New York: Cambridge University Press.

Gray, Julia, and Raymond P. Hicks. 2014. "Reputations, Perceptions, and International Economic Agreements." *International Interactions* 40(3): 325–49.

Green, Jessica F. 2013. *Rethinking Private Authority: Agents and Entrepreneurs in Global Environmental Governance*. Princeton, NJ: Princeton University Press.

Greif, Avner. 1992. "Institutions and International Trade: Lessons from the Commercial Revolution." *American Economic Review* 82(2): 128–33.

Greif, Avner. 1993. "Contract Enforceability and Economic Institutions in Early Trade: The Maghribi Traders' Coalition." *American Economic Review* 83(3): 525–48.

Greif, Avner, Paul Milgrom, and Barry R. Weingast. 1994. "Coordination, Commitment, and Enforcement: The Case of the Merchant Guild." *Journal of Political Economy* 102(4): 745–76.

Grittersová, Jana. 2014. "Transfer of Reputation: Multinational Banks and Perceived Creditworthiness of Transition Countries." *Review of International Political Economy* 21(4): 878–912.

Grittersová, Jana. 2017. *Borrowing Credibility: Global Banks and Monetary Regimes*. Ann Arbor: University of Michigan Press.

Grossman, Emiliano, and Cornelia Woll. 2014. "Saving the Banks: The Political Economy of Bailouts." *Comparative Political Studies* 47(4): 574–600.

G-20. 2008. "Declaration of the Summit on Financial Markets and the World Economy." White House Archives, 15 November 2008. https://georgewbush-whitehouse.archives.gov/news/releases/2008/11/20081115-1.html.

Gurowitz, Amy. 1999. "Mobilizing International Norms: Domestic Actors, Immigrants, and the Japanese State." *World Politics* 51(3): 413–45.

Gutterman, Ellen, and Ian Roberge. 2019. "Chapter 29: The Financial Action Task Force: Fighting Transnational Organized Crime, Money Laundering, and the Limits of Experimentalist Governance." In *Handbook of Organised Crime and Politics*, edited by Felia Allum and Stan Gilmour. Northampton, MA: Edward Elgar.

Guzman, Andrew T. 2007. *How International Law Works: A Rational Choice Theory*. Oxford: Oxford University Press.

Guzman, Andrew T., and Timothy L. Meyer. 2010. "International Soft Law." *International Soft Law* 2(1): 171–225.

Guzman, Andrew T., and Beth A. Simmons. 2005. "Power Plays and Capacity Constraints: The Selection of Defendants in World Trade Organization Disputes." *Journal of Legal Studies* 34(2): 557–98.

Haas, Ernst B. 1980. "Why Collaborate? Issue-Linkage and International Regimes." *World Politics* 32(3): 357–405.

Haas, Ernst B. 1990. *When Knowledge Is Power*. Berkeley: University of California Press.

Haas, Peter M. 2009. "Introduction: Epistemic Communities and International Policy Coordination." *International Organization* 46(1): 1–35.

Hadfield, Gillian K., and Barry R. Weingast. 2012. "What Is Law? A Coordination Model of the Characteristics of Legal Order." *Journal of Legal Analysis* 4(2): 471–514.

Hafner-Burton, Emilie M. 2008. "Sticks and Stones: Naming and Shaming the Human Rights Enforcement Problem." *International Organization* 62(4): 689–716.

Hafner-Burton, Emilie M., Miles Kahler, and Alexander H. Montgomery. 2009 (July). "Network Analysis for International Relations." *International Organization* 63: 559–92.

Hafner-Burton, Emilie M., and Alexander H. Montgomery. 2006. "Power Positions: International Organizations, Social Networks, and Conflict." *Journal of Conflict Resolution* 50(1): 3–27.

Hafner-Burton, Emilie M., and Alexander H. Montgomery. 2009. "Globalization and the Power Politics of International Economic Networks." In *Networked Politics: Agency, Power, and Government,* edited by Miles Kahler. Ithaca, NY: Cornell University Press.

Hafner-Burton, Emilie M., and Kiyoteru Tsutsui. 2005. "Human Rights in a Globalizing World: The Paradox of Empty Promises." *American Journal of Sociology* 110(5): 1373–1411.

Hafner-Burton, Emilie M., and Kiyoteru Tsutsui. 2007. "Justice Lost! The Failure of International Human Rights to Matter Where Needed Most." *Journal of Peace Research* 44(4): 407–25.

Haggard, Stephan, and Sylvia Maxfield. 1996. "The Political Economy of Financial Internationalization in the Developing World." *International Organization* 50(1): 35–68.

Hainmueller, Jens, Jonathan Mummolo, and Yiqing Xu. 2019. "How Much Should We Trust Estimates from Multiplicative Interaction Models? Simple Tools to Improve Empirical Practice." *Political Analysis* 27(2): 163–92.

Hawkins, Darren G., David A. Lake, Daniel L. Nielson, and Michael J. Tierney. 2006. "Delegation under Anarchy: States, International Organizations, and Principal-Agent Theory." In *Delegation and Agency in International Organizations,* edited by Darren G. Hawkins, David A. Lake, Daniel L. Nielson, and Michael J. Tierney. New York: Cambridge University Press.

Hayes, Ben. 2013 (May). "How International Rules on Countering the Financing of Terrorism Impact Civil Society." Transnational Institute (website). https://www.tni.org/my/node/1452.

Healy, Paul M., and Krishna G. Palepu. 2001 (September). "Information Asymmetry, Corporate Disclosure, and the Capital Markets: A Review of the Empirical Disclosure Literature." *Journal of Accounting and Economics* 31:405–40.

Helfer, Laurence R., and Anne-Marie Slaughter. 1997. "Toward a Theory of Effective Supranational Adjudication." *Yale Law Journal* 107(2): 273–391.

Helfer, Laurence R., and Erik Voeten. 2014. "International Courts as Agents of Legal Change: Evidence from LGBT Rights in Europe." *International Organization* 68(1): 77–110.

Helleiner, Eric. 1994. *States and the Reemergence of Global Finance.* Ithaca, NY: Cornell University Press.

Helleiner, Eric. 1998. "Electronic Money: A Challenge to the Sovereign State?" *Journal of International Affairs* 51(2): 387–409.

Helleiner, Eric. 2008. "Political Determinants of International Currencies: What Future for the US Dollar?" *Review of International Political Economy* 15(3): 354–78.

Helleiner, Eric. 2010. "What Role for the New Financial Stability Board? The Politics of International Standards after the Crisis." *Global Policy* 1(3): 282–90.

Helleiner, Eric. 2011. "Understanding the 2007–2008 Global Financial Crisis: Lessons for Scholars of International Political Economy." *Annual Review of Political Science* 14:67–87.

Helleiner, Eric. 2014. *The Status Quo Crisis: Global Financial Governance after the 2008 Meltdown.* Oxford: Oxford University Press.

Helleiner, Eric, and Tony Porter. 2010. "Making Transnational Networks More Accountable." *Economics, Management, and Financial Markets* 5(2): 158–73.

Henkin, Louis. 1979. *How Nations Behave.* 2nd ed. New York: Columbia University Press.

Herrmann, Sabine, and Dubravko Mihaljek. 2010 (July). "The Determinants of Cross-Border Bank Flows to Emerging Markets: New Empirical Evidence on the Spread of Financial Crises." BIS Working Paper, 1–42. https://www.bis.org/publ/work315.pdf.

Hirschman, Albert. 1970. *Exit, Voice, and Loyalty.* Cambridge, MA: MIT Press.

Ho, Daniel E. 2002. "Compliance and International Soft Law: Why Do Countries Implement the Basel Accord?" *Journal of International Economic Law* 5(3): 647–88.

Ho, Daniel E., Kosuke Imai, Gary King, and Elizabeth A. Stuart. 2007. "Matching as Non-parametric Preprocessing for Reducing Model Dependence in Parametric Causal Inference." *Political Analysis* 15(03): 199–236.

Holder, William E. 2003. "The International Monetary Fund's Involvement in Combating Money Laundering and the Financing of Terrorism." *Journal of Money Laundering Control* 6(4): 383–87.

Honig, Dan, and Catherine Weaver. 2019. "A Race to the Top? The Aid Transparency Index and the Normative Power of Global Performance Assessments." *International Organization* 73(3): 579–610.

Horn, Henrik, Petros C. Mavroidis, and Hakan Nordstrom. 1999. "Is the Use of the WTO Dispute Settlement System Biased?" CEPR Discussion Papers. https://cepr.org/active/publications/discussion_papers/dp.php?dpno=2340.

Hülsse, Rainer. 2008. "Even Clubs Can't Do without Legitimacy: Why the Anti–Money Laundering Blacklist Was Suspended." *Regulation and Governance* 2(4): 459–79.

Hülsse, Rainer, and Dieter Kerwer. 2007. "Global Standards in Action: Insights from Anti–Money Laundering Regulation." *Organization* 14(5): 625–42.

Hurd, Ian. 1999. "Legitimacy and Authority in International Politics." *International Organization* 53(2): 379–408.

Hurd, Ian. 2017. *How to Do Things with International Law.* Princeton, NJ: Princeton University Press.

Huth, Paul K., Sarah E. Croco, and Benjamin J. Appel. 2011. "Does International Law Promote the Peaceful Settlement of International Disputes? Evidence from the Study of Territorial Conflicts since 1945." *American Political Science Review* 105(2): 415–36.

Huth, Paul K., Sarah E. Croco, and Benjamin J. Appel. 2013. "Bringing Law to the Table: Legal Claims, Focal Points, and the Settlement of Territorial Disputes since 1945." *American Journal of Political Science* 57(1): 90–103.

Ikenberry, G. John, and Charles A. Kupchan. 1990. "Socialization and Hegemonic Power." *International Organization* 44(3): 283–315.

IMF. 2007. *Thailand: Detailed Assessment Report on Anti–Money Laundering and Combating the Financing of Terrorism.* Paris: FATF/OECD.

IMF Legal Department. 2011 (May). *Anti–Money Laundering and Combating the Financing of Terrorism (AML/CFT): Report on the Review of the Effectiveness of the Program.* International Monetary Fund, 1–97.

IMF and World Bank. 2016 (December). "Development of Local Currency Bond Markets: Overview of Recent Developments and Key Themes." Staff Note for the G20 IFAWG, 1–33.

International Chamber of Commerce. 2017. *Rethinking Trade and Finance 2017.* Paris: ICC.

Jacob, Marc. 2014. *Precedents and Case-Based Reasoning in the European Court of Justice: Unfinished Business.* Cambridge: Cambridge University Press.

Jacobsson, Bengt. 2000. "Standardization and Expert Knowledge." In *A World of Standards*, edited by Nils Brunsson, Bengt Jacobsson, and associates. Oxford: Oxford University Press.

Jakobi, Anja P. 2013. *Common Goods and Evils? The Formation of Global Crime Governance*. Oxford: Oxford University Press.

Jakobi, Anja P. 2015. "Global Networks against Crime: Using the Financial Action Task Force as a Model?" *International Journal* 70(3): 391–407.

Jakobi, Anja P. 2018. "Governing Illicit Finance in Transnational Security Spaces: The FATF and Anti–Money Laundering." *Crime, Law and Social Change* 69(2): 173–90.

James, Scott C., and David A. Lake. 1989. "The Second Face of Hegemony: Britain's Repeal of the Corn Laws and the American Walker Tariff of 1846." *International Organization* 43(1): 1–29.

Jamieson, Craig. 2006 (April). "Reputation Damage: The Price Riggs Paid." World Check (website). https://www.world-check.com/media/d/content_whitepaper_reference/whitepaper-3.pdf.

Jensen, Nathan M. 2008. *Nation-States and the Multinational Corporation: A Political Economy of Foreign Direct Investment*. Princeton, NJ: Princeton University Press.

Jerven, Morten. 2013. *Poor Numbers: How We Are Misled by African Development Statistics and What to Do about It*. Ithaca, NY: Cornell University Press.

Jo, Hyeran, Brian J. Phillips, and Joshua Alley. 2020. "Can Blacklisting Reduce Terrorist Attacks?" In *The Power of Global Performance Indicators*, edited by Judith G. Kelley and Beth A. Simmons. New York: Cambridge University Press.

Johns, Leslie, and Rachel L. Wellhausen. 2016. "Under One Roof: Supply Chains and the Protection of Foreign Investment." *American Political Science Review* 110(1): 31–51.

Johnston, Alastair Iain. 2001. "Treating International Institutions as Social Environments." *International Studies Quarterly* 45(4): 487–515.

Kahneman, Daniel. 2003. "A Psychological Perspective on Economics." *American Economic Review* 93(2): 162–68.

Kapstein, Ethan B. 1989. "Resolving the Regulator's Dilemma: International Coordination of Banking Regulations." *International Organization* 43(2): 323–47.

Kapstein, Ethan B. 1992. "Between Power and Purpose: Central Bankers and the Politics of Regulatory Convergence." *International Organization* 43(2): 323–47.

Kapstein, Ethan B. 1994. *Governing the Global Economy: International Finance and the State*. Cambridge, MA: Harvard University Press.

Karlsson-Vinkhuyzen, Sylvia I., and Antto Vihma. 2009. "Comparing the Legitimacy and Effectiveness of Global Hard and Soft Law: An Analytical Framework." *Regulation and Governance* 3(4): 400–420.

Katzenstein, Peter J. 2009. "Mid-Atlantic: Sitting on the Knife's Sharp Edge." *Review of International Political Economy* 16:122–35.

Katzenstein, Peter J., Robert O. Keohane, and Stephen D. Krasner. 1998. "International Organization and the Study of World Politics." *International Organization* 52(4): 645–85.

Katzenstein, Peter J., and Stephen C. Nelson. 2013. "Reading the Right Signals and Reading the Signals Right: IPE and the Financial Crisis." *Review of International Political Economy* 20(5): 1101–31.

Keck, Margaret E., and Kathryn Sikkink. 1998. *Activists beyond Borders: Advocacy Networks in International Politics*. Ithaca, NY: Cornell University Press.

Keefer, Philip, and David Stasavage. 2003. "The Limits of Delegation: Veto Players, Central Bank Independence, and the Credibility of Monetary Policy." *American Political Science Review* 97(3): 407–23.

Keleman, R. Daniel, and Terence K. Teo. 2014. "Law, Focal Points, and Fiscal Discipline in the United States and the European Union." *American Political Science Review* 108(2): 355–70.

Kelley, Judith G. 2017. *Scorecard Diplomacy: Grading States to Influence Their Reputation and Behavior*. New York: Cambridge University Press.

Kelley, Judith G., and Beth A. Simmons. 2015. "Politics by Number: Indicators as Social Pressure in International Relations." *American Journal of Political Science* 59(1): 55–70.

Kelley, Judith G., and Beth A. Simmons. 2019. "Introduction: The Power of Global Performance Indicators." *International Organization* 73(3): 491–510.

Kelley, Judith G., Beth A. Simmons, and Rush Doshi. 2019. "The Power of Ranking: The Ease of Doing Business Report as a Form of Social Pressure." *International Organization* 73(3): 611–43.

Keohane, Robert O. 1984. *After Hegemony: Cooperation and Discord in the World Political Economy*. Princeton, NJ: Princeton University Press.

Keohane, Robert O., and Helen V. Milner. 1996. *Internationalization and Domestic Politics*. Cambridge: Cambridge University Press.

Keohane, Robert O., and Joseph S. Nye. 1977. *Power and Interdependence: World Politics in Transition*. Boston: Little, Brown.

Keynes, John Maynard. 1936. *The General Theory of Employment Interest and Money*. London: Macmillan.

Kijima, Rie, and Phillip Y. Lipscy. 2020. "International Assessments and Educational Policy: Evidence from an Elite Survey." In *The Power of Global Performance Indicators*, edited by Judith G. Kelley and Beth A. Simmons. New York: Cambridge University Press.

Kirshner, Jonathan. 2003. "Money Is Politics." *Review of International Political Economy* 10(4): 645–60.

Kirshner, Jonathan. 2007. *Appeasing Bankers: Financial Caution on the Road to War*. Princeton, NJ: Princeton University Press.

Kirshner, Jonathan. 2014a. *American Power after the Financial Crisis*. Ithaca, NY: Cornell University Press.

Kirshner, Jonathan. 2014b. "Same as It Ever Was? Continuity and Change in the International Monetary System." *Review of International Political Economy* 21(5): 1007–16.

Kirton, John J., Marina Larionova, and Paolo Savona. 2010. *Making Global Economic Governance Effective: Hard and Soft Law Institutions in a Crowded World*. London: Ashgate.

Kocher, M. G., and S. T. Trautmann. 2013. "Selection into Auctions for Risky and Ambiguous Prospects." *Economic Inquiry* 51:882–95.

Koliev, Faradj, Thomas Sommerer, and Jonas Tallberg. 2020. "Reporting Matters: Performance Indicators and Compliance in the International Labor Organization." In *The Power of Global Performance Indicators*, edited by Judith G. Kelley and Beth A. Simmons. New York: Cambridge University Press.

Krugman, Paul. 2010 (April 25). "Berating the Raters." *New York Times*. https://www.nytimes.com/2010/04/26/opinion/26krugman.html.

Kucik, Jeffrey, and Kryzysztof J. Pelc. 2016. "Do International Rulings Have Spillover Effects? The View from Financial Markets." *World Politics* 68(4): 713–51.

Kurzer, Paulette. 1993. *Business and Banking: Political Change and Economic Integration in Western Europe*. Ithaca, NY: Cornell University Press.

Lagarde, Christine. 2016 (July). "Relations in Banking—Making It Work for Everyone." Speech to New York Fed, 1–9.

Lake, David A. 1993. "Leadership, Hegemony, and the International Economy: Naked Emperor or Tattered Monarch with Potential?" *International Studies Quarterly* 37(4): 459–89.

Lake, David A. 2009a. *Hierarchy in International Relations.* Ithaca, NY: Cornell University Press.

Lake, David A. 2009b. "Open Economy Politics: A Critical Review." *Review of International Organizations* 4(3): 219–44.

Lall, Ranjit. 2012. "From Failure to Failure: The Politics of International Banking Regulation." *Review of International Political Economy* 19(4): 609–38.

Lall, Ranjit. 2020. "Assessing International Organizations: Competition, Collaboration, and the Politics of Funding." In *The Power of Global Performance Indicators*, edited by Judith G. Kelley and Beth A. Simmons. New York: Cambridge University Press.

Lane, Philip R., and Gian Maria Milesi-Ferretti. 2017. "International Financial Integration in the Aftermath of the Global Financial Crisis." IMF Working Paper WP/17/115. https://www.imf.org/en/Publications/WP/Issues/2017/05/10/International-Financial-Integration-in-the-Aftermath-of-the-Global-Financial-Crisis-44906.

Laurence, Henry. 2001. *Money Rules: The New Politics of Finance in Britain and Japan.* Ithaca, NY: Cornell University Press.

Lebovic, James H., and Erik Voeten. 2009. "The Cost of Shame: International Organizations and Foreign Aid in the Punishing of Human Rights Violators." *Journal of Peace Research* 46(1): 79–97.

Lee, Melissa M., and Aila M. Matanock. 2020. "Third-Party Policymakers and the Limits of the Influence of Indicators." In *The Power of Global Performance Indicators*, edited by Judith G. Kelley and Beth A. Simmons. New York: Cambridge University Press.

Leong, Angela Veng Mei. 2007. "Chasing Dirty Money: Domestic and International Measures against Money Laundering." *Journal of Money Laundering Control* 10(2): 140–56.

Levi, Michael. 2002. "Money Laundering and Its Regulation." *Annals of the American Academy of Political Science and Social Science* 582:181–94.

Levi, Michael. 2015. "Money for Crime and Money from Crime: Financing Crime and Laundering Crime Proceeds." *European Journal on Criminal Policy and Research* 21(2): 275–97.

Levi, Michael, and W. Gilmore. 2002. "Terrorist Finance, Money Laundering and the Rise of Mutual Evaluation: A New Paradigm for Crime Control." In *Financing Terrorism*, edited by M. Pieth. Dordrecht: Kluwer.

Levi, Michael, and Peter Reuter. 2006. "Money Laundering." *Crime and Justice* 34(1): 289–375.

Levi-Faur, David. 2005. "The Global Diffusion of Regulatory Capitalism." *Annals of the American Academy of Political and Social Science* 598(1): 1232.

Loffler, Gunter. 2005. "Avoiding the Rating Bounce: Why Rating Agencies Are Slow to React to New Information." *Journal of Economic Behavior and Organization* 56(3): 365–81.

Madsen, Frank. 2009. *Transnational Organized Crime.* New York: Routledge.

Mansfield, Edward D, Helen V. Milner, and B. Peter Rosendorff. 2002. "Why Democracies Cooperate More: Electoral Control and International Trade Agreements." *International Organization* 56(3): 477–513.

March, James G., and Johan P. Olsen. 1998. "The Institutional Dynamics of International Political Orders." *International Organization* 52(4): 943–69.

March, James G., and Herbert W. Simon. 1958. *Organizations*. New York: Wiley.

Martin, Lisa L. 1992. "Interests, Power, and Multilateralism." *International Organization* 46(4): 765–92.

Martin, Lisa L. 2000. *Democratic Commitments: Legislatures and International Cooperation*. Princeton, NJ: Princeton University Press.

Martin, Lisa L. 2011. "Against Compliance." Working paper. https://papers.ssrn.com/sol3/papers.cfm?abstract_id=1900163.

Martin, Lisa L., and Beth Simmons. 2012. "International Organizations and Institutions." In *Handbook of International Relations*, edited by Walter Carlsnaes, Thomas Risse, and Beth Simmons. London: SAGE.

Masciandaro, Donato. 2005. "False and Reluctant Friends? National Money Laundering Regulation, International Compliance and Non-cooperative Countries." *European Journal of Law and Economics* 20:17–30.

Mattli, Walter, and Ngaire Woods. 2009. *The Politics of Global Regulations*. Princeton, NJ: Princeton University Press.

McAdams, Richard H. 2005. "The Expressive Power of Adjudication." *University of Illinois Law Review* (5): 1043–1122.

McAdams, Richard H., and Janice Nadler. 2005. "Testing the Focal Point Theory of Legal Compliance: The Effect of Third-Party Expression in an Experimental Hawk/Dove Game." *Journal of Empirical Legal Studies* 2(1): 87–123.

McKeen-Edwards, Heather, and Tony Porter. 2013. *Transnational Financial Associations and the Governance of Global Finance: Assembling Wealth and Power*. New York: Routledge.

McNamara, Kathleen R. 2008. "A Rivalry in the Making? The Euro and International Monetary Power." *Review of International Political Economy* 15(3): 439–59.

Mearsheimer, John. 1995. "The False Promise of International Institutions." *International Security* 19(3): 5–49.

Medina, Leandro, and Fredrich Schneider. 2018. "Shadow Economies around the World: What Did We Learn over the Last 20 Years?" IMF Working Paper No. 18/17.

Merry, Sally Engle. 2011. "Measuring the World." *Current Anthropology* 52(S3): S83–S95.

Milgrom, Paul R., Douglass C. North, and Barry R. Weingast. 1990. "The Role of Institutions in the Revival of Trade: The Law Merchant, Private Judges, and the Champagne Fairs." *Economics and Politics* 2(1): 1–23.

Mitsilegas, Valsamis. 2003. "Countering the Chameleon Threat of Dirty Money: 'Hard' and 'Soft' Law in the Emergence of a Global Regime against Money Laundering and Terrorist Finance." In *From Transnational Organized Crime: Perspectives on Global Security*, edited by Adam Edwards and Peter Gill. London: Routledge.

Molyneux, Philip, Yener Altunbas, and Edward Gardener. 1996. *Efficiency in European Banking*. Chichester: Wiley.

Moody's. 2016 (24 February). Cross-Sector—Panama: Panama's Removal from the Money Laundering Grey List Is Credit Positive for the Sovereign and Banks. *Moody's Credit Ratings*.

Moravcsik, Andrew. 1995. "Explaining International Human Rights Regimes: Liberal Theory and Western Europe." *European Journal of International Relations* 1(2): 157–89.

Morris, Stephen, and Hyun Song Shin. 2002. "Social Value of Public Information." *American Economic Review* 92(5): 1521–34.

Morrow, James D. 2007. "When Do States Follow the Laws of War?" *American Political Science Review* 101(3): 559–72.

Morse, Julia C. 2019. "Blacklists, Market Enforcement, and the Global Regime to Combat Terrorist Financing." *International Organization* 73(3): 511–45.

Moschella, Manuela. 2013. "Designing the Financial Stability Board: A Theoretical Investigation of Mandate, Discretion, and Membership." *Journal of International Relations and Development* 16(3): 380–405.

Mosley, Layna. 2000. "Room to Move: International Financial Markets and National Welfare States." *International Organization* 54(4): 737–73.

Mosley, Layna. 2003a. *Global Capital and National Governments*. New York: Cambridge University Press.

Mosley, Layna. 2003b. "Attempting Global Standards: National Governments, International Finance, and the IMF's Data Regime." *Review of International Political Economy* 10(2): 331–62.

Mosley, Layna, and David Singer. 2009. "The Global Financial Crisis: Lesson and Opportunities for International Political Economy." *International Interactions* 35(4): 420–29.

Mummolo, Jonathan, and Erik Peterson. 2018. "Improving the Interpretation of Fixed Effects Regression Results." *Political Science Research and Methods* 6(4): 829–35.

Nance, Mark T. 2015. "Naming and Shaming in Financial Regulation: Explaining Variation in the Financial Action Task Force on Money Laundering." In *The Politics of Leverage in International Relations: Name, Shame, and Sanction*, edited by H. Richard Friedman. New York: Palgrave Macmillan.

Nance, Mark T. 2018a. "The Regime That FATF Built: An Introduction to the Financial Action Task Force." *Crime, Law and Social Change* 69:109–29.

Nance, Mark T. 2018b. "Re-thinking FATF: An Experimentalist Interpretation of the Financial Action Task Force." *Crime, Law, and Social Change* 69(2): 131–52.

Nance, Mark T., and M. Patrick Cottrell. 2014. "A Turn toward Experimentalism? Rethinking Security and Governance in the Twenty-First Century." *Review of International Studies* 40(2): 277–301.

Naylor, Robin Thomas. 1999. "Wash-Out: A Critique of Follow-the-Money Methods in Crime Control Policy." *Crime, Law, and Social Change* 32(1): 1–57.

Newman, Abraham, and David Bach. 2014. "The European Union as Hardening Agent: Soft Law and the Diffusion of Global Financial Regulation." *Journal of European Public Policy* 21(3): 430–52.

Newman, Abraham, and Elliot Posner. 2016. "Transnational Feedback, Soft Law, and Preferences in Global Financial Regulation." *Review of International Political Economy* 23(1): 123–52.

Newman, Abraham L., and Elliot Posner. 2018. *Voluntary Disruptions: International Soft Law, Finance, and Power*. New York: Oxford University Press.

Niepmann, Friederike, and Tim Schmidt-Eisenlohr. 2017. "International Trade, Risk and the Role of Banks." *Journal of International Economics* 107(C): 111–26.

Norloff, Carla. 2014. "Dollar Hegemony: A Power Analysis." *Review of International Political Economy* 21(5): 1042–70.

Norman, Ben, Rachel Shaw, and George Speight. 2011 (June). "The History of Interbank Settlement Arrangements: Exploring Central Banks' Role in the Payment System." Bank of England Working Paper, 1–33.

North, Douglass C., and Barry R. Weingast. 1989. "Constitutions and Commitment: The Evolution of Institutions Governing Public Choice in Seventeenth-Century England." *Journal of Economic History* 49(4): 803–32.

Oates, Wallace E. 1972. *Fiscal Federalism*. New York: Harcourt Brace Jovanovich.

Oatley, Thomas. 2011. "The Reductionist Gamble: Open Economy Politics in the Global Economy." *International Organization* 65(2): 311–41.

Oatley, Thomas, and Robert Nabors. 1998. "Redistributive Cooperation: Market Failure, Wealth Transfers, and the Basel Accord." *International Organization* 52(1): 35–54.

Obstfeld, M. 2012. "Financial Flows, Financial Crises, and Global Imbalances." *Journal of International Money and Finance* 31:469–80.

Opp, Christian C., Marcus M. Opp, and Milton Harris. 2013. "Rating Agencies in the Face of Regulation." *Journal of Financial Economics* 108(1): 46–61.

Pagliari, Stefano, and Eric Helleiner. 2010. "Crisis and the Reform of International Financial Regulation." In *Global Finance in Crisis: The Politics of International Financial Regulation*, edited by Eric Helleiner, Stefano Pagliari, and Hubert Zimmerman. New York: Routledge.

Palan, Ronen. 2003. *The Offshore World: Sovereign Markets, Virtual Places, and Nomad Millionaires*. Ithaca, NY: Cornell University Press.

Peinhardt, Clint, and Todd Sandler. 2015. *Transnational Cooperation: An Issue-Based Approach*. New York: Oxford University Press.

Pelc, Krzystof J. 2014. "The Politics of Precedent in International Law: A Social Network Application." *American Political Science Review* 108(3): 547–64.

Pepinsky, Thomas B. 2013. "The Domestic Politics of Financial Internationalization in the Developing World." *Review of International Political Economy* 20(4): 848–80.

Perlman, Rebecca L. 2020. "The Domestic Impact of International Standards." *International Studies Quarterly* 64(3): 600–608.

Pierson, Paul. 1993. "When Effect Becomes Cause: Policy Feedback and Political Change." *World Politics* 45(4): 595–628.

Pierson, Paul. 2006. "Public Policies as Institutions." In *Rethinking Political Institutions*, edited by Ian Shapiro, Stephen Skowronek, and Daniel Galvin. New York: New York University Press.

Pinheiro-Alves, Ricardo, and João Zambujal-Oliveira. 2012. "The Ease of Doing Business Index as a Tool for Investment Location Decisions." *Economics Letters* 117(1): 66–70.

Pinker, Steven, Martin A. Nowak, and James J. Lee. 2008 (January). "The Logic of Indirect Speech." *Proceedings of the National Academy of Sciences of the United States of America (PNAS)* 105(3): 833–38.

Pokalova, Elena. 2015. "Legislative Responses to Terrorism: What Drives States to Adopt New Counterterrorism Legislation?" *Terrorism and Political Violence* 27(3): 474–96.

Porter, Tony, and Duncan Wood. 2002. "Reform without Representation? The International and Transnational Dialogue on the Global Financial Architecture." In *Debating the Global Financial Architecture*, edited by Leslie Elliott Armijo. New York: SUNY Press.

Posner, Elliot. 2009. "Making Rules for Global Finance: Transatlantic Regulatory Cooperation at the Turn of the Millennium." *International Organization* 63(4): 665–99.

Poszar, Zoltan, Tobias Adrian, Adam Ashcraft, and Hayley Boesky. 2010. *Shadow Banking*. Federal Reserve Bank of New York Staff Report no. 458.

Powell, Emilia Justyna, and Sara McLaughlin Mitchell. 2007. "The International Court of Justice and the World's Three Legal Systems." *Journal of Politics* 69(2): 397–415.

Pratt, Tyler. 2018. "Deference and Hierarchy in International Regime Complexes." *International Organization* 72(3): 561–90.

Putnam, Robert D. 1988. "Diplomacy and Domestic Politics: The Logic of Two-Level Games." *International Organization* 42(3): 427–60.

Quadir, Regina. 2012 (February 14). "The Great Flood of 2011, Thailand: A Firsthand Account." Centers for Disease Control and Prevention Blog. https://blogs.cdc. gov/publichealthmatters/2012/02/the-great-flood-of-2011-thailand-a-firsthand-account-3/.

Quaglia, Lucia. 2019. "The Politics of State Compliance with International 'Soft Law' in Finance." *Governance* 32(1): 45–62.

Raustiala, Kal. 1997. "States, NGOs, and International Environmental Institutions." *International Studies Quarterly* 41:719–40.

Raustiala, Kal. 2002. "The Architecture of International Cooperation: Transgovernmental Networks and the Future of International Law." *Virginia Journal of International Law* 43(1): 1–90.

Raustiala, Kal, and David G. Victor. 1998. "Conclusions." In *The Implementation and Effectiveness of International Environmental Commitments*, edited by David Victor, Kal Raustiala, and Eugene B. Skolniko. Cambridge, MA: MIT Press.

Rawlings, Greg, and Brigitte Unger. 2008. "Competing for Criminal Money." *Global Business and Economics Review* 10(3): 331–52.

Rethel, Lena. 2011. "Whose Legitimacy? Islamic Finance and the Global Financial Order." *Review of International Political Economy* 18(1): 75–98.

Reuter, Peter, and Edwin M. Truman. 2004. *Chasing Dirty Money: The Fight against Money Laundering*. Washington, DC: Institute for International Economics.

Risse, Thomas, and Kathryn Sikkink. 1999. "The Socialization of International Human Rights Norms into Domestic Practices: Introduction." In *The Power of Human Rights: International Norms and Domestic Change*, edited by Thomas Risse, Stephen C. Ropp, and Kathryn Sikkink. New York: Cambridge University Press.

Risse-Kappen, Thomas. 1995. *Bringing Transnational Actors Back In*. Cambridge: Cambridge University Press.

Roberge, Ian. 2009. "Bringing the United States Back." In "A Response to Rainer Hülsse's 'Creating Demand for Global Governance . . .'" *Global Society* 23:177–81.

Roberge, Ian. 2011. "Financial Action Task Force." In *The Handbook of Transnational Governance: Institutions and Innovations*, edited by Thomas Hale and David Held. Cambridge, MA: Polity.

Roberts, Jordan, and Juan Tellez. 2020. "Freedom House's Scarlet Letter: Assessment Power through Transnational Pressure." In *The Power of Global Performance Indicators*, edited by Judith G. Kelley and Beth A. Simmons. New York: Cambridge University Press.

Rodrik, Dani. 1997 (Summer). "Sense and Nonsense in the Globalization Debate." *Foreign Policy* 107: 19–37.

Rogo, Kenneth. 1985. "The Optimal Degree of Commitment to an Intermediate Monetary Target." *Quarterly Journal of Economics* 100:1169–89.

Rosenbluth, Frances, and Ross Schaap. 2003. "The Domestic Politics of Banking Regulation." *International Organization* 57(2): 307–36.

Rosendorff, B. Peter, and Helen V. Milner. 2001. "The Optimal Design of International Trade Institutions: Uncertainty and Escape." *International Organization* 55(4): 829–57.

Rubenfeld, Samuel. 2011 (11 November). "FATF Removes Ukraine from Blacklist, Updates on Argentina." *Wall Street Journal*.

Sabel, Charles F., and Jonathan Zeitlin. 2010. *Experimentalist Governance in the European Union: Towards a New Architecture*. New York: Oxford University Press.

Sansonetti, R. 2000. "The Mutual Evaluation Process: A Methodology of Increasing Importance at International Level." *Journal of Financial Crime* 7(3): 218–26.

Sarin, R. K., and M. Weber. 1993. "Effects of Ambiguity in Market Experiments." *Management Science* 39:602–15.

Schafer, Armin. 2006. "A New Form of Governance? Comparing the Open Method of Co-ordination to Multilateral Surveillance by the IMF and the OECD." *Journal of European Public Policy* 13(1): 70–88.

Schelling, Thomas. 1960. *The Strategy of Conflict*. Cambridge, MA: Harvard University Press.

Schott, Paul Allen. 2003. *Reference Guide to Anti–Money Laundering and Combating the Financing of Terrorism*. Washington, DC: World Bank.

Schueth, Sam. 2015. "Winning the Rankings Game: The Republic of Georgia, USAID, and the Doing Business Project." In *Ranking the World: Grading States as a Tool of Global Governance*, edited by Alexander Cooley and Jack Snyder. New York: Cambridge University Press.

Schultz, Kenneth A., and Barry R. Weingast. 2003. "The Democratic Advantage: Institutional Foundations of Financial Power in International Competition." *International Organization* 57(1): 3–42.

Searle, John. 1975. "Indirect Speech Acts." In *Volume Three: Speech Acts*, edited by Peter Cole and Jerry L. Morgan. New York: Academic Press.

Searle, John. 1979. *Expression and Meaning: Studies in the Theory of Speech Acts*. Cambridge: Cambridge University Press.

Shaffer, Gregory C., and Mark A. Pollack. 2009. "Hard vs. Soft Law: Alternatives, Complements, and Antagonists in International Governance." *Minnesota Law Review* 94:706–99.

Sharman, J. C. 2005. "South Pacific Tax Havens: From Leaders in the Bottom to Laggards in the Race to the Top?" *Accounting Forum* 29(3): 311–23.

Sharman, J. C. 2006. *Havens in a Storm: The Struggle for Global Tax Regulation*. Ithaca, NY: Cornell University Press.

Sharman, J. C. 2008. "Power and Discourse in Policy Diffusion: Anti–Money Laundering in Developing States." *International Studies Quarterly* 52(3): 635–56.

Sharman, J. C. 2009. "The Bark Is the Bite: International Organizations and Blacklisting." *Review of International Political Economy* 16(4): 573–96.

Sharman, J. C. 2011. *The Money Laundry: Regulating Criminal Finance in the Global Economy*. Ithaca, NY: Cornell University Press.

Shin, Hyun Song. 2014. "The Second Phase of Global Liquidity and Its Impact on Emerging Economies." In *Volatile Capital Flows in Korea: Current Policies and Future Responses*, edited by Kyuil Chung, Soyoung Kim, Hail Park, Changho Choi, and Hyun Song Shin. New York: Palgrave Macmillan.

Shor, Eran. 2017. "The Spatial Diffusion of Counterterrorist Legislation, 1970–2011." *Social Problems* 64(1): 106–32.

Sica, Vincent. 2000. "Cleaning the Laundry: States and the Monitoring of the Financial System." *Millennium: Journal of International Studies* 29(1): 47–72.

Simmons, Beth A. 1998. "Compliance with International Agreements." *Annual Review of Political Science* 1(1): 75–93.

Simmons, Beth A. 2000a. "International Law and State Behavior: Commitment and Compliance in International Monetary Affairs." *American Political Science Review* 94(4): 819.

Simmons, Beth A. 2000b. "International Efforts against Money Laundering." In *Commitment and Compliance: The Role of Non-binding Norms in the International Legal System*, edited by D. Shelton. Oxford: Oxford University Press.

Simmons, Beth A. 2001. "The International Politics of Harmonization: The Case of Capital Market Regulation." *International Organization* 55(3): 589–620.

Simmons, Beth A. 2009. *Mobilizing for Human Rights. International Law in Domestic Politics.* New York: Cambridge University Press.

Simmons, Beth A., and Zachary Elkins. 2004. "The Globalization of Liberalization: Policy Diffusion in the International Political Economy." *American Political Science Review* 98(1): 171–89.

Simmons, Beth A., Frank Dobbin, and Geoffrey Garrett. 2006. "Introduction: The International Diffusion of Liberalism." *International Organization* 60(4): 781–810.

Singer, David Andrew. 2004. "Capital Rules? The Domestic Politics of International Regulatory Harmonization." *International Organization* 58(3): 531–65.

Singer, David Andrew. 2007. *Regulating Capital: Setting Standards for the International Financial System.* Ithaca, NY: Cornell University Press.

Skagerlind, Helena Hede. 2020. "The Power of Indicators in Global Development Policy: The Millennium Development Goals." In *The Power of Global Performance Indicators,* edited by Judith G. Kelley and Beth A. Simmons. New York: Cambridge University Press.

Slaughter, Anne-Marie. 1995. "International Law in a World of Liberal States." *European Journal of International Law* 6(3): 503–38.

Slaughter, Anne-Marie. 2004. *A New World Order.* Princeton, NJ: Princeton University Press.

Snow, Arthur. 2011. "Ambiguity Aversion and the Propensities for Self-Insurance and Self-Protection." *Journal of Risk and Uncertainty* 42:27–43.

Standard & Poor's. 2014. *Guide to Credit Rating Essentials: What Are Credit Ratings and How Do They Work?* New York: McGraw-Hill Financial.

Steinberg, Richard H. 2002. *The Greening of Trade Law: International Trade Organizations and Environmental Issues.* Lanham, MD: Rowman & Littlefield.

Stephen, Matthew D. 2015. "'Can You Pass the Salt?' The Legitimacy of International Institutions and Indirect Speech." *European Journal of International Relations* 21(4): 768–92.

Stone, Randall W. 2011. *Controlling Institutions: International Organizations and the Global Economy.* New York: Cambridge University Press.

Suchman, Mark C. 1995. "Managing Legitimacy: Strategic and Institutional Approaches." *Academy of Management Review* 20(3): 571–610.

Takats, Elod, and Stefan Avdjiev. 2014. "Cross-Border Bank Lending during the Taper Tantrum: The Role of Emerging Market Fundamentals." *BIS Quarterly Review.* https://econpapers.repec.org/article/bisbisqtr/1409g.htm.

Tomz, Michael. 2007. *Reputation and International Cooperation: Sovereign Debt across Three Centuries.* Princeton, NJ: Princeton University Press.

Trautmann, Stefan T., and Gijs van de Kuilen. 2015. "Chapter 3: Ambiguity Attitudes." In *The Wiley Blackwell Handbook of Judgment and Decision Making,* edited by Gideon Keren and George Wu. West Sussex: John Wiley & Sons.

Trautmann, Stefan T., F. M. Vieider, and P. P. Wakker. 2008. "Cause of Ambiguity Aversion: Known versus Unknown Preferences." *Journal of Risk and Uncertainty* 36:225–43.

Tsingou, Eleni. 2008. "Transnational Private Governance and Basel II." In *Transnational Private Governance and Its Limits,* edited by J. Graz and A. Nolke. London: Routledge.

Tsingou, Eleni. 2010. "Global Financial Governance and the Developing Anti–Money Laundering Regime: What Lessons for International Political Economy?" *International Politics* 47(6): 617–37.

Tsingou, Eleni. 2015. "Club Governance and the Making of Global Financial Rules." *Review of International Political Economy* 22(2): 225–56.

Underhill, Geoffrey R. D., and Xiaoke Zhang. 2008. "Setting the Rules: Private Power, Political Underpinnings, and Legitimacy in Global Monetary and Financial Governance." *International Affairs* 84(3): 535–54.

Unger, Brigitte, and Joras Ferwerda. 2008. "Regulating Money Laundering and Tax Havens: The Role of Blacklisting." Tjalling C. Koopmans Research Institution Discussion Paper Series, 1–35. https://www.uu.nl/sites/default/files/rebo_use_dp_2008_08-12.pdf.

UNODC (United Nations Office on Drugs and Crime). 2011. *In-Depth Evaluation of the United Nations Global Programme against Money Laundering, Proceeds of Crime and the Financing of Terrorism (GPML).* New York: United Nations.

US Department of Justice. 2012 (December). "HSBC Holdings Plc. and HSBC Bank USA N.A. Admit to Anti–Money Laundering and Sanctions Violations, Forfeit 1.256 Billion in Deferred Prosecution Agreement." https://www.justice.gov/opa/pr/hsbc-holdings-plc-and-hsbc-bank-usa-na-admit-anti-money-laundering-and-sanctions-violations.

US Department of State. 2011. *International Narcotics Control Strategy Report.* Vol. 2. Washington, DC: US Department of State, 1–383.

US Department of State. 2012. *International Narcotics Control Strategy Report.* Vol. 2. Washington, DC: US Department of State.

US Department of State. 2019. *International Narcotics Control Strategy Report.* Vol. 2. Washington, DC: US Department of State, 1–198.

Vabulas, Felicity. Forthcoming. "Informality in International Political Economy." In *The Oxford Handbook of International Political Economy,* edited by Jon Pevehouse and Leonard Seabrooke. Oxford: Oxford University Press.

Vabulas, Felicity, and Duncan Snidal. 2013. "Organization without Delegation: Informal Intergovernmental Organizations (IIGOs) and the Spectrum of Intergovernmental Arrangements." *Review of International Organizations* 8(2): 193–220.

Vabulas, Felicity, and Duncan Snidal. 2020. "Cooperation under Autonomy: Building and Analyzing the Informal Intergovernmental Organizations 2.0 Dataset." *Journal of Peace Research.* https://journals.sagepub.com/doi/full/10.1177/0022343320943920.

Vajs, Stephen. 2014 (February). "Government Debt Issuance: Issues for Central Banks." In *The Role of Central Banks in Macroeconomic and Financial Stability,* edited by M. S. Mohanty. Bank for International Settlements, BIS Papers No. 76.

Van Duyne, Petrus C. 1998. "Money-Laundering: Pavlov's Dog and Beyond." *Howard Journal of Criminal Justice* 37(4): 359–74.

Van Fossen, Anthony B. 2003. "Money Laundering, Global Financial Instability, and Tax Havens in the Pacific Islands." *Contemporary Pacific* 15(2): 237–75.

Verdier, Pierre-Hugues. 2009. "Transnational Regulatory Networks and Their Limits." *Yale Journal of International Law* 34:113–231.

Verhage, Antoinette. 2011. *The Anti Money Laundering Complex and the Compliance Industry.* New York: Routledge.

Vinuales, Jorge E. 2008. "The Contribution of the International Court of Justice to the Development of International Environmental Law: A Contemporary Assessment." *Fordham International Law Journal* 32(1): 232–58.

Voeten, Erik. 2005. "The Political Origins of the UN Security Council's Ability to Legitimize the Use of Force." *International Organization* 59(3): 541.

Vogel, Steven. 1996. *Freer Markets, More Rules*. Ithaca, NY: Cornell University Press.

Volgy, Thomas J., Elizabeth Fausett, Keith A. Grant, and Stuart Rodgers. 2008. "Identifying Formal Intergovernmental Organizations." *Journal of Peace Research* 45(6): 837–50.

Von Stein, Jana. 2005. "Do Treaties Constrain or Screen? Selection Bias and Treaty Compliance." *American Political Science Review* 99(4): 611–22.

Von Stein, Jana. 2008. "The International Law and Politics of Climate Change: Ratification of the United Nations Framework Convention and the Kyoto Protocol." *Journal of Conflict Resolution* 52(2): 243–68.

Walter, Andrew. 2008. *Governing Finance: East Asia's Adoption of International Standards*. Ithaca, NY: Cornell University Press.

Walter, Andrew. 2010. "Chinese Attitudes toward Global Financial Regulatory Cooperation: Revisionist or Status Quo?" In *Global Finance in Crisis: The Politics of International Regulatory Change*, edited by Eric Helleiner, Stefano Pagliari, and Hubert Zimmerman. London: Routledge.

Warde, Ibrahim. 2007. *The Price of Fear: The Truth behind the Financial War on Terror*. New York: Palgrave Macmillan.

Weingast, Barry R. 1997. "The Political Foundations of Democracy and the Rule of Law." *American Political Science Review* 91(2): 245–63.

Whitaker, Beth Elise. 2007. "Exporting the Patriot Act? Democracy and the 'War on Terror' in the Third World." *Third World Quarterly* 28(5): 1017–1032.

Wilf, Meredith. 2016. "Credibility and Distributional Effects of International Banking Regulations: Evidence from US Bank Stock Returns." *International Organization* 70(4): 763–96.

Williams, Morvin G. 2016. "De-risking/De-banking: The Reality Facing Caribbean Financial Institutions." Central Bank of the Bahamas Working Paper. https://cdn.centralbankbahamas.com/documents/2019-06-12-05-15-04-De-Risking-De-Banking-the-Reality-Facing-Caribbean-Financial-Institutions.pdf.

Williams, Phil. 2003. "Transnational Organized Crime and the State." In *The Emergence of Private Authority in Global Governance*, edited by Rodney Bruce Hall and Thomas J. Biersteker. Cambridge: Cambridge University Press.

World Bank. 2017. "Thailand Economic Monitor 2017." http://pubdocs.worldbank.org/en/823661503543356520/Thailand-Economic-Monitor-August-2017.pdf.

World Bank. 2018 (April). "Financial Inclusion on the Rise, but Gaps Remain, Global Findex Database Shows." https://www.worldbank.org/en/news/press-release/2018/04/19/financial-inclusion-on-the-rise-but-gaps-remain-global-findex-database-shows.

Yan, Meilan, Maximilian J. B. Hall, and Paul Turner. 2012. "A Cost-Benefit Analysis of Basel: Some Evidence from the UK." *International Review of Financial Analysis* 25:73–82.

Young, Kevin L. 2012. "Transnational Regulatory Capture? An Empirical Examination of the Transnational Lobbying of the Basel Committee on Banking Supervision." *Review of International Political Economy* 19(4): 663–88.

Young, Oran R. 1979. *Compliance and Public Authority: A Theory with International Applications*. New York: Routledge.

Zarate, Juan C. 2013. *Treasury's War: The Unleashing of a New Era of Financial Warfare*. Washington, DC: Public Affairs.

Zaring, David. 1998. "International Law by Other Means: The Twilight Existence of International Financial Regulatory Organizations." *Texas International Law Journal* 38:281–330.

Zaring, David. 2004. "Informal Procedure, Hard and Soft, in International Administration." *Chicago Journal of International Law* 5(2): 547–603.

Zaring, David. 2019. *The Globalized Governance of Finance.* Cambridge: Cambridge University Press.

Zoppei, Verena. 2015. "Money Laundering: A New Perspective in Assessing the Effectiveness of the AML Regime." *European Review of Organized Crime* 2(1): 130–48.

Index